C

ON POMPE *⌐JMMAND*
(DE IMPERIO), 27-49

Cicero,
On Pompey's Command
(De Imperio), 27-49

Latin text, study aids with vocabulary, commentary, and translation

Ingo Gildenhard,
Louise Hodgson, *et al.*

http://www.openbookpublishers.com

This is the fourth volume of the Classics Textbooks series:

ISSN: 2054-2437 (Print)
ISSN: 2054-2445 (Online)

ISBN Paperback: 978-1-78374-077-2
ISBN Hardback: 978-1-78374-078-9
ISBN Digital (PDF): 978-1-78374-079-6
ISBN Digital ebook (epub version): 978-1-78374-080-2
ISBN Digital ebook (mobi version): 978-1-78374-081-9
DOI: 10.11647/OBP.0045

Cover image: *Bust of Cicero*, Vatican Museums. Photograph by Anna Gatti, 2014. CC BY

All paper used by Open Book Publishers is SFI (Sustainable Forestry Initiative), and PEFC (Programme for the Endorsement of Forest Certification Schemes) Certified.

Printed in the United Kingdom and United States by Lightning Source for Open Book Publishers

Contents

1. Preface and Acknowledgements

This commentary has its origins in a neat coincidence: for the years 2015-2017, the prose text of the OCR Latin AS-Level specifications comes from a speech by Cicero, the *pro* (or *de*) *lege Manilia* ('In support of/ About the law of Manilius') or (our preference) *de imperio Cn. Pompei* ('On the command of Gnaeus Pompeius') that, for the last few years, has also been one of the set texts first-year Classics students read at the University of Cambridge. (Given that it is now part of the OCR examination, it's off the Cambridge syllabus from 2015.)

Here was a perfect opportunity to link up the study of Latin at school and university. In the summer of 2013 a group of our so-called 'Prelims' – undergraduates who arrive at Cambridge without having studied Latin or Greek at school and spend a 'preliminary year' bringing their Latin up to A-level standards, before starting our regular three-year degree programme – signed up to hammering out a commentary on the OCR set text. And in autumn 2013, they were joined by a group of first-year undergraduates who arrived at Cambridge with A-level Latin, happened to have their first-term Latin literature supervision channelled to King's College, and thus got co-opted into the commentary project. All contributed key ideas and inspiring draft versions to the final product. The student co-authors, and their College affiliation, are George Lord (Christ's); Molly Richards (Clare); Nnenda Chinda and Rachel Franks (Downing); Hannah Philp (Emmanuel); Charlotte Frude, Grace Miller, Heather Shorthouse, and Samantha Tarling (Fitzwilliam); Jake Cohen-Setton, Eleanor Hussey, Billy Robinson, and Pete Westcott (Jesus); Qasim Alli, Ashley Chhibber, Reece Edmends, Naomi Farhi, and Harry Strawson (King's); Emily Dean, Charlotte Furniss-Roe, Alice Greenwood, and Georgie Illingworth (Murray Edwards); and Bryony Hutchinson and Alex Nelson (St. Catherine's).

Last but not least, Louise Hodgson, who received her doctorate from Durham University in 2013 for a dissertation on the political culture of the late Roman republic, generously agreed to do the heavy lifting on the Introduction and the Further Resources and kindly vetted the rest of the volume.

The commentary, then, is a work of multiple authorship. I personally claim credit for a tweak here, an editorial intervention there; any remaining mistakes or oversights are also mine, all mine, though fortunately their number has been vastly reduced (once more) by John Henderson, OBP's *summus lector*. It would require a Cicero to sing his praises, so let me simply say that you'll find his *virtus, humanitas, ingenium,* and *urbanitas* sparkling on every page, not least the Introduction.

Ingo Gildenhard, King's College Cambridge

PS: The portion of the speech set for the AS-examination (§§ 27-45) covers most of Cicero's portrait of the perfect general but leaves out the end (§§ 46-49). We are convinced that most, if not all, students would wish to read the full account and have therefore included these additional paragraphs in the present edition.

2. Introduction: why does the set text matter?

Fig. 1 V. Foppa, *The Young Cicero Reading*, c.1464. Photograph by Sailko, 2011.
Image from Wikimedia, CC BY-SA 3.0. http://commons.wikimedia.org/wiki/File:Vincenzo_
foppa,_giovane_che_legge_cicerone,_dal_banco_mediceo_di_milano_03.JPG

Born in 106 BC, Cicero reached his political maturity during a nasty period in Roman history: the reign of Sulla (82-79 BC).[1] The dictator introduced a new practice into Roman politics: the mass-slaughter of Roman citizens by Roman citizens – and not just on the battlefield. Once Sulla had crushed armed resistance in the first full-blown civil war that Rome experienced (it proved trend-setting...), he proceeded to 'proscriptions' – the drafting of lists that contained the names of alleged enemies of the *res publica*, who then could be killed on sight. (*Mutatis mutandis*, such 'hit lists' seem to have remained in fashion ever since...) He used this procedure to purge the Roman elite of his personal enemies: several thousands lost their lives, slaughtered in cold blood. As Plutarch puts it in his *Life of Sulla* (31.1): 'Sulla now [sc. after his appointment to the dictatorship] busied himself with slaughter and filled the city with deaths without number or limit.'

Cicero seems to have found Sulla's civic bloodshed deeply disturbing. Arguably, his entire political career and intellectual efforts unfolded under the banner: 'History Must Not Repeat Itself! Proscriptions? Never Again!'[2] History, of course, *did* repeat itself: in 43 BC, the second triumvirate of Caesar Octavianus (a.k.a. Octavian, the future *princeps* Augustus), Mark Antony, and Lepidus again opted to 'proscribe' enemies: and their most famous victim was none other than Cicero. Ironically, Cicero lost his head at the hands of a clique he himself had helped to bring to power *via* his initial support of the young Octavian and his uncompromising stance towards Mark Antony in his last set of speeches, the *Philippics*. These constituted his last-ditch effort of a lifetime dedicated to the fight against the political 'monsters' (his idiom) that he perceived as threats to his beloved *res publica*, which he identified with the senatorial tradition of republican government. His speeches and treatises (and there are lots of them!) are filled with outbursts against 'the tyrants' of the late republic, who abused

---

1   His earliest surviving speech, in defence of Publius Quinctius in a civil law suit, dates to 81.
2   So Flower (2006).

power, allegedly aimed at kingship, and sought to bring down the state: Verres, Catiline, Clodius, Caesar, Mark Antony – with Sulla figuring as the archetype of them all.

Cicero, then, went down in history as the incarnation of the free republic. (This is no exaggeration: after Brutus had sunk his dagger into Caesar on the Ides of March 44, he lifted his bloodied weapon in the air and called out: 'Cicero!') Yet in 66 BC, Cicero gave a speech, the *pro lege Manilia* or *de imperio Gnaei Pompei*, in support of a bill designed to give extraordinary powers to one of Sulla's most notorious lieutenants, whom many suspected of desiring to pick up the mantle of the former dictator. The *lex* proposed by the tribune Manilius transferred supreme command of the war between Rome and Mithridates VI, the king of Pontus, to Gnaeus Pompeius (or 'Pompey'), already then known as 'the Great' (*Magnus*) – but also, less flatteringly, as *adulescens carnifex* ('youthful butcher'), a sobriquet he acquired for his role in the civil wars on Sulla's side. Admittedly, Mithridates, the 'poison king', whom one scholar has hailed as 'Rome's deadliest enemy', had proved himself a real nuisance in Rome's attempt to establish imperial control over Asia Minor (roughly present-day Turkey).[3] Hostilities dated back to the 80s and included the genocidal slaughter of 80,000 Roman citizens and their Italian allies during the 'Asiatic Vespers' in 88 BC. But despite some recent setbacks, there was arguably no strategic need to appoint Pompey (or anyone else) with the help of extraordinary measures. Indeed, one could forgive those members of Rome's ruling elite who screamed a 'Déjà vu!' in protest: one of the past commanders who had had a go at Mithridates was none other than Sulla, who after a few inconsequential victories abandoned the campaign in order to march on Rome and sort out his internal enemies. Wasn't Pompey a second Sulla in the making? Had he not just celebrated an unprecedented success over the pirates of the Mediterranean with the help of another extraordinary command, proposed by the tribune Gabinius? Had not Gaius Piso, in the debate over the mandate against the pirates, threatened Pompey with a senatorial *sparagmos* ('a tearing to pieces') if he continued to aim at kingship?[4] Wouldn't a further victory over Mithridates inflate him from Magnus to Maximus for sure and enable him to march on Rome with the same autocratic ambitions as his mentor Sulla?

---

3   For a biography that pays due attention to the lurid and the sensational see Mayor (2009).

4   Plutarch, *Life of Pompey* 25.4. For a literary description of a *sparagmos* see your verse set text, the Pentheus-episode from Ovid's *Metamorphoses*.

The bill did not *require* Cicero's support. No one forced him to speak, and it was hugely popular with the people anyway. All thirty-five tribes passed the bill, Plutarch reports (*Life of Pompey* 30). Besides, several senatorial peers much more distinguished than Cicero at the time had already spoken in its favour. So even if he felt strongly about Pompey's appointment, he could have just kept his silence – instead of pushing at an open door that led him straight into a potential minefield: as he concedes in his peroration (§ 71, the last paragraph of the speech) his intervention may well have made him some enemies. Not only that – he decided to compound the problem (and amplify his voice) by disseminating a *written* version after the oral performance in the forum – again a deliberate choice: Cicero only published a selection of the speeches he gave. How truly amazing to find Cicero advocating concentration of power in one pair of hands, thus setting a precedent for some version or other of Caesar and Augustus!

In light of all this, you may legitimately ask: *why* in the world did he throw his (rhetorical) weight behind this bill, orally and, especially, in writing? And further: *how* did he manage to square his endorsement of the *lex Manilia* (which meant elevating Pompey above everyone else and giving him extraordinary powers) with his republican principles and convictions? (*If* he managed to do so: you'll have to be the judge of that!) To make headway with these questions, we need to ask ourselves what was in it for Cicero at this particular moment in his career – and take a close look at his portrait of the perfect general (i.e. the 'meat' of the set text).

The *pro lege Manilia* was Cicero's first persuasive speech to the people of Rome. He delivered it in 66 BC, at the age of 39, the year he was praetor, so an important serving magistrate, one step from the top post of consul. At the time, he was best known for his stunningly successful prosecution of the pretty awful Gaius Verres in 70 BC, as recorded (with a considerable dose of artistic licence) in his *Verrine Orations*. But in order to climb the highest rank of the *cursus honorum* ('the course of offices'), i.e. the consulship, he had to start making his voice heard in the civic arena. The bill proposed by Manilius proved just the ticket for Cicero's debut. And Cicero knew how to make an entry. Here is the opening paragraph of the speech (*Man.* 1):

> Quamquam mihi semper frequens conspectus vester multo iucundissimus, hic autem locus ad agendum amplissimus, ad dicendum ornatissimus est visus, Quirites, tamen hoc aditu laudis, qui semper optimo cuique maxime patuit, non mea me voluntas adhuc, sed vitae meae rationes ab ineunte aetate susceptae prohibuerunt. Nam cum antea per aetatem nondum huius

auctoritatem loci attingere auderem statueremque nihil huc nisi perfectum ingenio, elaboratum industria adferri oportere, omne meum tempus amicorum temporibus transmittendum putavi.

[Although it has at all times given me a special pleasure to behold your crowded assembly, and this place in particular has seemed to me to afford the amplest scope for action, the fairest stage for eloquence, nonetheless, fellow-citizens, this approach to fame, which the best have ever found most widely open, has hitherto been barred to me, not certainly by any wish of mine, but by that scheme of life which, from my earliest years, I had laid down for myself. For previously, seeing that I was debarred by my youth from aspiring to this proud position and was resolved to bring here nothing but the mature outcome of my talent, the finished product of my industry, I considered that my every hour should be devoted to my friends in their hours of peril.]

The moment is dramatic: Cicero, the acknowledged 'king of the *courts*' (that's what his devotion to imperiled friends refers to), delivers his first-ever speech to the citizens of Rome, the *Quirites*, from the *rostra*, the speaker's platform from which Roman magistrates negotiated with the Roman people (a procedure called *agere cum populo*; cf. *ad agendum, sc. cum populo*). Before Cicero settles down to business (his promotion of Manilius' bill and its beneficiary, i.e. Pompey), he uses the occasion to position *himself* vis-à-vis his audience (cf. *mihi, vester, mea ... voluntas, me, vitae meae rationes*).[5] The opening sentence is autobiographical with an apologetic subtext, arising from the need to justify *why* this is his first-ever *contio*-appearance. Cicero begins by stressing in superlative mode (*iucundissimus, amplissimus, ornatissimus,* though with his usual subjective hedge in *mihi ... est visus*) that his absence from the *contio*-scene had nothing to do with lack of esteem for the people of Rome or this particular institution. Rather, he butters up his audience with an elaborate *captatio benevolentiae*. He claims that, for him, of all the most agreeable things the most agreeable thing 'by far' (*multo*: a strategically placed ablative of the measure of difference) has always been a crowded (cf. *frequens*) citizen-assembly. And he adds to this rose-tinted view a more 'objective' recognition of the constitutional importance of this place and setting.

Such flattery of course only renders the question more acute as to why Cicero has never gotten round to actually delivering a speech here – until

---

5   For '*ego*' (and its inflections) as a main theme of the speech see MacKendrick (1995).

now. The second half of the sentence, introduced by *tamen* (with the direct address to the citizens functioning as pivot), tries to provide an answer. But the answer we get is curious, to say the least. Cicero sets up an opposition, or at least tension, between his inclination (*voluntas*) and the plan that from his earliest youth has informed his life (*vitae meae rationes*). While he was quite willing to step up, this mysterious plan *prevented* him from doing so (*prohibuerunt*). The final word of the sentence comes very much as a surprise. What *was* this plan, his audience will have started to wonder, that kept Cicero away from the speaker's platform? For an answer, we have to wait for the next sentence.

Before this surprise ending to his opening sentence, Cicero embeds his own career-choices within Rome's political culture more generally: *aditus laudis*, the gateway to fame, refers to the key ambition of every member of Rome's ruling elite, namely public recognition in the form of *laus* and *gloria*, attained through the holding of public office in the service of the *res publica* and, simultaneously or subsequently, military commands. The Roman citizens elected their magistrates, and a public career was in principle open to any citizen rich enough to pursue it; but in practice most of the candidates who successfully stood for office hailed from families that could boast ancestors who had held magistracies in the past. Against this reality, Cicero, a so-called 'new man' (*homo novus*), i.e. someone without politically successful ancestors in his family tree, validates inborn talent (and hence merit): he claims that especially (cf. *maxime*) the best (cf. *optimo cuique*), by stepping up to the *rostra*, could make a career for themselves and acquire renown in Rome. This conflicts with Roman common sense: Joe Public would have thought that 'the best' would look to performing feats in warfare to acquire fame and recognition rather than seeking out the *rostra*. Obliquely, Cicero here ranks the *orator* ('public speaker') above the *imperator* ('general')!

What follows is even more mind-boggling: Cicero claims that only after he had turned himself into a *perfect* orator, by means of a combination of innate talent and the most strenuous training, did he consider it appropriate to appear in such a hallowed place as the *rostra* to address such a worthy audience as the Roman people! The reason why he hasn't spoken before, it now emerges, are his own exacting standards: the Roman people deserve nothing but the best. Cicero didn't appear on the *rostra* before he had been crowned 'king of eloquence': this implies that all the other, lesser speakers hold the people in less respect than he does – since they offer less than perfect oratory, falling below Ciceronian standards of *ingenium, labor* (cf. *e-labor-atum* and the explicit reference to *meus labor* in § 2), and *industria*.

Put differently, Cicero begins with the *perfectus orator* (himself) before moving on to the *summus imperator* (Pompey). He and Pompey thereby emerge as a complementary pair, each outstanding in his respective sphere – a complementarity Cicero would come back to some years later when he suggested to Pompey (who was none too pleased) that his suppression of the Catilinarian Conspiracy at home (*domi*) as *dux togatus* ('a military leader dressed in the toga', i.e. Rome's civic apparel) compared favourably with Pompey's victory over Mithridates abroad on campaign (*militiae*). The set up also underscores the 'power of definition' that comes with Cicero's command of eloquence: in sketching a portrait of Pompey as perfect general, he simultaneously uses his understanding of the perfect general to define Pompey – what, *according to Cicero*, Pompey *should be* like. Playing (panegyric) adviser to those in power was a role Cicero rather fancied – and also tried later to play with Caesar and Octavian.

In the *pro lege Manilia*, to be sure, this aspect remains rather oblique. Cicero is at pains to stress that his principal motivation for stepping up is the wellbeing of the *res publica* and the Roman people. This, at least, is what he pronounces at the very end of the speech (§ 70):

> testorque omnis deos, et eos maxime qui huic loco temploque praesident, qui omnium mentis eorum qui ad rem publicam adeunt maxime perspiciunt, me hoc neque rogatu facere cuiusquam, neque quo Cn. Pompei gratiam mihi per hanc causam conciliari putem, neque quo mihi ex cuiusquam amplitudine aut praesidia periculis aut adiumenta honoribus quaeram;

> [And I call all the gods to witness – most especially the guardians of this hallowed spot who clearly see into the hearts of all who enter upon public life – that I am acting thus neither in deference to any man's request nor with any idea of winning for myself by my support of this cause the favour of Gnaeus Pompeius, nor in the hope of gaining for myself from any man's high position either protection from dangers or aids to advancement.]

No, his motives, Cicero goes on to say, are entirely unselfish, focused exclusively on public welfare – at significant personal cost (§ 71):

> Quam ob rem quicquid in hac causa mihi susceptum est, Quirites, id ego omne me rei publicae causa suscepisse confirmo; tantumque abest ut aliquam mihi bonam gratiam quaesisse videar, ut multas me etiam simultates partim

obscuras, partim apertas intellegam mihi non necessarias, vobis non inutilis suscepisse.

[Wherefore any effort I may have made in this cause, citizens, I protest has been made in the cause of my country; and far from seeming to have sought any popularity for myself, I am aware of having even incurred many enmities, some overt and some secret, which I might have avoided, though not without some detriment to you.]

Is Cicero protesting too much? Is he trying to pre-empt the impression that he had been bought or was just trying to muscle in on the bill to secure the gratitude and future goodwill of Pompey? Does the explicit denial not give the game away? Do we have to cancel out the negatives to get at the truth? What happens if we fiddle a bit with the prose: 'I am acting thus ~~neither~~ in deference to ~~any~~ *a* man's request ~~nor~~ *and* with ~~any~~ *the* idea of winning for myself by my support of this cause the favour of Gnaeus Pompeius, ~~nor~~ in the hope of gaining for myself from ~~any man's~~ *someone's* high position ~~either~~ protection from dangers ~~or~~ *and* aids to advancement' – would that come closer to the truth? How cynical is *your* reading of these concluding – *politician's* – paragraphs?

In this context we may note that not only the people, but also the 'knights', Rome's 'moneyed elite', Cicero's own social order with which he seems to have entertained mutually beneficial terms of reciprocity in his climb up the *cursus honorum*,[6] were very much in favour of Pompey's appointment. They had commercial interests in the region and sought a quick conclusion to the hostilities so they could pursue business and 'farm' taxes. Indeed, a passage in Velleius Paterculus (2.33.1), a historian writing during the reign of Tiberius, allows the inference that Manilius had been bribed by the knights to propose the bill.[7] Whether this is true or not (and whether Cicero was in their pocket or not), there seem to have been a range of self-interested reasons for him to lend his rhetorical muscle to an initiative that was popular with the people (without being unanimously opposed by the senate), enabled him to jump on the MAJOR bandwagon in town (Gnaeus Pompeius MAGNUS), and was bound to find favour with his most loyal political supporters. Did it, does it, matter that this move, which could only bump up his own chances of up-coming election into the big time, meant

---

6   Berry (2003).
7   MacKendrick (1995) 11.

a mode of panegyric elevation of a single individual difficult to reconcile with republican principles?

After this peek at the beginning and end of the speech (and Cicero's possible motivations for mounting the speaker's platform), it's time to get the speech as a whole into view, with a particular emphasis on his portrait of the perfect general (§§ 27-49), most of which (= §§ 27-45) is included in your set text. Here is a basic outline:[8]

Paragraphs	Part of the oration
1-5	I. *Exordium and narratio*
6-50	II. *Confirmatio I*
6-19	1. *de genere belli*
20-6	2. *de magnitudine belli*
27-49	3. *de imperatore deligendo*
28	a. *scientia rei militaris*
29-42	b. *virtus*
43-6	c. *auctoritas*
47-8	d. *felicitas*
49-50	4. Sum-up
51-63	III. *Refutatio*
64-71	IV. *Confirmatio II and Peroratio*

The structure is straightforward. Cicero starts with a few words by way of introduction (§§ 1-3 = *exordium*) and briefly covers some key points of the current military situation in Asia Minor (§§ 4-6 = *narratio*). In §§ 6-50 he gives his reasons why the bill should pass: the type of war (§§ 6-19) and the scope of the war (§§ 20-6) call for a perfect general (§§ 27-49), and the only one who fits the bill is therefore Pompey, the greatest general of all times. After summing up his argument (§§ 49-50), Cicero considers and dismisses objections to the appointment of Pompey (§§ 51-63 = *refutatio*), reasserts the desirability of the bill (§§ 64-68) and signs off with a rousing conclusion (§§ 69-71 = *peroratio*). The set text (§§ 27-45) hits on the very centre of the speech, i.e. Cicero's portrait of the perfect general and his four principal qualities, all of which (so Cicero claims) Pompey embodies: knowledge of military matters (*scientia rei militaris*), overall excellence (*virtus*), commanding

---

8   For a more detailed outline see MacKendrick (1995) 3-6.

respect (*auctoritas*), and divinely sponsored success (*felicitas*). Let's take a look at each of these qualities in turn.

Scientia militaris (§ 28)

In § 28 Cicero surveys Pompey's career, tracing his transition from school to army, from GI to general, from general to greatest military commander of all times. A stint in the army around the age of twenty was routine for a Roman aristocrat with political ambitions. Cicero, too, served his time – as it happens also under Pompey's father Strabo.[9] But after his stint in the armed forces, he went off on a study trip to Greece and devoted himself to excellence in (courtroom) oratory – knowing full well of course that military achievement was the highway to public office in Rome with a monopoly on *gloria*. Decades later, finally obliged to serve as pro-consul of Cilicia in 51 BC, i.e. the very region supposedly 'pacified' and turned into a Roman province by Pompey in the 60s, Cicero won a couple of minor military encounters against uppity tribes, was hailed as *imperator* by his troops, and did his futile best to convince the senate to grant him a triumph. But what was little more than a fortuitous accident for Cicero, i.e. holding a military command and at least staking a claim to celebrate a triumph, was a profession for Pompey, who triumphed thrice in the course of his career. His rise to the top did perhaps not happen quite as quickly as Cicero's star-struck way of putting it in § 28 suggests; and it was facilitated by such factors as the premature death of his father (leaving Pompey in charge of the extended social networks of the family), the chaos of the civil wars, and his willingness to proceed by means of unconstitutional measures, which included the raising of a private army that he put at the disposal of Sulla.[10] In Cicero's survey of Pompey's career, these scary details are carefully airbrushed.[11]

---

9   There is no evidence that the two met then and there.

10   Caesar Octavianus, the future *princeps* Augustus, proudly followed in his footsteps. See the opening of his *Res Gestae*: *Annos undeviginti natus exercitum privato consilio et privata impensa comparavi, per quem rem publicam a dominatione factionis oppressam in libertatem vindicavi* ('In my nineteenth year, on my own initiative and at my own expense, I raised an army with which I set free the state, which was oppressed by the domination of a faction'). See further Hodgson (2014).

11   To enable you to read between the lines and properly appreciate Cicero's artful 'silences' in his account of where Pompey's astounding *scientia militaris* came from, we have supplied a detailed biography under 'Further Resources', which should offer a neat opportunity for a 'compare and contrast' exercise with the set text.

One peculiar feature of Cicero's praise of Pompey's unmatched *scientia militaris* is his insistence that it is grounded in actual experience, rather than the perusal of books: *plura bello gessit quam ceteri legerunt* ('he has conducted more campaigns than the rest have read of'). It is worth questioning this piece of praise a bit, especially as it comes from Cicero.[12] Depending on *the reader*, it could imply very few military feats indeed; if, on the other hand, the reader Cicero has in mind is someone like himself (who had surely perused all the major Greek and Roman historiographers and most of the minor ones as well) the praise turns into panegyric hyperbole. It is perhaps unsurprising that the earliest attestation of the contrast comes from Cicero, whose first-hand experience of military life was notoriously limited, but who was a voracious reader. As John Henderson puts it: 'The ludicrous presumption that Cicero's worth listening to when he comes on as expert on imperial strategy in the field – as if he knows anything about campaigning, soldiers and fighting, local barons and militias, anything he didn't read in books or from reports of his colleagues and rivals – has to be underlined. Do we want a foreign office full of champion debaters or people who have been in a helicopter or used a field latrine, etc. etc.?'

Virtus (§§ 29-42)

By the late republic, if not since time immemorial, the term *virtus* possessed a range of meanings. It could signify 'martial prowess', refer to various other 'excellences', or designate *ethical* excellence in a technical philosophical sense. It moreover served as a generic label for an entire set of desirable qualities or values in contrast to the semantics of other, more sharply defined value terms such as *fortitudo* ('bravery'). We thus also find it in the plural (*omnes virtutes*) or similar phrases (*omne genus virtutis*). This range of meanings came in handy: since, by etymological definition, each Roman *vir* worth his masculine mettle wanted to lay claim to *vir-tus*, it must have been agreeable that there were different versions of *virtus* to choose from.[13]

---

12 He seems to have been quite fond of it: see his speech *pro Fonteio* 43, where he praises the defendant as someone to be numbered among *non litteris homines ad rei militaris scientiam sed rebus gestis ac victoriis eruditos* ('men who gained their military knowledge not from text-books but from their operations and their victories'). The contrast famously recurs in the speech the historian Sallust put into the mouth of Marius, where the readers come from the established nobility, and the doers are new men like himself (*Bellum Iugurthinum* 85.13).

13 As the author of the *Rhetorica ad Herennium* puts it (3.6): *nemo erit qui censeat a virtute*

In fact, there are reasons to suppose that it was in part its privileged status in the Roman system of values, which turned *virtus* into such a protean concept: the Romans tussled over its definition and proprietorship. A ready example of individuals or groups trying to spin *virtus* in their own image are the controversial views over whether *virtus* ran in families and could thus be handed down like a heirloom from one generation to the next or whether (the potential for) *virtus* occurred randomly throughout society or at least its upper echelon. The former was the preferred view of the nobility, which had a vested interest in naturalizing historical achievement, the latter that of *homines novi* ('new men'), who liked to style themselves as the standard-bearers of an excellence that the degenerate offspring of once-great families no longer managed to uphold – according to the formula '*novus homo-prisca virtus*' ('new man – ancient excellence').[14] New men naturally did not all agree either on what, precisely, 'ancient excellence' consisted in. Marius and Cicero, for example, were both 'new men'; but they could not have differed more radically in their preferred definition of *virtus*. Marius emphasized military *virtus*, whereas Cicero preferred to foreground other aspects, such as 'civic ethics' (well aware of the fact that Roman common sense was with Marius on this).[15] The different nuances and variants of *virtus* in Roman culture mean that each individual instance of the term requires careful inspection in order to spot the ideological agenda that is afoot, and this is doubly true for as innovative a treatment as Cicero's in the *pro lege Manilia*.

The section on *virtus* is by far the longest of the four. It neatly falls into two halves: §§ 29-35 (= 7 paragraphs); and §§ 36-42 (= 7 paragraphs). The exact symmetry is programmatic: each half has equal weight. Cicero sets up the partition in § 29, where he distinguishes between the *virtutes* of a military commander that are commonly recognized as such and a further set that could be considered 'handmaidens' of the first, but turn out to be equally essential for winning the war against Mithridates. Those in the first set are all aspects of the *virtus bellandi* ('martial prowess') and have to

---

recedendum ('no one will propose the abandonment of *virtus*') – even though the orator will spin what *virtus* actually is and means to suit his agenda.

14 Wiseman (1971) 113.

15 A related controversy concerned the question as to whether *virtus* ultimately boiled down to natural endowment or whether (and if so to what extent and how) it was teachable. Against a strictly 'biological' conception of *virtus*, educators of all stripes have had a professional stake in upholding the belief that, at least in part, excellence can be taught or that innate talent is, at any rate, insufficient by itself for attaining perfection.

do with the nuts and bolts of successful warfare. Cicero specifies *labor in negotiis* ('effort in public affairs'), *fortitudo in periculis* ('courage in dangers'), *industria in agendo* ('care in operating'), *celeritas in conficiendo* ('speed in finishing') and *consilium in providendo* ('good judgement in exercising forethought'). Those in the second set all foreground ethical qualities – qualities, in other words, that shape socio-political interactions outside the combat zone, but are important to generate trust in Roman rule and marshal support for Rome's war-efforts among the allies. Cicero specifies *innocentia* ('integrity'), *temperantia* ('moderation'), *fides* ('trustworthiness'), *facilitas* ('ease in interpersonal relations'), *ingenium* ('outstanding talent'), and *humanitas* ('human kindness').[16] It is probably fair to say (and Cicero concedes as much in § 29) that many in the audience would not have intuitively thought of the qualities in the second set as essential attributes of *virtus imperatoria* and hence hallmarks of the perfect general. Cicero, in other words, does something decidedly unorthodox. Why?

To begin with, he argues that the entire portfolio of *virtutes*, both the 'tough' ones and the 'soft' ones, are necessary to win this particular war. Those in the first set are necessary to crush Mithridates on the battlefield; those in the second to win the 'hearts and minds' of the local population and thus create the conditions for a permanent peace (or 'pacification'). There is an eerie contemporary relevance to Cicero's argument. The fact that he also had some ulterior motives for making it (see below) should not obfuscate the possibility that he may actually have a point: recent history has again shown that it is much easier to crush combatants with superior military force than to genuinely 'pacify' a region by winning over the local populations.

Secondly, Cicero's insistence that Pompey combined outstanding *virtus* in the traditional sense of martial prowess with ethical integrity, social humility, and overall moderation was bound to assuage fears that he would turn into a second Sulla: someone known for his *temperantia* would not make an immoderate grab for absolute power in Rome like the former dictator, surely? (Whether Pompey actually possessed the qualities Cicero here ascribes to him is of secondary importance for the rhetorical agenda of the speech: but it is an interesting question for you to pursue and debate.)

---

16 *Ingenium* (which is something like 'innate talent' and does not presuppose a wider social context) does not quite fit in with the others: for a possible explanation why Cicero included it in the list see our commentary on § 42.

And finally, the emphasis on 'soft' qualities that are equally desirable in the sphere of warfare (*militiae*) as they are at home in the sphere of domestic politics (*domi*) enables Cicero to outline a portfolio of *virtutes*, to which he too can stake a claim, as well as coming across as a wised-up political analyst. With the second set, he partially assimilates his *summus imperator* ('the perfect general') to the *summus orator* ('the perfect orator/statesman'), who was – as he obliquely hinted at in the opening paragraph of the speech – none other than himself. This crafty scheme of self-promotion, which enables Cicero to bask in Pompey's reflected glory (and, conversely, make Pompey beholden to a set of excellences Cicero himself held dear), comes out most forcefully in § 42, where Cicero claims that *dicendi gravitas et copia* ('weighty and abundantly eloquent oratory') possesses *quaedam dignitas imperatoria* ('a certain dignity characteristic of a general'). While ostensibly claiming this quality for Pompey, no-one had a greater gift for weighty and abundantly eloquent oratory than Marcus Tullius Cicero. Put differently, as with so many definitions of *virtus* that of Cicero, too, is at least in part a mirror image of the author and certainly branded as his design.

Auctoritas (§§ 43-46)

Let's start with an attempt at definition: 'Some exceptions notwithstanding, *auctoritas* in Roman Republican usage denoted a socially legitimized power that did not amount to binding commands and did not rely on means of enforcement. It presumed a likely obedience to social superiors (or acknowledged experts) in a society that presupposed a hierarchical order in all its segments, an obedience that emanated from the bottom-up.'[17] That's quite a mouthful – and more a gloss than a definition. But the Greek historiographer Cassius Dio, for one, would have appreciated the difficulty of pinning down *auctoritas* more precisely. He encountered the same quandary upon reporting that the Augustan senate, when a poorly attended session was not quorate to pass a piece of legislation, would state its opinion in what he terms 'an act of *auctoritas*' (expressing a senatorial preference that carries the weight of the prestige attached to this particular body but was not legally binding, in short: 'an ineffective resolution').[18]

---

17 Nippel (2007) 27.
18 Balsdon (1951) 43.

Writing in his native tongue, he has to concede that Greek lacks a term to render *auctoritas* adequately (55.3.4-5):

ἐβουλεύοντο μὲν καὶ ἥ γε γνώμη συνεγράφετο, οὐ μέντοι καὶ τέλος τι ὡς κεκυρωμένη ἐλάμβανεν, ἀλλὰ αὐκτώριτας ἐγίγνετο, ὅπως φανερὸν τὸ βούλημα αὐτῶν ᾖ. τοιοῦτον γάρ τι ἡ δύναμις τοῦ ὀνόματος τούτου δηλοῖ· ἑλληνίσαι γὰρ αὐτὸ καθάπαξ ἀδύνατόν ἐστι.

[... the senators would proceed with their deliberations and their decision would be recorded, though it would not go into effect as if regularly passed, but instead, their action was what was termed *auctoritas*, the purpose of which was to make known their will. For such is the general force of this word; to translate it into Greek by a term that will always be applicable is impossible.]

Dio is right. His inability to translate *auctoritas* is a symptom of the fact that Greek and Roman culture evolved quite distinct vocabularies and ways of thinking about the phenomenon that we would refer to as 'power' – which we may loosely define, for present purposes, as 'the (value-neutral) ability to impose one's will in a given situation'. Interestingly enough, Ulrich Gotter has argued that just as Greek has no straightforward lexical equivalent for Latin *auctoritas*, Latin (unlike Greek) has no straightforward lexical equivalent to English 'power' (or the equivalent Greek terms *archê* and *kratos*).[19] Surveying the range of terms to do with power – in the main: *potestas* ('a socially or institutionally sanctioned form of power that attached to social roles (such as the *pater familias*) and public offices'), *imperium* ('the right to issue orders that attached to certain public offices'), *auspicium* ('the right to consult the will of the gods that attached to certain public offices'), *auctoritas* ('prestige derived from past achievements'), *dignitas* ('social rank and standing'), *opes* ('unsanctioned means to impose one's will on others'), *potentia* ('unsanctioned means to impose one's will on others'), and *vis* ('illegitimate use of force') – he notes that none of them signifies 'power' in the abstract, general sense of the English word (or *archê* and *kratos* in Greek):

---

19 The Greek terms have continued to define the way Western culture understands and categorizes political systems: they are part of mon-archy = 'power' (-archy from *archê*) is in the hands of 'one' (*monos* in Greek); aristo-cracy = power (-cracy from *kratos*) is in the hands of 'the best' (*aristoi* in Greek); or demo-cracy = power (-cracy from *kratos*) is in the hands of the people (*demos* in Greek). Question: in whose hands does power lie in a 'republic' (from Latin *res publica* = 'the public thing', 'civic affairs')?

all of these notions were deeply rooted in a normative discourse. Generally speaking, they can be divided into *acceptable* and *unacceptable* forms of asserting one's will. It is true that *potentia, opes,* and *vis* are as unspecific as equivalent Greek terms. But they all carry highly negative connotations, implying as they do the *irregular* or *illegitimate* potential for, or assertion of, power. The other terms refer to *legitimate* forms of commanding or enforcing obedience and, in principle, can be reduced to the complementary pair of *potestas* and *auctoritas. Dignitas* provided *auctoritas* with legitimacy. And *imperium* and *auspicium* were specifications of *potestas.* The semantic range of neither *potestas* nor *auctoritas* is sufficiently abstract and general to render adequately any of the Greek terms for power.[20]

These observations deserve pondering in their own right, not least because the Greek and Roman ways of thinking about and conceptualizing power have left such a deep imprint on Western thought more generally, in the wider context of the classical tradition.[21] And they also offer an excellent, broader frame for a more specific discussion of *auctoritas* and its place within Rome's political culture.

The centre of *auctoritas* in republican Rome was the senate – a body consisting of former office-holders (i.e. former holders of public *potestas*), who here brought to bear their collected experience and wisdom on public affairs, especially those to do with international diplomacy or warfare. The senate had no executive powers (they relied on magistrates to enact their advice or recommendations) or legislative rights (the privilege to pass laws rested with the people). And yet, they were a significant, at times *the* significant, force in the administration of the *res publica*, especially when it stood more or less united – owing to the prestige and respect they commanded, in short because of their collective *auctoritas* (as well as, of course, other sources of influence such as social networks and wealth). 'In most cases ... *auctoritas senatûs* ... meant that the magistrates were supposed to present all issues of public importance to the senate and then follow the advice given to them by the senate. It is impossible to define whether this advice was binding in a *de iure* or a *de facto* sense... Or, as Mommsen put it: "*auctoritas* as a term which evades any strict definition corresponds to the senate's powerful position which is very effective on the one hand

---

20 Gotter (2008) 199; *acceptable, unacceptable, irregular, illegitimate,* and *legitimate* are our italics to help underscore the point that none of the Latin terms captures the abstract, value-neutral sense of 'power' in English or *archê* and *kratos* in Greek.

21 See Silk, Gildenhard and Barrow (2014), especially § 26 ('Forms of Government').

but cannot be defined in legal terms on the other hand. *Auctoritas* is more advice than command but it is advice that one cannot properly avoid".'[22]

In his *philosophical* (!) writings, Cicero too identified the senate as the principal 'site' of *auctoritas* in Roman politics. In the 'balanced' constitution he outlines in the *de Re Publica* ('On the Commonwealth'), written in the late 50s, the magistrates had *potestas*, the people represented *libertas* ('liberty'), and the senate possessed *auctoritas*.[23] Likewise in the ideal constitution he outlines in the subsequent *de Legibus* ('On the Laws'), where he specifies that *potestas* ought to lie 'with the people' (*in populo*) and *auctoritas* 'with the senate' (*in senatu*).[24]

The senate could exercise its *auctoritas* as a collective best when it stood united. That was not the case with the *lex Manilia*. Some distinguished senators, such as Quintus Hortensius and Quintus Catulus, former consuls both and hence beacons of *auctoritas*, opposed the bill. As a counterweight, Cicero calls upon the *auctoritas* of those senators who supported the legislation (§ 68):

> quod si *auctoritatibus* hanc causam, Quirites, confirmandam putatis, est vobis *auctor* vir bellorum omnium maximarumque rerum peritissimus, P. Servilius, cuius tantae res gestae terra marique exstiterunt ut, cum de bello deliberetis, *auctor* vobis gravior esse nemo debeat; est C. Curio, summis vestris beneficiis maximisque rebus gestis, summo ingenio et prudentia praeditus, est Cn. Lentulus in quo omnes pro amplissimis vestris honoribus summum consilium, summam gravitatem esse cognovistis, est C. Cassius, integritate, veritate, constantia singulari. qua re videte horumne *auctoritatibus* illorum orationi qui dissentiunt respondere posse videamur.

> [And if you think that our side of the argument, citizens, should be confirmed by *authorities*, you have the *authority* of Publius Servilius, a man of the greatest skill in all wars, and in affairs of the greatest importance, who has performed such mighty achievements by land and sea, that, when you are deliberating about war, no one's *authority* ought to have more weight with you. You have the *authority* of Caius Curio, a man who has received great kindnesses from you, who has performed great exploits, who is endowed with the highest abilities and wisdom; and of Cnaeus Lentulus, in whom all of you know there is (as, indeed, there ought to be from the ample honours which you have heaped upon him) the most eminent wisdom, and the

---

22 Nippel (2007) 18. The concluding reference is to Mommsen, *Römisches Staatsrecht*, vol. III/2, 1034.

23 See *de Re Publica* 2.57.

24 *de Legibus* 3.28.

greatest dignity of character; and of Caius Cassius, a man of extraordinary integrity, and valour, and virtue. Consider, therefore, whether we do not seem by the *authority* of these men to give a sufficient answer to the speeches of those men who differ from us.]

But this is not the only way in which *auctoritas* figures in the *pro lege Manilia*. At the beginning of the speech, Cicero identifies the people (!) as the ultimate source of *auctoritas* in Roman politics – right in the teeth of his own constitutional theory! Cicero starts by saying that he did not dare to intrude upon *the authority of this place* (*huius auctoritatem loci*) until he had honed his eloquence to perfection (§ 1). He follows this by acknowledging that his efforts in the law courts have received their most honourable reward in *the people's approbation* (*ex vestro iudicio*), with his election to the praetorship (§ 2). This serves him as point of departure for some more general statements about the reciprocity between magistrates and the people (§ 2):

Nam cum propter dilationem comitiorum ter praetor primus centuriis cunctis renuntiatus sum, facile intellexi, Quirites, et *quid de me iudicaretis*, et quid aliis praescriberetis. *Nunc cum et auctoritatis in me tantum sit, quantum vos honoribus mandandis esse voluistis*, et ad agendum facultatis tantum, quantum homini vigilanti ex forensi usu prope cotidiana dicendi exercitatio potuit adferre, *certe et si quid auctoritatis in me est, apud eos utar qui eam mihi dederunt*, et si quid in dicendo consequi possum, eis ostendam potissimum, qui ei quoque rei fructum *suo iudicio* tribuendum esse duxerunt.

[For when, on account of the adjournment of the comitia, I was three times elected the first praetor by all the centuries, I easily perceived, O Romans, *what your opinion of me was* (*quid de me iudicaretis*), and what conduct you enjoined to others. Now, when there is that authority in me which you, by conferring public offices on me (*nunc cum et auctoritatis in me tantum sit, quantum vos honoribus mandandis esse voluistis*), have chosen that there should be, and all that facility in pleading which almost daily practice in speaking can give a vigilant man who has habituated himself to the forum, at all events, if I have any authority (*certe et si quid auctoritatis in me est*), I will employ it before those who have given it to me (*apud eos utar qui eam mihi dederunt*); and if I can accomplish anything by speaking, I will display it to those men above all others, who have thought fit, by their decision (*suo iudicio*), to confer honours on that qualification.]

Here Cicero identifies the decision or approval (*iudicium, iudicare*) of the Roman people, who voted him into public office, as the (one and only) source of his *auctoritas* – and endows the place itself where magistrates interact with the citizen body with 'authority' (*auctoritas*). This is curious:

technically speaking, his election to the praetorship has given him *potestas* ('power associated with public office'), not *auctoritas*. So what is going on here? The solution to the riddle can be found in Cicero's portrait of the perfect general – one of whose four principal hallmarks is precisely *auctoritas*. And in § 43 Cicero reiterates the idea that the ultimate source of *auctoritas* is the people – though now with reference to Pompey: the 'judgements' of the Roman people, he claims, i.e. their decisions to vote Pompey into office or grant him extraordinary commands, represent Pompey's greatest source of *auctoritas*; and he leaves no doubt that Pompey will honour this investment with extraordinary service on behalf of the people. By some minor conceptual fiddling at the outset of the speech, where he uses *auctoritas* instead of *potestas* (and thereby transfers a quality conventionally associated with the senate to the people), Cicero manages to set up a triangular relationship between Pompey, the perfect general (and his *auctoritas*), himself, the perfect orator (and his self-proclaimed *auctoritas*), and his audience, the Roman people (according to the Cicero of the *pro lege Manilia*, the ultimate source of any *auctoritas*).[25]

Still, the most graphic image of *auctoritas* in the speech is not the *auctoritas* of the people (despite Cicero's conceptual alchemy), or that of individual senators (let alone the senate as a whole) but that of the perfect military commander and hence of Pompey. As §§ 43-46 of the set text suggests, it was enormous – and arguably incompatible with the central importance of senatorial *auctoritas*, which was designed to envelop short-term elected officials after their year in office: the key constraint of a club with life-time membership with strict rules for rising up the ranks 'in house' – all of which Pompey bypassed with supreme sangfroid in his rise to the top (see our commentary on § 28). In this context, you may wish to chew over what Augustus said in the *Res Gestae Divi Augusti* ('The Deeds of the Divine Augustus'): once he had become *princeps* in 27 BC, he surpassed everyone in *auctoritas*, even though the *potestas* attached to the magistracies he held did not exceed that of his colleagues in office: *post id tempus auctoritate omnibus praestiti, potestatis autem nihilo amplius habui quam ceteri qui mihi*

---

25 The insistence on the people as the ultimate source of prestige, and on the obligation of service Cicero feels he has incurred by winning a public election, fits into his self-promotion as a *homo novus* ('a new man' without any consuls in his lineage). Unlike the 'arrogant' established senatorial families, he does not consider election to high public office as part of his birthright; rather, he presents success at election as grounded entirely in the judgement of the people of Rome, who, with their votes, express approval for merit.

quoque in magistratu conlegae fuerunt (34.3).[26] This raises the question: what are the conditions in which *auctoritas* (the prestige and respect ascribed to an individual to the point that one follows him willingly) turns into a proto-autocratic form of power?

Felicitas (§§ 47-48)

The fourth quality of Cicero's portrait of the perfect general is *felicitas*, which can be glossed with 'divinely sponsored success'. To be sure, along with the tail end of the section on *auctoritas* Cicero's treatment of *felicitas* has not made it into the set text. Yet to exclude it from consideration entirely carries risk. The effect on your understanding of Cicero's agenda would in all likelihood resemble the attempt to sit on a four-legged chair from which one leg has been removed: it's bound to be shaky. Cicero placed *felicitas* in the last, climactic position for a reason. If *scientia militaris* and *virtus* are qualities very much focused on the individual (his biography/education, his personal talents), the notion of *auctoritas* presupposed a wider socio-political context; *felicitas*, in turn, widens the horizon still further: as divinely sponsored luck/success, it implies a supernatural frame of reference. Cicero thus proceeds from individual to community to the world at large.

Now public discourse in many, if not most societies (including postmodern ones, such as our own) often takes it for granted that one or more supernatural beings exist, are extraordinarily powerful (if not omnipotent), and show an interest in human affairs.[27] As Simon Jenkins noted not too long ago in *The Guardian*: 'Religious institutions are manifestly alive and kicking in both national and international politics. World leaders, even democrats such as Tony Blair and George Bush, appeal to supernatural entities to validate their politics.'[28] Republican Rome was no exception: references to the gods are standard in Roman oratory, and prayers frequent. The term *orator* itself has religious connotations: its etymological affinity with *orare* (to pray) situates the speaker and his discourse within a supernatural context.[29] The platform from which members of the ruling

---

26 For Augustus and *auctoritas* see Galinsky (1996), Chapter 1: 'A Principal Concept: *Auctoritas*'.

27 The following is based on Gildenhard (2011) 266-67.

28 Friday June 30, 2006, 34.

29 See Pina Polo (1996) 19, as well as, on the semantics of *oratio* more generally, Gavoille (2007).

elite addressed the populace during public assemblies was a sacred space;[30] and the senate frequently met in temples. In Cicero's speeches, too, the gods figure prominently. Invocations of the *di immortales* regularly occur at charged moments of pathos or outrage; numerous orations of his begin or end in prayers; and strategic oaths underscore his truthfulness or non-partisan devotion to the good of the commonwealth.

Like all belief-systems, Rome's civic religion, i.e. the religious beliefs and practices that formed an integral part of Roman politics and had co-evolved with the political culture of the *res publica*, had certain preferences: it endorsed some ways of configuring the divine sphere and frowned on others. The area of most concern to us here is the question to what extent a human being could resemble, perhaps even turn into, a god: any such 'boundary crossing' was irreconcilable with the principle of oligarchic equality that underwrote the republican tradition of senatorial government. Republican Rome did not even have a cult for Romulus, the city's founder, and the first time a human being underwent deification after his death (as happened to Julius Caesar), the *res publica* was well on its way to becoming a monarchy.

Rome's *civic* religion, then, maintained a strict divide between the human and the divine. Attempts at crossing the boundary, in whatever form, while feasible in theory (there existed, in principle, no *religious* objections to humans becoming gods: in literary texts, it happened all the time), were *politically* incorrect moves in the field of power.[31] Still, for outstanding aristocrats, to tiptoe across, or, as the case may be, boldly step over the dividing line of human and divine or to claim a special relationship with a supernatural being or, more generally, the supernatural sphere formed tempting means of self-promotion during the last centuries of the republic. Inspiration came from the East, in both theory and practice. Poets and other litterateurs cultivated a variety of Greek literary genres that explored different forms in which humans could become 'godlike', including outright apotheosis. In the context of imperial expansion, the Romans also encountered the cults that bestowed religious honours upon living rulers – a practice that had started to proliferate in the wake of Alexander the Great.[32]

---

30 At *Man.* 70, for instance, Cicero calls on those gods, *qui huic loco temploque praesident* ('who guard this sacred place').

31 Feeney (1998) 108-10.

32 Habicht (1970), Price (1984), Badian (1996), Mikalson (1998) (esp. ch. 3: 'Twenty years of the divine Demetrios Poliorcetes'), Chaniotis (2003). Flower (2006) 31-4 offers a useful reminder that the transition from deified human to disgraced dead could be a quick one.

The perceived divinity of (royal) power had little to do with the proclivity of Eastern subjects to emote irrationally about their kings, as some ancient sources (including Cicero: see our commentary on § 41) imply. Rather the Hellenistic ruler cult constituted an ideological form and social practice by which kings justified their reign and cities negotiated their existence within the domineering presence of 'a supra-poliadic power', i.e. a power bigger than the individual city-states or *poleis*.[33]

Given that the award of cultic honours to (potential) benefactors was part and parcel of the diplomatic activities of Greek city-states, it is hardly surprising that Romans too (including Pompey) received religious adulation when they started to flex their muscle in the Greek East. From the early second century onwards, Greek cities granted select Roman magistrates cultic worship.[34] A situation of cultural schizophrenia ensued: one and the same individual could be both godlike in Greece and all too human in Rome. The civil conflicts of the late republic accelerated the development of novel forms of religious self-promotion. Matters came (again) to a head with Sulla. His claim to permanent *felicitas* (he had himself called Sulla *Felix*) was incompatible with fundamental tenets of Rome's civic religion since it signalled a privileged and personal relationship with the gods.[35] His rise to the dictatorship demonstrated for all to see that a darling of the gods did not fit into the political culture of the republic. At the same time, his maverick self-promotion as the recipient of special supernatural support raised the stakes in the game of competitive emulation: any aristocrat who did *not* lay claim to similar privileges would implicitly concede that he was only second best.

By identifying *felicitas* as a crucial quality of the perfect general and ascribing an outstanding degree of divine support to Pompey, Cicero makes a significant concession to the expectation that superior military leadership evinces supernatural qualities and privileges. At the same time, he tries hard to accommodate this idea within republican parameters. The

---

33 Ma (2003) 179, with reference to Price (1984); further Stevenson (1996) on the social ideals that informed the elevation of human beings to divine status, Ma (1999/2002) and Chaniotis (2003).

34 Price (1984) 40-7 surveys the evidence of Greek cults of the goddess Roma and individual Roman officials in the Hellenistic period.

35 Classen (1963) 330. In his autobiography, Sulla suggested that he could sidestep the protocols of Roman *religio*, such as collective negotiation of the meaning of divine signs; statements such as that he liked to converse in private with a *daimon* by night made a mockery of this principle. For Sulla's (religious) self-promotion see e.g. Ramage (1991) and Lewis (1991).

divine favouritism that he claims for Pompey is rather more muted than that on which Hellenistic rulers or, indeed, Sulla insisted (for details, see our commentary on §§ 47-48). Cicero tries his hardest to lay down a *cordon sanitaire* between Pompey on the one hand and the Hellenistic kings and Sulla on the other, as he co-opts the registers of distinction defined by the dictator to authorize and validate Pompey's appointment, while bending over backwards to set him apart as well (for details of his conceptual gymnastics, see our commentary on §§ 47–48). Pompey thus emerges as a 'republican Sulla' as it were, a general with the same *felicitas* but without the penchant for the tyrannical exercise of power.

In Cicero's portrait of the perfect general and his endorsement of Pompey as one such, the most important tic of his rhetoric is the theme of singularity. Pompey, it seems, has outgrown the standard terms of aristocratic competition. He is the unheard-of peak, the new pinnacle, the quintessence of Roman excellence and all the excellences – *summa enim omnia sunt in uno* [*sc. Cn. Pompeio*]: everything desirable is present in this one man, and to the highest degree (cf. § 36)! It thus stands to reason that the Roman people would wish to stake everything (*omnia*) on him alone (*in uno Cn. Pompeio*); others warn that such a move is fraught with risk (see § 59). Both supporters and opponents of the bill were trying to seize upon the essential twinning of the polarity *omnia – in uno*, whether to promote or to demonize it. Cicero, for one, pumps up the volume: in giving shape to this *summus et perfectus imperator* (§ 36), he not only draws on Roman traditions, but brings into play idioms and imagery derived from Hellenistic kingship ideology. The speech advocates a variant of the 'theology of victory' that Eastern potentates promoted, features encomiastic themes reminiscent of Greek treatises 'On Kingship', and may even be alluding to Xenophon's *Cyropaideia*, in many ways the prototype of writings on the good king.[36] At times it sounds like Cicero is speaking at the court of Alexander *the Great*, Pompeius *Magnus*' Greek role model, rather than the Roman forum.[37]

Yet however much he is laying it on with a trowel, there are also protestations of restraint, however feeble, as Cicero tries to drape his *Magnus*,

---

36 See Fears (1981) for the 'composite of themes and ideas' of the Roman 'theology of victory' (797) and its Hellenistic background, Haake (2003) on *peri-basileias* (= 'On Kingship') treatises and Gruber (1988) for the likely influence of Xenophon on Cicero, including an analysis of the differences between the *Cyropaideia* and Hellenistic kingship ideology.

37 For the shadow that Alexander the Great cast over Roman politics see Spencer (2002), including a discussion of Pompey's systematic imitation and emulation of the Macedonian world-conqueror from early on.

Maior, Maximus rhetoric beneath a republican veneer. As Rufus Fears puts it: 'In its structure, language, and content the work is heavily influenced by Hellenistic encomiastic traditions; and the speech may quite properly be used as a primary source for the role and imagery of the theology of victory in Hellenistic panegyric. However, it is also quite clearly a political document, and in it we see the total accommodation of the theology of victory to exigencies of Roman political life.'[38] Or, to rephrase the point more simply: Pompey is no Sulla. Superman will control himself! (Just look at his 'soft virtues', which Cicero parades in §§ 36-43...)

History proves that, with respect to Pompey, Cicero was right. In 61 BC, Pompey returned to Italy and Rome, 'having conquered Mithridates, Syria and Jerusalem, reorganized the provinces, and built up a network of client states between Roman territory and the Parthian Empire. Pompey returned, in other words, from a tour of duty as a Roman Alexander, fighting his way into the territory that was still physically and intellectually dominated by Alexander's campaigns. But he seems to have stopped short of overt royal aspirations, making an effort instead to work within the traditional framework of power.'[39] Upon landing at Brundisium, he dismissed his troops.[40]

In the event, then, Cicero was correct in divining that Pompey would not turn into a second Sulla. In this respect, his calculated risk paid off. At the same time, in the form of the *pro lege Manilia* he imported Greek kingship ideology into Rome. The necessary revisions he undertook to make it more compatible with Roman aristocratic sensibilities resulted in a hybrid idiom of praise in which autocratic and republican elements intermingle. Historical reality caught up with Cicero's 'visionary' rhetoric soon enough. In a sense, the *pro lege Manilia* constitutes the blueprint for royal panegyric in a republican key that would define much of Roman imperial discourse – whether in the form of Cicero's speech *pro Marcello* (delivered in 46 BC), in which he praises the dictator Caesar for his 'self-restrained omnipotence', in Augustus' notion of the *princeps* as a *primus inter pares* ('the first among equals') who rules on the basis of his *auctoritas*, or in Trajan's self-promotion as *civilis princeps* ('an emperor beholden to the

---

38 Fears (1981) 797.
39 Spencer (2002) 19.
40 Matters are of course not so simple; naturally, there was a sequel: see our sketch of Pompey's subsequent career in 'Further Resources'.

principles that defined the political culture of the long-dead republic'), as articulated, above all, in the Cicero update of Pliny's *Panegyricus*.

The set text, then, offers plenty of talking points of abiding interest. Here are some (you will no doubt think of others):

- Spotting spin, not least personal agendas in rhetoric that proclaims exclusive devotion to the common good (an ability that ought to come in especially handy in election years).

- 'Eggs in one basket': how to differentiate forms of power (and its concentration) from republican principles.

- (Rome's) imperial expansion and the chicken coming home to roost.

- The qualities required of an outstanding general and statesman, and the potential desirability that those in command balance strategic with cultural and socio-political intelligence.

- The relationship between statesmen who do things with words and those who do things with swords.

- The longevity of (published) discourse, unintended consequences, and the ironies of history, or: how could the speech of an arch-republican turn into the blueprint for an imperial/autocratic ideology?

In short, the set text offers fraught stuff galore: have fun and mean it!

3. Latin text
with study questions
and vocabulary aid

27: THE ONLY WAY IS POMPEY

Satis mihi multa verba fecisse videor, qua re esset hoc bellum genere ipso necessarium, magnitudine periculosum. Restat ut de imperatore ad id bellum deligendo ac tantis rebus praeficiendo dicendum esse videatur. Utinam, Quirites, virorum fortium atque innocentium copiam tantam haberetis, ut haec vobis deliberatio difficilis esset, quemnam potissimum tantis rebus ac tanto bello praeficiendum putaretis! Nunc vero – cum sit unus Cn. Pompeius, qui non modo eorum hominum qui nunc sunt gloriam, sed etiam antiquitatis memoriam virtute superarit – quae res est quae cuiusquam animum in hac causa dubium facere possit?

Study Questions:

- What type of clause does *qua re* introduce? Why is *esset* in the imperfect subjunctive?
- What kind of ablatives are *genere ipso* and *magnitudine*?
- Which word in the *ut...videatur* clause governs the preposition *de*?
- Explain the constructions of *deligendo, praeficiendo,* and *dicendum esse.*
- What type of clause does *Utinam* introduce?
- Identify and explain the tense and mood of *haberetis.*
- What kind of clause is *ut...difficilis esset*?
- What case are *tantis rebus* and *tanto bello*? How do they fit into the sentence?
- *putaretis* governs an indirect statement: identify the subject accusative and the infinitive.
- What is the position of *unus* in relation to the noun it modifies (*Cn. Pompeius*)?
- On what noun does the genitive phrase *eorum hominum* depend?
- Parse *superarit.*
- What kind of ablative is *virtute*?
- *quae res est quae...*: explain the uses of *quae* (2x).
- Why is *possit* in the subjunctive?
- Why does Cicero consider the kind of war under discussion inevitable (*necessarium*) and its scope perilous (*periculosum*)? (NB: To answer this question you have to read the speech from the beginning.)
- Who are the *Quirites* whom Cicero addresses? What is their role in the political system of late republican Rome?
- In the stretch *ut haec ... putaretis!* a number of alliterations occur: *deliberatio, difficilis; potissimum, praeficiendum, putaretis; tantis, tanto.* What (if anything) do they emphasize?

satis (indeclinable)	enough, sufficient
qua re (also: *quare*)	in what way, why (interrogative or relative adverb)
genus, generis, n.	kind, type
resto, -are, -iti	to remain (to be dealt with)
deligo, -igere, -egi, -ectum	to pick out in preference to the rest, choose
praeficio, -icere, -eci, -ectum	to put in charge (of), set over
utinam (particle, used to reinforce wishes expressed by the subjunctive)	'how I wish that', 'if only'
fortis, -tis, -te	robust, vigorous, brave, resolute
innocens, -ntis	blameless, upright, virtuous; harmless
copia, -ae, f.	plentiful supply, abundance
quisnam, quaenam, quidnam	[*quis* + *nam*] who/what
potissimum (adverb)	especially, above all, preferably
unus, -a, -um	one, a single; (here) only, alone
Cn.	abbreviation of Gnaeus
quisquam, quicquam	any (single) person, anyone (at all)
dubius, -a, -um	uncertain what to do, hesitant

Stylistic Appreciation: Discuss the way in which Cicero positions himself vis-à-vis the audience in this paragraph. You may wish to focus on personal pronouns (*mihi, vobis*), Cicero's use of qualifying words or phrases (*satis, videor, videatur*), his preference for passive or impersonal constructions, as well as rhetorical questions and assertions.

Discussion Point: Cicero argues that the citizens do not really have a choice: there is only one! Is that (ever) true? And do you think that everyone in Cicero's original audience would have agreed? Who might have registered a protest?

28: THE PERFECT GENERAL, POMPEY THE KID, AND MR. EXPERIENCE

Ego enim sic existimo, in summo imperatore quattuor has res inesse oportere: scientiam rei militaris, virtutem, auctoritatem, felicitatem. Quis igitur hoc homine scientior umquam aut fuit aut esse debuit? qui e ludo atque e pueritiae disciplinis, bello maximo atque acerrimis hostibus, ad patris exercitum atque in militiae disciplinam profectus est; qui extrema pueritia miles in exercitu fuit summi imperatoris, ineunte adulescentia maximi ipse exercitus imperator; qui saepius cum hoste conflixit quam quisquam cum inimico concertavit, plura bella gessit quam ceteri legerunt, plures provincias confecit quam alii concupiverunt; cuius adulescentia ad scientiam rei militaris non alienis praeceptis sed suis imperiis, non offensionibus belli sed victoriis, non stipendiis sed triumphis est erudita. Quod denique genus esse belli potest, in quo illum non exercuerit fortuna rei publicae? Civile, Africanum, Transalpinum, Hispaniense, servile, navale bellum, varia et diversa genera et bellorum et hostium, non solum gesta ab hoc uno, sed etiam confecta nullam rem esse declarant in usu positam militari, quae huius viri scientiam fugere possit.

Study Questions:

- What kind of construction does *existimo* govern?
- Explain how *scientiam rei militaris, virtutem, auctoritatem, felicitatem* fit into the syntax of the sentence.
- What kind of ablative is *hoc homine*?
- Explain the construction of *qui* (3x) and *cuius*.
- What kind of ablative is *extrema pueritia*?
- What construction is *ineunte adulescentia*?
- *maximi ipse exercitus imperator*: which words are in the nominative, which in the genitive?
- Parse *saepius*.
- What is the difference between a *hostis* and an *inimicus*?
- What kind of ablative are *alienis praeceptis, suis imperiis, offensionibus, victoriis, stipendiis,* and *triumphis*?
- What is the subject of the relative clause *in quo illum non exercuerit fortuna rei publica*? Discuss its placement in the clause.
- Parse *exercuerit* and explain the mood.
- What are the subjects of *declarant* (the main verb of the last sentence)?
- *declarant* introduces an indirect statement: identify the subject accusative and the infinitive.
- What is the antecedent of the relative pronoun *quae*?
- Parse *possit* and explain the mood.

existimo, -are, -avi, -atum	to think, judge, suppose (that)
quattuor (indeclinable)	four
insum, inesse, infui	to be present (in), be possessed (by)
oportet, -êre, -uit	it is proper, right, requisite; it is demanded
scientia, ae f.	knowledge
virtus, -utis, f.	the quality typical of a true man; excellence, ability; moral excellence, virtue
auctoritas, -atis, f.	commanding influence, authority, prestige
felicitas, -atis, f.	good fortune (as a result of divine favour)
igitur	in that case, then
debeo, -êre, -ui, -itum	to be under an obligation; should, ought
sciens, -ntis	aware, conscious, knowledgeable
ludus, -i, m.	sport, play, game; place of instruction
pueritia, -ae, f.	childhood, boyhood
disciplina, -ae, f.	teaching, instruction, training
militia, ae, f.	military service; warfare
proficiscor, -ci, profectus sum	to set out, leave, depart (from... to...)
extremus, -a, -um	situated at the edge; end of
ineo, -ire, -ii/ivi, -itum	to come in, enter upon, begin
adulescentia, -ae, f.	(young) adulthood
confligo, -gere, -xi, -ctum	to collide, clash; do battle, fight; argue
concerto, -are, -avi, -atum	to contend, fight, vie with; argue, dispute
lego, -ere, legi, lectum	to pick out; to read
provincia, -ae, f.	1. special function/task assigned to a magistrate
	2. a provincial command
	3. a territory outside Italy under direct Roman control, a province
conficio, -icere, -eci, -ectum	to do, perform; make; produce, cause; finish off, complete; overwhelm, undo
concupisco, -iscere, -ivi/ii, -itum	to conceive a strong desire for, covet
alienus, -a, -um	not one's own; of/belonging to others
praeceptum, -i, n. (from *praecipio*)	a piece of advice, teaching; instruction
imperium, -i, n.	the right of command invested in Roman high office
offensio, -onis, f.	the action of striking against; setback, mishap; affront, outrage
stipendium, -ii, n.	a cash payment, esp. to soldiers; a year or season of military service, campaign
erudio, -ire, -ivi/ii, -itum	to instruct, train, educate (*ad*: in)
exerceo, -ere, -ui, -itum	to train by practice, exercise; occupy
fortuna, -ae, f.	good *or* bad fortune; vicissitudes
Fortuna, -ae, f.	the goddess Fortune

Transalpinus, -a, -um	situated in the region beyond the Alps [from the point of view of Rome]
Hispaniensis, -is, -e	of or concerning Spain and its people
servilis, -is, -e	of, belonging to, involving slaves
usus, -us, m.	application, use; practical experience
in usu	in one's experience
in usu poni/esse	to be in common use
fugio, fugere, fugi	to run away, flee from, escape

Stylistic Appreciation: What are the rhetorical devices Cicero uses to convey a sense of Pompey's comprehensive knowledge of military matters?

Discussion Point: Consider the four qualities that Cicero views as essential attributes of the perfect general: *scientia rei militaris, virtus, auctoritas, felicitas*. Are they still relevant qualities for military commanders today? Which qualities would *your* perfect general have?

Fig. 2 *Roman statue of Pompey,* in Villa Arconati a Castellazzo di Bollate (Milan).
Photograph by Guido Bertolotti, 2007. Image from Wikimedia.
http://commons.wikimedia.org/wiki/File:PompeoMagno.jpg

29: HIS EXCELLENCE (AND EXCELLENCES)

Iam vero virtuti Cn. Pompei quae potest oratio par inveniri? Quid est quod quisquam aut illo dignum aut vobis novum aut cuiquam inauditum possit adferre? Neque enim illae sunt solae virtutes imperatoriae, quae vulgo existimantur, labor in negotiis, fortitudo in periculis, industria in agendo, celeritas in conficiendo, consilium in providendo; quae tanta sunt in hoc uno, quanta in omnibus reliquis imperatoribus, quos aut vidimus aut audivimus, non fuerunt.

Study Questions:

- How does the dative *virtuti* fit into the sentence?
- What is the subject of the opening question?
- Identify and explain the mood of *possit*.
- Discuss Cicero's manipulation of the term '*virtus*' in this paragraph, starting with the switch from singular (*virtuti*) to plural (*virtutes*).
- Parse *quae* in the sentence *quae tanta sunt in hoc uno...* What is its antecedent?
- Cicero here lists those qualities of a general that are commonly thought of as such, but also claims that there are others: what are they? And how do they compare to *labor in negotiis, fortitudo in periculis, industria in agendo, celeritas in conficiendo*, and *consilium in providendo*?
- Why does Cicero distinguish between *imperatores* he and his audience have seen (*vidimus*) and those they have only heard of (*audivimus*)? Comment on the use of the first person plural verbs (*vidimus, audivimus*).

Stylistic Appreciation: What are the lexical and rhetorical devices Cicero uses in this paragraph to elevate Pompey's claim to *virtus* above that of everyone else?

Discussion Point:

- *vir-tus* is related to *vir* ('man'): its basic meaning is 'manliness'. What did manliness comprise in late republican Rome? What does 'being a man' mean in 21st century Britain? What are the similarities, what the differences?

- Do you have to be a man to exhibit *virtus*?

iam	at this point, now - in a transition to a new topic
(often strengthened by *vero*):	further, besides
par, paris	matching, equal
+ dative	measuring up to, equal to, adequate
invenio, -enire, -eni, -entum	to encounter, come upon; discover, learn; to devise
inauditus, -a, -um	unheard (of)
adfero, -rre, attuli, allatum	to bring, fetch; adduce, relate
imperatorius, -a, -um	of or belonging to a commanding officer
vulgo (adv.)	in a way common to all, publicly, commonly
existimo, -are, -avi, -atum	to form or hold an opinion of, judge; to think, suppose (that)
negotium, -(i)i, n.	work, business; (pl.) public affairs
industria, -ae, f.	diligence, application, industry
provideo, -idere, -idi, -isum	to see in advance, see beforehand, to exercise forethought

30: WITNESSES TO THE TRUTH!

Testis est Italia, quam ille ipse victor L. Sulla huius virtute et subsidio confessus est liberatam. Testis est Sicilia, quam multis undique cinctam periculis non terrore belli, sed consilii celeritate explicavit. Testis est Africa, quae magnis oppressa hostium copiis eorum ipsorum sanguine redundavit. Testis est Gallia, per quam legionibus nostris iter in Hispaniam Gallorum internecione patefactum est. Testis est Hispania, quae saepissime plurimos hostes ab hoc superatos prostratosque conspexit. Testis est iterum et saepius Italia, quae cum servili bello taetro periculosoque premeretur, ab hoc auxilium absente expetivit, quod bellum exspectatione eius attenuatum atque imminutum est, adventu sublatum ac sepultum.

Study Questions:

- Identify the subject accusative and the infinitive of the indirect statement introduced by *confessus est*.
- What noun does *multis* agree with? What noun does *magnis* agree with? What is the rhetorical effect of the placement of *multis* and *magnis* in their respective clauses?
- What kind of ablative are *terrore* and *celeritate*?
- On what noun does *eorum ipsorum* depend? And what noun does it refer back to?
- What is the subject of the relative clause *per quam legionibus nostris iter in Hispaniam Gallorum internecione patefactum est*?
- Identify and explain the case of *legionibus nostris*.
- What kind of genitive is *Gallorum*? What noun does it depend on?
- What kind of ablative is *ab hoc*?
- Parse *saepius*.
- In the sentence *quae cum servili bello taetro periculosoque premeretur, ab hoc auxilium absente expetivit*, is the *cum* a preposition or a conjunction?
- Explain the construction of *quod* (in the last sentence of the paragraph).
- Consider the references to 'blood' and 'slaughter' in this paragraph and sketch out the vision of Roman geopolitics that Cicero endorses here.
- Is there a logic to the sequence in which Cicero calls up his geographical witnesses?

Stylistic Appreciation: What rhetorical effect does the repetition of *Testis est...* at the beginning of each sentence create?

Discussion Point: Does it matter that some of the wars to which Cicero here alludes were civil wars? Which ones are they? *How* does he allude to them?

subsidium, -(i)i, n.	reinforcement, support; assistance, help
confiteor, -fiteri, -fessus sum	to admit, confess
undique (adverb)	from all sides or directions
cingo, -gere, -xi, -ctum	to surround, encircle
explico, -are, -avi/-ui, -atum/-itum	to free from, extricate
opprimo, -imere, -essi, -essum	to press on/against, smother, overpower, crush
redundo, -are, -avi, -atum	[*re-* + *undo*] to overflow, pour out
iter, itineris, n.	path, road; journey
internecio, -onis, f.	total destruction of life, massacre
patefacio, -facere, -feci, -factum	to make visible, reveal; to open, make accessible
prosterno, -ernere, -ravi, -ratum	to lay low, strike down, defeat utterly
conspicio, -icere, -exi, -ectum	to catch sight of, see, witness, discern
taeter, -tra, -trum	foul, horrible; morally offensive, vile
expeto, -ere, -ivi/-ii, -itum	to ask for, request, beg; seek after, try to obtain
exspectatio, -onis, f.	the state of waiting in suspense; expectation
attenuo, -are, -avi, -atum	to make thin/slender, weaken, reduce
imminuo, -uere, -ui, -utum	to reduce in amount or size, diminish
adventus, -us, m.	arrival
tollo, -ere, sustuli, sublatum	to raise, lift; remove, take away, get rid of
sepelio, -elire, -elivi/-elii, -ultum	to bury; submerge, overcome

31: PACIFYING THE POND, OR: POMPEY AND THE PIRATES

Testes nunc vero iam omnes orae atque omnes exterae gentes ac nationes, denique maria omnia, cum universa, tum in singulis oris omnes sinus atque portus. quis enim toto mari locus per hos annos aut tam firmum habuit praesidium, ut tutus esset, aut tam fuit abditus, ut lateret? quis navigavit, qui non se aut mortis aut servitutis periculo committeret, cum aut hieme aut referto praedonum mari navigaret? hoc tantum bellum, tam turpe, tam vetus, tam late divisum atque dispersum quis umquam arbitraretur aut ab omnibus imperatoribus uno anno aut omnibus annis ab uno imperatore confici posse?

Study Questions:

- Identify all words in the nominative in the opening sentence (*testes nunc vero iam ... atque portus*). What is the verb of the sentence?
- Explain the case of *toto mari*.
- What kind of *ut*-clauses are *ut tutus esset* and *ut lateret*?
- Compare and contrast the *quis* that introduces the second sentence (*quis enim toto maris locus...*) with the *quis* that introduces the third sentence (*quis navigavit...*): what is the difference?
- Explain the tense and mood of *committeret*.
- What kind of ablative is *hieme*?
- What kind of ablative is *referto ... mari*?
- Parse *praedonum*.
- What are the subject and the verb of the last sentence (*hoc tantum bellum ... confici posse*)? What is the rhetorical effect of their placement?
- Explain the tense and mood of *arbitraretur*.
- Identify the subject accusative and the verb of the indirect statement introduced by *arbitraretur*.
- What kind of ablative are *ab omnibus imperatoribus* and *ab uno imperatore*?
- What kind of ablative are *uno anno* and *omnibus annis*?
- Parse *confici* and explain its function in the sentence.
- In the opening sentence Cicero sketches a notional map of the entire Mediterranean coastline: how much of it was under Roman control at the time of his speech?
- What does the clause *cum aut hieme aut referto praedonum mari navigaret* tell us about ancient sea-faring?
- How and why does the accusative object of the final sentence (*hoc tantum bellum, tam turpe, tam vetus, tam late divisum atque dispersum*) rhetorically mirror the subject of the first sentence (*testes nunc vero iam omnes orae atque omnes exterae gentes ac nationes, denique maria omnia, cum universa, tum ... omnes sinus atque portus*)?
- Identify and appreciate the magnificent chiasmus in the final sentence.

vero	moreover, indeed
nunc	(here introducing the final, climactic item in Cicero's list of witnesses:) as it is
ora, -ae, f.	coast
exter, -era, -erum	foreign
gens, -tis, f.	nation, people, ethnicity; a (Roman) clan
natio, -onis, f.	people, nation, ethnicity
denique	finally, at last
mare, -ris, (ablative: *mari*), n.	the sea
cum... tum...	(correlating two circumstances, with *tum* indicating the more noteworthy one) both... and..., as well as
universus, -a, -um	the whole of, entire
singuli, -ae, -a (plural)	each one of, every single
praesidium, -(i)i, n.	defence, protection, stronghold
abditus, -a, -um	hidden from sight, concealed; remote, secluded
lateo, -ere, -ui	to hide, be concealed, escape notice
committo, -ittere, -isi, -issum	to bring into contact with; expose to
hiems, -mis, f.	winter; winter weather; storm
refertus, -a, -um (here + genitive)	crammed or stuffed full of
praedo, -onis, m.	pirate
turpis, -is, -e	offensive, disgusting, shameful, disgraceful
vetus, -eris	old, veteran, long-standing, chronic
late (adverb)	over a large area, widely
divido, -idere, -isi, -isum	to separate, divide, distribute
dispergo, -gere, -si, -sum	to spread about, scatter, disperse
conficio, -icere, -eci, -ectum	to do, perform, accomplish; bring to completion

Stylistic Appreciation: Analyse the rhetorical design of the first sentence (*Testis est ... sinus atque portus*): how does its form reinforce its theme?

Discussion Point: What does the claim 'Pompey brought the war against the pirates to an end' imply? How did he do it?

32: THE PIRATES OF THE MEDITERRANEAN

Quam provinciam tenuistis a praedonibus liberam per hosce annos? quod vectigal vobis tutum fuit? quem socium defendistis? cui praesidio classibus vestris fuistis? quam multas existimatis insulas esse desertas, quam multas aut metu relictas aut a praedonibus captas urbes esse sociorum? Sed quid ego longinqua commemoro? Fuit hoc quondam, fuit proprium populi Romani, longe a domo bellare, et propugnaculis imperii sociorum fortunas, non sua tecta defendere. Sociis ego nostris mare per hos annos clausum fuisse dicam, cum exercitus vestri numquam Brundisio nisi hieme summa transmiserint? Qui ad vos ab exteris nationibus venirent captos querar, cum legati populi Romani redempti sint? Mercatoribus tutum mare non fuisse dicam, cum duodecim secures in praedonum potestatem pervenerint?

Study Questions:

- Explain the syntax of *liberam*.
- What kind of dative is *vobis*?
- What kind of dative is *cui*?
- What kind of dative is *praesidio*?
- Identify and explain the case of *classibus vestris*.
- Explain the difference between the *quam* in *quam provinciam* and the *quam* in *quam multas*.
- Identify the components of the indirect statement introduced by *existimatis*.
- What kind of ablative is *metu*?
- Parse *longinqua*.
- What kind of ablative is *propugnaculis*?
- Identify and explain the case of *sociis ... nostris*.
- What kind of ablative is *Brundisio*?
- What kind of ablative is *hieme summa*?
- Why is *venirent* in the imperfect subjunctive?
- What is the subject accusative and the infinitive of the indirect statement introduced by *querar*?
- *legati populi Romani*: which noun is in the nominative plural, which in the genitive singular?
- Try to imagine what an *urbs capta* entails.
- Explore the ways in which Cicero plays with 'centre' (Rome) and 'periphery' in this paragraph.
- What does Cicero mean when he says that 'twelve axes' (*duodecim secures*) fell into the hands of the pirates?
- With reference to phrases that refer to aggressive or defensive military measures, try to describe the picture of Rome's imperial presence in the Mediterranean that Cicero is painting here.

vectigal, -alis, n.	revenue
tutus, -a, -um	safe, secure, protected from danger
praesidium, -(i)i, n.	defence, protection
classis, -is, f.	a naval force, fleet; a class or grade
metus, -us, m. (f.)	fear, alarm, apprehension
longinquus, -a, -um	situated at a distance, far-off, remote
commemoro, -are, -avi, -atum	to recall, mention, relate
quondam (adv.)	formerly, in ancient days; some day
proprius, -a, -um	one's own, personal, peculiar to, special
bello, -are, -avi, -atum	to wage war, fight
propugnaculum, -i, n.	a bulwark, rampart, defence
fortuna, -ae, f.	fortune, chance, prosperity
in plural:	wealth, property
tectum, -i, n.	roof; house, dwelling
claudo, -dere, -si, -sum	to close, shut; blockade
legatus, -i, m.	an ambassador, envoy; legate
redimo, -imere, -emi, -emptum	to buy back, ransom, rescue
mercator, -oris, m.	merchant, trader
duodecim (indeclinable)	twelve
securis, -is, f.	an axe
pervenio, -enire, -eni, -entum	to come to, arrive at, to pass into the hands of, to come under the control of

Stylistic Appreciation: The paragraph contains nine rhetorical questions. Can you identify sets and patterns?

Discussion Point: How would you define the way in which Cicero interacts with his audience in this paragraph?

33: PIRATES *ANTE PORTAS*!

Cnidum aut Colophonem aut Samum, nobilissimas urbes, innumerabilesque alias captas esse commemorem, cum vestros portus atque eos portus, quibus vitam et spiritum ducitis, in praedonum fuisse potestate sciatis? An vero ignoratis portum Caietae celeberrimum ac plenissimum navium inspectante praetore a praedonibus esse direptum? ex Miseno autem eius ipsius liberos, qui cum praedonibus antea bellum gesserat, a praedonibus esse sublatos? Nam quid ego Ostiense incommodum atque illam labem atque ignominiam rei publicae querar, cum prope inspectantibus vobis classis ea, cui consul populi Romani praepositus esset, a praedonibus capta atque oppressa est? Pro di immortales! tantamne unius hominis incredibilis ac divina virtus tam brevi tempore lucem adferre rei publicae potuit, ut vos, qui modo ante ostium Tiberinum classem hostium videbatis, nunc nullam intra Oceani ostium praedonum navem esse audiatis?

Study Questions:

- Identify and explain the mood of *commemorem*.
- Identify the subject accusatives and the infinitives of the indirect statements introduced by *commemorem, sciatis,* and *ignoratis*.
- What does Cicero mean by *vitam et spiritum*?
- What construction are *inspectante praetore* and *inspectantibus vobis*?
- Look at the verbs *captas esse, esse direptum, esse sublatos, capta* (sc. *est*), *oppressa est*. What do you notice about their voice? Is there a rationale for Cicero's 'choice of voice' here? How does it change after *pro di immortales!*?
- *cui consul…praepositus est*: what case is *cui* and why? What is the antecedent?
- Does Cicero choose his moment for the exclamation *pro di immortales* well?
- What noun does *tantam(ne)* agree with? What is the rhetorical effect of its placement in the sentence?
- Explore the tension between 'mortal' and 'immortal' in the phrase *unius hominis incredibilis ac divina virtus*.
- What is the rhetorical effect of Cicero's relentless references to pirates in this paragraph (*in praedonum ... potestate; a praedonibus; cum praedonibus; a praedonibus; a praedonibus; nullam ... praedonum navem*)?
- Discuss Cicero's reference to seeing and spectatorship in this paragraph.
- Can you place the locations Cicero mentions here (Cnidus, Colophon, Samos, Caieta, Misenum, Ostia, the straits of Gibraltar) on a map? Is there a logic to the order in which they occur?

Cnidus, -i, m.	Cnidus (a town in the extreme South-West of Caria)
Colophon, -onis, m.	Colophon (a city in Ionia)
Samos, -i, f.	Samos (an island off the coast of Asia Minor)
- acc. *-um* or *-on*	
spiritus, -us, m.	the action of breathing, respiration; breath (of life)
scio, -ire, -ii/-ivi, -itum	to know, be aware of
ignoro, -are, -avi, -atum	to have no knowledge of, be ignorant of
celeber, -bris, -bre	much used, busy, frequented; famed, celebrated, distinguished
inspecto, -are, -avi, -atum	to look at, watch, observe; look on
diripio, -ipere, -ipui, -eptum	to pull to pieces, tear to shreds to seize as plunder, loot
liberi, -um (or *-orum*), m. pl.	sons and daughters, children
tollo, -ere, sustuli, sublatum	to pick up, take away, remove, carry off
Ostiensis, -is, -e	of or belonging to Ostia
incommodum, -i, n.	detriment, harm, disadvantage; misfortune, trouble, set-back
labes, -is, f.	disaster, defect; stain upon honour or reputation, disgrace
ignominia, -ae, f.	disgrace
queror, -ri, -stus	to regret, complain, grumble, protest
prope	in close proximity, near by; (modifying a hyperbole): almost, pretty well
praepono, -onere, -osui, -ositum	to place in front; to put in charge of
modo (adverb)	only recently
ostium, -(i)i, n.	a door, aperture, opening; mouth
- *ostium Oceani*	the strait of Gibraltar

Stylistic Appreciation: How does Cicero maintain the supernatural colouring he introduces in his discourse with the exclamation *pro di immortales!* in the subsequent sentence?

Discussion Point: Why does Cicero refer to the pirates' attack on Ostia as a national disgrace? What qualifies as a 'national disgrace' nowadays?

34: POMPEY'S CRUISE CONTROL (I): 'I HAVE A FLEET – AND NEED FOR SPEED'

Atque haec qua celeritate gesta sint, quamquam videtis, tamen a me in dicendo praetereunda non sunt. Quis enim umquam aut obeundi negotii aut consequendi quaestus studio tam brevi tempore tot loca adire, tantos cursus conficere potuit, quam celeriter Cn. Pompeio duce tanti belli impetus navigavit? qui nondum tempestivo ad navigandum mari Siciliam adiit, Africam exploravit, in Sardiniam cum classe venit, atque haec tria frumentaria subsidia rei publicae firmissimis praesidiis classibusque munivit.

Study Questions:

- What kind of clause does *qua* introduce?
- What kind of ablative is *a me*? What is unusual about it?
- Explain the construction *Cn. Pompeio duce*.
- Explain the syntax of *qui* (in *qui nondum...*).
- Explain the syntax of *navigandum*.
- For most nouns in the fourth declension, the nominative singular, the genitive singular, the nominative plural, and the accusative plural all end in -*us*. Can you identify the three fourth-declension nouns in the paragraph and their respective cases? (One is in the nominative singular, one in the genitive singular, one in the accusative plural.)

Stylistic Appreciation: How does Cicero convey Pompey's extraordinary speed of operation in his prose?

Discussion Point: What according to Cicero are Pompey's priorities?

gero, -rere, -ssi, -stum	to bear, carry, perform, do
praetereo, -ire, -ii/-ivi, -itum	to pass by, go past; omit, pass over
obeo, -ire, -ivi/-ii, -itum	to meet with, visit; to attend
consequor, -qui, -cutus	to come after, follow; pursue; reach, achieve
quaestus, -us, m.	the acquisition of income, production of profit
studium, - (i)i, n.	zeal, enthusiasm, eagerness; pursuit
impetus, -us, m.	force, impetus; charge, assault; vigorous effort
tempestivus, -a, -um	seasonable; ready; suitable, opportune
frumentarius, -a, -um	of or concerned with corn; corn-
subsidium, -(i)i, n.	reserves; a supply kept in reserve
munio, -ire, -ivi/-ii, -itum	to fortify, guard from attack, safeguard

35: POMPEY'S CRUISE CONTROL (II): 'I HAVE A FLEET – AND NEED FOR SPEED'

Inde cum se in Italiam recepisset, duabus Hispaniis et Gallia Transalpina praesidiis ac navibus confirmata, missis item in oram Illyrici maris et in Achaiam omnemque Graeciam navibus Italiae duo maria maximis classibus firmissimisque praesidiis adornavit, ipse autem, ut Brundisio profectus est, undequinquagesimo die totam ad imperium populi Romani Ciliciam adiunxit: omnes, qui ubique praedones fuerunt, partim capti interfectique sunt, partim unius huius se imperio ac potestati dediderunt. Idem Cretensibus, cum ad eum usque in Pamphyliam legatos deprecatoresque misissent, spem deditionis non ademit obsidesque imperavit. Ita tantum bellum, tam diuturnum, tam longe lateque dispersum, quo bello omnes gentes ac nationes premebantur, Cn. Pompeius extrema hieme apparavit, ineunte vere suscepit, media aestate confecit.

Study Questions:

- Identify the various clauses and constructions that make up the first long sentence (*Inde cum ... Ciliciam adiunxit*): what are the subjects, what the main verbs? How are they linked? How many ablative absolutes can you spot? How many subordinate clauses can you bracket off?
- Identify and explain the case of *Brundisio*.
- Can you explain how the Romans hit upon the verbal monstrosity *undequinquagesimus, -a, -um* to express '49th'?
- Parse *dediderunt* and identify its accusative object.
- Parse *idem*.
- Explain the construction *obsides imperavit*. What other constructions does the verb *impero, imperare* govern?
- Analyse the rhetorical design of *Cn. Pompeius extrema hieme apparavit, ineunte vere suscepit, media aestate confecit.*
- What kinds of ablative are *extrema hieme, ineunte vere, media aestate*?
- Cicero continues with his geopolitical discourse: can you place all the locations he mentions (including Illyria, Cilicia, and Pamphylia) on a map?

Stylistic Appreciation: This is the last of several paragraphs that Cicero devotes to Pompey's campaign against the pirates. What are the rhetorical means by which he generates a sense of closure?

Discussion Point: Why did the Cretans prefer to surrender to Pompey, who was far away in Pamphylia, rather than to another Roman general in their vicinity?

inde (adverb)	from that place, thence, from there
recipio, -ipere, -epi, -eptum	to admit, receive, acquire, accept
se recipere	to turn back, withdraw, retire; return, get back
item (adverb)	similarly, likewise
adorno, -are, -avi, -atum	to get ready, prepare; equip, furnish; adorn
proficiscor, -icisci, -ectus	to set out, depart
undequinquagesimus, -a, -um	forty-ninth
adiungo, -gere, -xi, -ctum (here with *ad*)	to connect, link, attach; annex, acquire
ubique (adverb)	in any place whatever, anywhere; everywhere
partim (adverb)	partly
interficio, -ficere, -feci, -fectum	to kill, destroy
dedo, -ere, -idi, -itum (reflexive)	to give (oneself) up, surrender
legatus, -i, m.	an ambassador, envoy, delegate; legate
deprecator, -oris, m.	one who pleads for clemency, intercessor
usque (adverb)	all the way to, as far as (with *ad* or *in* + acc.)
deditio, -onis, f.	surrender
adimo, -imere, -emi, -emptum	to remove, take away, deny, preclude
obses, -idis, m./(f.)	hostage; surety, pledge, guarantee
apparo, -are, -avi, -atum	to prepare, make ready, organize
ver, -ris, n.	spring

36: 'THOU ART MORE LOVELY AND MORE TEMPERATE': POMPEY'S SOFT SIDES

Est haec divina atque incredibilis virtus imperatoris: quid? ceterae, quas paulo ante commemorare coeperam, quantae atque quam multae sunt! Non enim bellandi virtus solum in summo ac perfecto imperatore quaerenda est, sed multae sunt artes eximiae huius administrae comitesque virtutis. Ac primum quanta innocentia debent esse imperatores! quanta deinde in omnibus rebus temperantia! quanta fide, quanta facilitate, quanto ingenio, quanta humanitate! quae breviter qualia sint in Cn. Pompeio consideremus: summa enim omnia sunt, Quirites, sed ea magis ex aliorum contentione quam ipsa per sese cognosci atque intellegi possunt.

Study Questions:

- What noun has to be supplied with *ceterae*?
- Identify and explain the case of *paulo*.
- In the sentence *multae sunt artes eximiae huius administrae comitesque virtutis*, which words are in the nominative plural, which in the genitive singular?
- What kind of ablative are *innocentia, temperantia, fide, facilitate, ingenio* and *humanitate*?
- What effect does the repetition of *quanta* generate?
- Why is the verb of the *qualia*-clause (*sint*) in the subjunctive?
- Identify and explain the mood of *consideremus*.
- Parse *cognosci* and *intellegi*.

Stylistic Appreciation: Cicero has reached a pivotal moment in his argument: after discussion of Pompey's prowess as military leader, he now focuses on his personal qualities more broadly. Discuss the stylistic devices he uses to emphasize their importance.

Discussion Point: Can you find contemporary parallels for Cicero's claim that good military leaders ought to possess 'soft qualities' of the kind he discusses here, to complement strategic or martial excellence?

paulum, -i, n.	a small amount, little, a little bit
ars, -tis, f.	skill, craftsmanship;
	personal characteristic, quality
	a systematic body of knowledge
eximius, -a, -um	outstanding, exceptional; special, distinct
administra, -ae, f.	a (female) assistant, 'hand-maiden'
comes, -itis, m./f.	companion, partner, associate
innocentia, -ae, f.	freedom from guilt, innocence;
	uprightness, integrity
temperantia, -ae, f.	self-control, moderation, restraint
fides, -ei, f.	trust, guarantee, promise, assurance;
	good faith, honesty, honour;
	trustworthiness, reliability
facilitas, -atis, f.	facility, ease; good nature, indulgence
ingenium, -(i)i, n.	natural disposition, natural abilities, talent
humanitas, -atis, f.	human nature; humane character, kindness
qualis, -is, -e (interrogative)	of what kind or quality
contentio, -onis, f.	exercise, effort; contention, competition;
	contrast, comparison

37: SPQR CONFIDENTIAL

Quem enim imperatorem possumus ullo in numero putare, cuius in exercitu centuriatus veneant atque venierint? quid hunc hominem magnum aut amplum de re publica cogitare, qui pecuniam ex aerario depromptam ad bellum administrandum aut propter cupiditatem provinciae magistratibus diviserit aut propter avaritiam Romae in quaestu reliquerit? Vestra admurmuratio facit, Quirites, ut agnoscere videamini, qui haec fecerint: ego autem nomino neminem; quare irasci mihi nemo poterit, nisi qui ante de se voluerit confiteri. Itaque propter hanc avaritiam imperatorum quantas calamitates, quocumque ventum est, nostri exercitus ferant, quis ignorat?

Study Questions:

- Parse *centuriatus*.
- Identify and explain the mood of *veneant atque venierint*.
- What is the main verb of the sentence *quid hunc hominem magnum aut amplum de re publica cogitare...*? (NB: it needs to be supplied from the previous sentence.) What construction does it govern?
- Identify and explain the mood of *diviserit* and *reliquerit*.
- What case is *Romae*?
- Parse, and explain the syntax of, *videamini*.
- Parse *voluerit*.
- What weirdo form is *ventum est*?
- Identify and explain the mood of *ferant*.
- *Vestra admurmuratio*: how do you explain Cicero's reference to unrest in the audience? Did he anticipate this murmur of outraged assent when drafting the speech? Did he add this bit after delivery, before disseminating the speech in writing – and how can we be sure that the *admurmuratio* actually happened? What is the effect of having a gesture to the original performance-context in the written version of the speech?
- Can you think of contemporary figures that (don't) live up to Cicero's injunction that public officials ought to *magnum et amplum de re publica cogitare*?

Stylistic Appreciation: How does Cicero generate an atmosphere of outraged collusion with his audience?

Discussion Point: What are the mechanisms by which ancient and modern governments ensure the proper use of public funds by elected officials? What laws against bribery and embezzlement existed in ancient Rome – as compared to contemporary Britain?

ullo in numero	of any account/in any esteem
centuriatus, -us, m.	the office of centurion
veneo, -ire, -ii (-itum)	[used as passive of *vendo*:] to be sold

Not to be confused with:

venio, venire, veni, ventum	to come
amplus, -a, -um	great, wide, spacious; glorious, magnificent
aerarium, -i, n.	(Rome's) public treasury
depromo, -ere, -prompsi, -promptum	to draw out/forth, fetch
divido, -ere, -visi, -visum	to separate, divide; distribute, apportion
quaestus, -us, m.	acquisition, profit, advantage
- pecuniam in quaestu relinquere	to let out money at interest
admurmuratio, -onis, f.	a murmuring, murmur (here: of disapproval)
agnosco, -noscere, -novi, -notum	to know well; declare, announce; recognize
nomino, -are, -avi, -atum	to call by name, name; mention, accuse
irascor, irasci, iratus	to be angry (at) (most frequently, as here, with dative)
confiteor, confiteri, confessus	to acknowledge, confess, avow

38: OF LOCUSTS AND LEECHES

Itinera, quae per hosce annos in Italia per agros atque oppida civium Romanorum nostri imperatores fecerint, recordamini: tum facilius statuetis, quid apud exteras nationes fieri existimetis. Utrum plures arbitramini per hosce annos militum vestrorum armis hostium urbes an hibernis sociorum civitates esse deletas? Neque enim potest exercitum is continere imperator, qui se ipse non continet, neque severus esse in iudicando, qui alios in se severos esse iudices non vult.

Study Questions:

- What kind of clause does *quae* introduce?
- Parse *recordamini* and *arbitramini*.
- Parse *facilius*.
- Identify and explain the tenses and moods (plural!) of *statuetis* and *existimetis*.
- What nouns (plural!) does *plures* agree with?
- What do you call the stylistic device on display in *in iudicando ... iudices*?
- Why could hosting a Roman winter-quarter prove so disastrous for allied communities? (Compare and contrast with modern-day protests by local communities *against* the closure of military bases in their region.)
- What is the timeframe of *per hosce annos*?

Stylistic Appreciation: In the *utrum... an...* clause, how do the elements in the *utrum*-part match up with the elements in the *an*-part?

Discussion Point: How does Cicero construe the relationship between 'army' and 'general' in this paragraph?

iter, itineris, n.	journey, march
-ce (*hosce*)	a deictic particle, usually 'enclitic'[1]
recordor, -ari, -atus	to think over, be mindful of, recollect
statuo, -uere, -ui, -utum	to place, fix, stand; to establish, decide, uphold
exter, extera, exterum	outside, external, foreign
existimo, -are, -avi, -atum	to value, esteem; form an opinion, judge; think
utrum... an...	(introducing a disjunctive question, the second alternative introduced by *an*): whether... or...
hiberna, -orum, n. pl.	winter encampment, winter quarters
contineo, -inere, -inui, -entum	to hold together, link, connect; keep within; to keep under control

---

1   'enclitic' is a linguistic term deriving from the Greek *enklinein* = 'to le⌐ on'; it is a word that does not stand on its own so gets attached to ('leans on') the preceding one.

39: POMPEY THE PEACEFUL, OR: IMPERIALISM WITH GLOVES

Hic miramur hunc hominem tantum excellere ceteris, cuius legiones sic in Asiam pervenerint, ut non modo manus tanti exercitus, sed ne vestigium quidem cuiquam pacato nocuisse dicatur? Iam vero quem ad modum milites hibernent cotidie sermones ac litterae perferuntur. Non modo ut sumptum faciat in militem nemini vis adfertur, sed ne cupienti quidem cuiquam permittitur. Hiemis enim, non avaritiae perfugium maiores nostri in sociorum atque amicorum tectis esse voluerunt.

Study Questions:

- What is *hic*? (Hint: it's *not* the demonstrative pronoun.)
- What case, number and gender is *cuius*? To whom does it refer?
- Identify and explain the mood of *pervenerint*.
- What declension (and what gender) are *manus* and *exercitus*? What case is *manus* in, what case *exercitus*?
- What type of clause does *ut* introduce?
- What construction does *dicatur* govern?
- What kind of clause is *quem ad modum milites hibernent*?
- Both *hiemis* and *avaritiae* are genitives dependent on *refugium*: but what type of genitive is *hiemis*, what type *avaritiae*?
- How many indirect statements can you find in this section? Can you identify the verbs introducing them, and find their subject accusatives?

Stylistic Appreciation: What are the rhetorical devices Cicero uses to emphasise the good behaviour of Pompey's forces in Asia?

Discussion Point: Cicero ends this section by invoking the normative force of the ancestors. Are 'older generations' by definition ethically superior – in ancient Rome and elsewhere in history?

miror, -ari, -atus	to be surprised, amazed, bewildered; marvel
manus, -us, f.	hand; *in the plural:* band, troop
ne... quidem	not even [negating the enclosed word]
vestigium, -(i)i, n.	footprint, track
pacatus, -a, -um	tranquil, peaceable, disposed to peace
paco, -are, -avi, -atum	to impose a settlement on, bring under control, subdue
noceo, -ere, -ui, -itum	(regularly with dative): to harm, injure
iam vero	further, now, besides
quem ad modum/quemadmodum	(interrogative) in what way? how? (relative) in the manner in which
hiberno, -are, -avi, -atum	to spend the winter (esp. of troops)
cotidie (adverb)	every day, daily
sermo, -onis, m.	speech, talk; conversation, dialogue; gossip
litterae, -arum, f.	letters
perfero, -rre, pertuli, perlatum	to carry/convey to, deliver; tolerate, endure
sumptus, -us, m.	expenditure, outlay, expense
- sumptum facere	to expend money
hiems/hiemps, -mis, f.	winter
avaritia, ae, f.	greed, avarice, rapacity
perfugium, -(i)i, n.	a place of refuge, shelter
tectum, -i, n.	roof, ceiling; house, dwelling

40: NO SIGHT-SEEING OR SOUVENIRS FOR THE PERFECT GENERAL

Age vero ceteris in rebus qua ille sit temperantia, considerate. Unde illam tantam celeritatem et tam incredibilem cursum inventum putatis? Non enim illum eximia vis remigum aut ars inaudita quaedam gubernandi aut venti aliqui novi tam celeriter in ultimas terras pertulerunt, sed eae res, quae ceteros remorari solent, non retardarunt: non avaritia ab instituto cursu ad praedam aliquam devocavit, non libido ad voluptatem, non amoenitas ad delectationem, non nobilitas urbis ad cognitionem, non denique labor ipse ad quietem; postremo signa et tabulas ceteraque ornamenta Graecorum oppidorum, quae ceteri tollenda esse arbitrantur, ea sibi ille ne visenda quidem existimavit.

Study Questions:

- Can you think of any reasons why the imperative form *Age* is singular whilst *considerate* (equally imperative) is plural?
- What kind of clause is *ceteris in rebus qua ille sit temperantia*?
- What kind of ablative is *qua... temperantia*?
- What kind of clause does *putatis* introduce?
- Parse *retardarunt*. What is its accusative object?
- What do you think of Cicero's use of synonyms such as *voluptatem* and *delectationem*? Do they complement each other (and if so how) or do they give the text a bloated wordiness?
- Identify the subject accusative and infinitive of the indirect statement introduced by *arbitrantur*.
- Identify and explain the case of *sibi*.
- How does the explanation of Pompey's speed Cicero gives in this paragraph affect our understanding of his previous praise of Pompey's speed as a facet of his martial prowess?

Stylistic Appreciation: Explore the rhetorical effect of negations in the passage.

Discussion Point: Describe and discuss the Romans' attitude to Greece that comes through in this paragraph. How does Pompey differ from the *ceteri*?

age (vero)!	(*a call for attention:*) come!
unde	from which place, whence, where
cursus, -us, m.	the action of running; charge, onrush, motion, movement, speed
	journey, voyage, passage
invenio, -enire, -eni, -entum	to encounter, meet; to find, discover, come by
eximius, -a, -um	outstanding, exceptional, remarkable
remex, -igis, m.	oarsman, rower
remoror, -ari, -atus	to wait, linger, dally; delay, hold up
retardo, -are, -avi, -atum	to hinder the progress of, hold up, inhibit
devoco, -are, -avi, -atum	to call down; to call away, summon, divert
amoenitas, -atis, f.	allurement, attraction, charm; pleasant spot
delectatio, -onis, f.	pleasure, delight
nobilitas, -atis, f.	renown, celebrity, distinction; nobility
cognitio, -onis, f.	the act of getting to know, study, investigation
quies, -etis, f.	rest, repose, relaxation
signum, -i, n.	sign; (here) statue
tabula, -ae, f.	board, plank, panel of wood; writing-tablet; painting
tollo, -ere, sustuli, sublatum	to pick up, carry off, remove, eliminate
ne... quidem	not even
viso, -ere, -i	to go and look, view, visit

41: SAINT POMPEY

Itaque omnes nunc in iis locis Cn. Pompeium sicut aliquem non ex hac urbe missum, sed de caelo delapsum intuentur; nunc denique incipiunt credere, fuisse homines Romanos hac quondam continentia, quod iam nationibus exteris incredibile ac falso memoriae proditum videbatur; nunc imperii vestri splendor illis gentibus lucem adferre coepit; nunc intellegunt non sine causa maiores suos tum, cum ea temperantia magistratus habebamus, servire populo Romano quam imperare aliis maluisse. Iam vero ita faciles aditus ad eum privatorum, ita liberae querimoniae de aliorum iniuriis esse dicuntur, ut is qui dignitate principibus excellit, facilitate infimis par esse videatur.

Study Questions:

- Parse *intuentur*.
- Explain the syntax of the infinitives *credere* and *fuisse*.
- What kind of ablative is *hac ... continentia*?
- What is the antecedent of *quod*?
- Identify the words in the nominative in the clause *quod iam nationibus exteris incredibile ac falso memoriae proditum videbatur*.
- Parse *falso* and *memoriae*: why can't *falso* modify *memoriae*?
- Who is the subject implied in *intellegunt*?
- Explain the tense of *videbatur*.
- In the *cum*-clause *cum ea temperantia magistratus habebamus*: who is the subject? What kind of ablative is *ea temperantia*? What case is *magistratus*?
- What kind of ablatives are *dignitate* and *facilitate*?
- What is the significance of the word *delapsum*? What impression does it give of Pompey?
- Who are the ancestors of the Eastern people who preferred to be subject to the Romans to ruling others?
- Discuss the way in which Cicero intertwines Pompey's *dignitas* ('social rank and standing in the community') and his *facilitas* ('accessibility') in the last sentence of the paragraph: why does he stress *facilitas* so much?

Stylistic Appreciation: Discuss how Cicero employs the temporal adverbs *quondam*, *iam* and *nunc* in his argument.

Discussion Point: Can you think of contemporary public figures who combine *dignitas* with *facilitas*?

intueor, -eri, -itus	to look at, watch; observe, see; consider; to look upon, regard as
delabor, -bi, -psus	to fall, drop; descend, glide down; slip
incipio, -ipere, -epi, -eptum	to begin
falsus, -a, -um	erroneous, untrue; incorrect, wrong
prodo, -ere, -idi, -itum	(here) to hand down, transmit
splendor, -oris, m.	brightness, brilliance, radiance; lustre; glory
coepi, -isse, -tum	to begin
malo, -lle, -lui	to wish rather, prefer
aditus, -us, m.	approach, access, right of entry
privatus, -i, m.	one who holds no public office; individual
querimonia, -ae, f.	an expression of grievance, complaint, protest
iniuria, -ae, f.	unlawful conduct, injustice, injury
excello, -ere, -ui	to be pre-eminent, surpass, excel
facilitas, -atis, f.	ease, facility, indulgence
infimus, -a, -um	lowest in position, most undistinguished, humblest
par, paris	matching, equal, similar, like

42: PEACE FOR OUR TIME

Iam quantum consilio, quantum dicendi gravitate et copia valeat, in quo ipso inest quaedam dignitas imperatoria, vos, Quirites, hoc ipso ex loco saepe cognovistis. Fidem vero eius quantam inter socios existimari putatis, quam hostes omnes omnium generum sanctissimam iudicarint? Humanitate iam tanta est, ut difficile dictu sit, utrum hostes magis virtutem eius pugnantes timuerint an mansuetudinem victi dilexerint. Et quisquam dubitabit quin huic hoc tantum bellum permittendum sit, qui ad omnia nostrae memoriae bella conficienda divino quodam consilio natus esse videatur?

Study Questions:

- Why is *valeat* in the subjunctive?
- What kind of ablative are *consilio, gravitate* and *copia*?
- What is the antecedent of the relative pronoun *quam*?
- Parse *generum*.
- Parse *iudicarint* and explain the mood.
- What kind of ablative is *humanitate*?
- What kind of clause is *ut difficile dictu sit*?
- Parse *dictu*.
- Parse *pugnantes*.
- *dicendi* (in the first sentence) goes with both *gravitate* and *copia; eius* (in the penultimate sentence) goes with both *virtutem* and *mansuetudinem*. What do you call this phenomenon?
- Explain the construction governed by the preposition *ad* (*ad omnia nostrae memoriae bella conficienda*).
- Why is *videatur* in the subjunctive?
- What does Cicero mean when he says that public oratory comprises *quaedam dignitas imperatoria*?

Stylistic Appreciation: Discuss the rhetorical effect of Cicero's use of *quantus, -a, -um* and *tantus, -a, -um*.

Discussion Point: Cicero argues that the secret of Pompey's ability to bring wars to a successful conclusion derives in large part from his 'soft qualities' – the reliability of his 'word' (*fides*) and his human kindness (*humanitas*). Is that a principle that holds true elsewhere in history?

gravitas, -atis, f.	weight, heaviness; dignity, importance, gravity
copia, -ae, f.	abundant power, wealth, riches, fullness, copiousness, multitude, abundance
valeo, -ere, -ui, -itum	to be strong; to have power, force, influence to avail, prevail, be strong, effective
insum, inesse, infui	to be in or upon; to be contained in, to be in, to belong to, to appertain to
dignitas, -atis, f.	dignity, greatness, grandeur, authority, rank
imperatorius, -a, -um	of or belonging to a general
cognosco, -ere, cognovi, cognitum	to become thoroughly acquainted with, to perceive, understand
genus, -eris, n.	birth, descent, origin; kind, type, character
sanctus, -a, -um	sacred, inviolable
mansuetudo, -inis, f.	mildness, gentleness, clemency
diligo, -ere, dilexi, dilectum	to value/esteem highly, love
permitto, -ere, permisi, permissum	to let go through; to give up, intrust, surrender, commit; to give leave, let, allow, suffer, grant, permit
quin (conjunction + subjunctive)	that
memoria, -ae, f.	memory, recollection the period of recollection, time
nascor, nasci, natus sum	to be born, to rise, to arise, to spring forth

43: RUMOUR AND RENOWN: POMPEY'S *AUCTORITAS*

Et quoniam auctoritas quoque in bellis administrandis multum atque in imperio militari valet, certe nemini dubium est quin ea re idem ille imperator plurimum possit. Vehementer autem pertinere ad bella administranda, quid hostes, quid socii de imperatoribus nostris existiment, quis ignorat, cum sciamus homines in tantis rebus, ut aut contemnant aut metuant, aut oderint aut ament, opinione non minus et fama quam aliqua ratione certa commoveri? Quod igitur nomen umquam in orbe terrarum clarius fuit? cuius res gestae pares? de quo homine vos, id quod maxime facit auctoritatem, tanta et tam praeclara iudicia fecistis?

Study Questions:

- Explain the grammar and syntax of *multum* and *plurimum*.
- What kind of ablative is *ea re*?
- Identify the subject accusative and the infinitive of the indirect statement introduced by *ignorat*.
- Identify and explain the mood of *existiment*.
- What kind of clause does *ut* introduce?
- What kind of ablative are *opinione, fama,* and *ratione*?
- Identify the subject accusative and the infinitive of the indirect statement introduced by *sciamus*.
- Parse *clarius*.
- What verb form has to be supplied in the clause *cuius res gestae pares?*
- What is *auctoritas*? How does it differ from *potestas* or *imperium*? Is Cicero right to claim that the reputation/prestige of the general matters in warfare?

Stylistic Appreciation: In the indirect statement dependent on *sciamus* Cicero switches into an 'anthropological register' with a statement about how humans behave in extreme situations. What is the rhetorical effect of this switch?

Discussion Point: Can you think of figures in your life who are formally invested with power of one sort or another because of their social role or office (= *potestas*) but have little or no *auctoritas* ('commanding respect') – or, conversely, of individuals who do not possess any formal powers but nevertheless command respect and obedience? How would you explain this?

quoniam	since, seeing that, inasmuch as, because
quoque	in the same way, too, likewise, no less
valeo, -ere, -ui, -itum	to be powerful, be well, be potent; to have the ability or power (with infinitive or internal accusative)
dubius, -a, -um	hesitant, undecided, doubtful, uncertain
quin (conjunction + subjunctive)	that
possum, posse, potui	to be able (to); to have power, influence, or importance
vehementer (adverb)	with great force, violently, firmly
pertineo, -ere, -ui	to extend, reach; pertain to, be a concern
contemno, -nere, -psi, -ptum	to regard with contempt, look down on; to disregard
metuo, -ere, -i	to fear, be afraid
odi, -isse	to hate, dislike
opinio, -onis, f.	opinion, belief; fancy, imagination
fama, -ae, f.	news, tidings; rumour, hearsay; public opinion; fame, glory, renown
commoveo, -overe, -ovi, -otum	to move, shake, agitate; to interest, stimulate, prompt, strike
clarus, -a, -um	loud, sonorous; bright, shining; celebrated, famous
par, paris	matching, equal, similar, like
praeclarus, -a, -um	very clear/bright; excellent, famous, celebrated

44: CASE STUDY I: THE SOCIO-ECONOMICS OF POMPEY'S *AUCTORITAS*

An vero ullam usquam esse oram tam desertam putatis, quo non illius diei fama pervaserit, cum universus populus Romanus referto foro completisque omnibus templis, ex quibus hic locus conspici potest, unum sibi ad commune omnium gentium bellum Cn. Pompeium imperatorem depoposcit? Itaque, ut plura non dicam neque aliorum exemplis confirmem, quantum auctoritas valeat in bello, ab eodem Cn. Pompeio omnium rerum egregiarum exempla sumantur: qui quo die a vobis maritimo bello praepositus est imperator, tanta repente vilitas annonae ex summa inopia et caritate rei frumentariae consecuta est unius hominis spe ac nomine, quantum vix in summa ubertate agrorum diuturna pax efficere potuisset.

Study Questions:

- *oram:* why does Cicero use this particular word as opposed to, say, *regionem*? What kind of implications does it have?
- What kind of construction does *putatis* introduce?
- Specify and explain the mood of *pervaserit*.
- What kind of construction are *referto foro* and *completis omnibus templis*?
- *hic locus:* what place in Rome is Cicero talking about?
- What kind of clause is *ut plura non dicam neque aliorum exemplis confirmem*?
- What kind of clause is *quantum auctoritas valeat in bello*?
- Specify and explain the mood of *sumantur*.
- Explain the syntax of *qui*.
- What kind of ablative is *a vobis*?
- On what words does the genitive *unius hominis* depend and what kinds (! plural intended) of genitive is it?
- What kind of ablatives are *spe* and *nomine*?
- Parse *potuisset* and explain the mood.
- *illius diei fama:* how does Cicero convey the atmosphere in Rome on this day?

an	introducing direct questions with a notion of surprise/indignation: 'can it really be that...?'
usquam	in any place, anywhere
pervado, -dere, -si, -sum	to cross, traverse; pervade, penetrate
refercio, -cire, -si, -tum	to cram or stuff full
forum, -i, n.	the forum
compleo, -ere, -evi, -etum	to fill, to occupy a space, throng
conspicio, -icere, -exi, -ectum	to see, stare at, watch, discern
deposco, -scere, -posci	to demand (peremptorily), ask for
confirmo, -are, -avi, -atum	to strengthen, corroborate
egregius, -ia, -ium	outstanding, excellent, splendid, pre-eminent
sumo, -mere, -mpsi, -mptum	to take, put on, seize, get, procure
maritimus, -a, -um	relating to the sea, naval
praepono, -onere, -osui, -ositum	to place in front, set in authority over, put in charge of
repente (adverb)	without warning, suddenly; in an instant
vilitas, -atis, f.	lowness of price, cheapness
annona, -ae, f.	(annual) marketable output, produce; the supply of corn; corn, food
inopia, -ae, f.	lack of wealth, poverty; dearth; shortage, scarcity
caritas, -atis, f.	dearness, high price; love, affection, esteem
res frumentaria	the corn-supply
consequor, -qui, -cutus	to go or come after, to follow
vix (adverb)	with difficulty, hardly, barely, just
ubertas, -atis, f.	productiveness, fruitfulness, fertility, abundance

Stylistic Appreciation: Discuss the ways in which Cicero relates Pompey to the Roman commonwealth (and the world as a whole) with reference to the comprehensive, superlative, and extreme expressions in the paragraph (e.g. *ullam ... oram, tam desertam, universus populus Romanus, omnibus templis, ad commune omnium gentium bellum, omnium rerum egregiarum exempla, tanta vilitas, ex summa inopia et caritate, in summa ubertate agrorum, diuturna pax*).

Discussion Point: Explore the correlation between the appointment of Pompey as general in the war against the pirates and the ensuing drop in the price of corn in Rome. Why is this 'cause-and-effect' relationship between a political decision and its economic consequences such a brilliant illustration of Pompey's *auctoritas*?

45: CASE STUDY II: POMPEY'S *AUCTORITAS* AND PSYCHO-LOGICAL WARFARE

Iam accepta in Ponto calamitate ex eo proelio, de quo vos paulo ante invitus admonui, cum socii pertimuissent, hostium opes animique crevissent, satis firmum praesidium provincia non haberet, amisissetis Asiam, Quirites, nisi ad ipsum discrimen eius temporis divinitus Cn. Pompeium ad eas regiones fortuna populi Romani attulisset. Huius adventus et Mithridatem insolita inflatum victoria continuit et Tigranem magnis copiis minitantem Asiae retardavit. Et quisquam dubitabit, quid virtute perfecturus sit, qui tantum auctoritate perfecerit? aut quam facile imperio atque exercitu socios et vectigalia conservaturus sit, qui ipso nomine ac rumore defenderit?

Study Questions:

- What kind of construction is *accepta in Ponto calamitate*?
- What kind of ablative is *paulo*?
- Parse *pertimuissent, crevissent* and *haberet*.
- Specify and explain the mood and tense of *amisissetis* and *attulisset*.
- What form is *divinitus*? What is the subject of the *nisi*-clause?
- What kind of ablative is *magnis copiis*?
- Parse *minitantem*.
- What kind of clauses do *quid* and *quam* introduce?
- What forms are *perfecturus sit* and *conservaturus sit*?
- Specify and explain the mood of *perfecerit* and *defenderit*.
- What are the accusative objects of *defenderit*?
- Explore how Cicero represents the complementary impact of the *virtus* and the *auctoritas* of Pompey.

Stylistic Appreciation: How does the syntax of the first sentence reinforce Cicero's themes and rhetorical agenda?

Discussion Point: What entity/force does Cicero refer to with *fortuna populi Romani*?

accipio, -ipere, -epi, -eptum	to receive, acquire, get
proelium, -(i)i, n.	battle
paulum, -i, n.	a small amount, little, a little bit
invitus, -a, -um	unwilling, reluctant
admoneo, -ere, -ui, -itum	to give a reminder to, to remind (of *or* that)
pertimesco, -escere, -ui	to become very scared, take excessive fright
ops, opis, f.	power, ability
plural:	domination, influence, resources
animus, -i, m.	mind; courage, spirit, morale
cresco, -ere, crevi, cretum	to be born, arise; develop, grow, increase
amitto, -ittere, -isi, -issum	to send away, dismiss; to forfeit, lose
discrimen, -inis, n.	a separating line, a point in which things differ; a decisive stage, critical point, crisis
divinitus (adverb)	by divine agency or inspiration, providentially
insolitus, -a, -um	unusual, unfamiliar
inflo, -are, -avi, -atum	to fill with air, puff out, inflate; cause to swell
minitor, -ari, -atus (+ dative)	to threaten (somebody/something)
retardo, -are, -avi, -atum	to hinder the progress of, inhibit
dubito, -are, -avi, -atum	to be in doubt, be uncertain
vectigal, -alis, n.	revenue
rumor, -oris, m.	noise, rumour, reputation, esteem

46: *AUCTORITAS* SUPREME

Age vero illa res quantam declarat eiusdem hominis apud hostes populi Romani auctoritatem, quod ex locis tam longinquis tamque diversis tam brevi tempore omnes huic se uni dediderunt: quod a communi Cretensium legati, cum in eorum insula noster imperator exercitusque esset, ad Cn. Pompeium in ultimas prope terras venerunt eique se omnes Cretensium civitates dedere velle dixerunt! Quid? idem iste Mithridates nonne ad eundem Cn. Pompeium legatum usque in Hispaniam misit? eum quem Pompeius legatum semper iudicavit, ii quibus erat molestum ad eum potissimum esse missum, speculatorem quam legatum iudicari maluerunt. Potestis igitur iam constituere, Quirites, hanc auctoritatem, multis postea rebus gestis magnisque vestris iudiciis amplificatam, quantum apud illos reges, quantum apud exteras nationes valituram esse existimetis.

Study Questions: .

- What word does *quantam* agree with?
- Parse *communi* and *legati*.
- Who is the *noster imperator*?
- Which words does the *-que* after *ei* connect?
- Parse *ei*.
- Explain the syntax of *se* and *omnes ... civitates*.
- Identify the subject accusative and the infinitive of the indirect statement dependent on *existimetis*.

Stylistic Appreciation: What are the stylistic devices Cicero uses to highlight Pompey's *auctoritas*?

Discussion Point: If you were a member of one of Rome's established senatorial families, how would you react to Cicero's rhetoric in this paragraph?

declaro, -are, -avi, -atum	to make known, declare, tell, reveal; testify to, show
dedo, -ere, -idi, -itum	to yield possession of, give up, surrender
commune, -is, n.	property of rights held in common; commonwealth, state, collective body
usque (ad/in) (adverb)	all the way (to), right up (to), as far (as)
molestus, -a, -um	troublesome, annoying, vexing
potissimum (adverb)	especially, above all
speculator, -oris, m.	a spy
constituo, -uere, -ui, -utum	to set up, establish, locate; arrange, agree on
valeo, -ere, -ui, -itum	to have strength, be powerful, have weight

47: *FELICITAS*, OR HOW NOT TO 'SULL(A)Y' POMPEY

Reliquum est ut de felicitate, quam praestare de se ipso nemo potest, meminisse et commemorare de altero possumus, sicut aequum est homines de potestate deorum, timide et pauca dicamus. Ego enim sic existimo, Maximo, Marcello, Scipioni, Mario, et ceteris magnis imperatoribus non solum propter virtutem, sed etiam propter fortunam saepius imperia mandata atque exercitus esse commissos. Fuit enim profecto quibusdam summis viris quaedam ad amplitudinem et ad gloriam et ad res magnas bene gerendas divinitus adiuncta fortuna. De huius autem hominis felicitate, de quo nunc agimus, hac utar moderatione dicendi, non ut in illius potestate fortunam positam esse dicam, sed ut praeterita meminisse, reliqua sperare videamur, ne aut invisa dis immortalibus oratio nostra aut ingrata esse videatur.

Study Questions:

- What is the object of *meminisse* and *commemorare*?
- Identify the subject accusative and infinitive of the indirect statement introduced by *existimo*.
- What is missing from the clause *sicut aequum est homines de potestate deorum* and has to be supplied from the surrounding text?
- Which name is conspicuously absent from Cicero's list of generals who enjoyed outstanding *fortuna*?
- Parse *saepius*.
- What noun does *quaedam* modify? What is the rhetorical effect of its placement in the sentence?

Stylistic Appreciation: Cicero declares that he wishes to speak about Pompey's *felicitas* '*timide et pauca*'. What are the rhetorical ploys by which he puts this principle into practice?

Discussion Point: *felicitas* indicates divine support. Can you think of contemporary politicians who appeal to the supernatural sphere as a source of support in governance?

reliquus, -qua, -quum	the rest of, the remaining
reliquum est	for the rest
praesto, -are, -iti (-avi), -atum (-itum)	to be outstanding/superior, excel; to make available, furnish, supply; vouch for
sicut	in the same way as, just as... (so)...
timide (adverb)	apprehensively, nervously
propter (preposition + accusative)	because of, on account of, thanks to
mando, -are, -avi, -atum	to hand over, deliver, entrust
committo, -ittere, -isi, -issum	to join, engage; entrust to; bring about
profecto (adverb)	without question, undoubtedly, assuredly
amplitudo, -inis, f.	size, bulk, extent; distinction, eminence, prestige
divinitus	by divine agency or inspiration
adiungo, -gere, -xi, -ctum	to connect, link up, attach to, assign
ago, agere, egi, actum	to drive
agere de	to speak about, treat, discuss
utor, uti, usus + ablative	to use, employ
moderatio, -onis, f.	moderation, restraint
praeteritus, -a, -um	that has occurred, been done; past, bygone
invisus, -a, -um	hateful, odious, disliked, unpopular
ingratus, -a, -um	ungrateful, thankless, unappreciative;
+ dative	unwelcome to, displeasing to, unpopular with

48: THE DARLING OF THE GODS

itaque non sum praedicaturus, quantas ille res domi militiae, terra marique, quantaque felicitate gesserit, ut eius semper voluntatibus non modo cives adsenserint, socii obtemperarint, hostes oboedierint, sed etiam venti tempestatesque obsecundarint: hoc brevissime dicam, neminem umquam tam impudentem fuisse, qui ab dis immortalibus tot et tantas res tacitus auderet optare, quot et quantas di immortales ad Cn. Pompeium detulerunt: quod ut illi proprium ac perpetuum sit, Quirites, cum communis salutis atque imperii, tum ipsius hominis causa, sicuti facitis, velle et optare debetis.

Study Questions:

- *non sum praedicaturus...* – What is the technical term for this literary technique, and what is the effect of employing it here?
- Parse *domi militiae* and *terra marique*.
- Identify and explain the mood of *gesserit*.
- Parse *obtemperarint* and *obsecundarint*.
- Identify and explain the mood of *auderet*.
- How does *quod ut illi proprium ac perpetuum sit* fit into the syntax of the sentence?

Stylistic Appreciation: Explore the ways in which Cicero hints at a quasi-divine status for Pompey without actually turning him into a god.

Discussion Point: What relationship between Pompey and the gods does Cicero posit in this paragraph?

praedico, -are, -avi, -atum	to make known, proclaim, declare
voluntas, -atis, f.	will, intention, disposition
adsentio, -tire, -si, -sum	to agree, assent, approve
obtempero, -are, -avi, -atum	to be submissive to, comply with, obey
oboedio, -ire, -ivi/-ii, -itum	to obey, submit to
obsecundo, -are, -avi, -atum	to act in compliance or support, fall in with
impudens, -ntis	shameless, impudent, brazen
tacitus, -a, -um	silent, quiet, secret
audeo, -ere, -sus	to dare, venture
opto, -are, -avi, -atum	to wish, desire, pray for
defero, -rre, detuli, delatum	to carry, convey, bring; transfer; confer, grant to
proprius, -a, -um	belonging, one's own, one's own property
perpetuus, -a, -um	continuous, permanent
causa (preposition + genitive)	because of, on account of

49: SUMMING UP

Quare cum et bellum sit ita necessarium, ut neglegi non possit, ita magnum, ut accuratissime sit administrandum, et cum ei imperatorem praeficere possitis, in quo sit eximia belli scientia, singularis virtus, clarissima auctoritas, egregia fortuna, dubitatis, Quirites, quin hoc tantum boni, quod vobis ab dis immortalibus oblatum et datum est, in rem publicam conservandam atque amplificandam conferatis?

Study Questions:

- What kind of *ut*-clause are *ut neglegi non possit* and *ut accuratissime sit administrandum*?
- Parse *ei*. What does it refer back to?
- Explain the subjunctive (*sit*) in the relative clause introduced by *in quo*.
- What kind of genitive is *boni*?

Stylistic Appreciation: What are the rhetorical devices Cicero uses to render his summing-up both clear and memorable?

Discussion Point: What relationship does Cicero construe between the gods and the Roman citizens?

neglego, -gere, -xi, -ctum	to disregard, ignore, do nothing about
accuratus, -a, -um	carefully performed or prepared, meticulous
praeficio, -icere, -eci, -ectum	to put in charge (of), set over
eximius, -a, -um	outstanding, exceptional, remarkable, special
singularis, -is, -e	alone, peculiar, special; remarkable, unusual
clarus, -a, -um	sonorous; bright, shining; celebrated, famous
egregius, -a, -um	outstanding, excellent, splendid
tantum, -i, n. (pronoun)	such a quantity, so much
bonum, -i, n.	any good, boon, advantage, blessing
offero, -rre, obtuli, oblatum	to put in the path of, provide, supply, offer
amplifico, -are, -avi, -atum	to enlarge, increase; extol, exalt, magnify
confero, -rre, contuli, collatum	to carry, convey; direct, aim; confer, bestow; to bring together; compare

4. Commentary

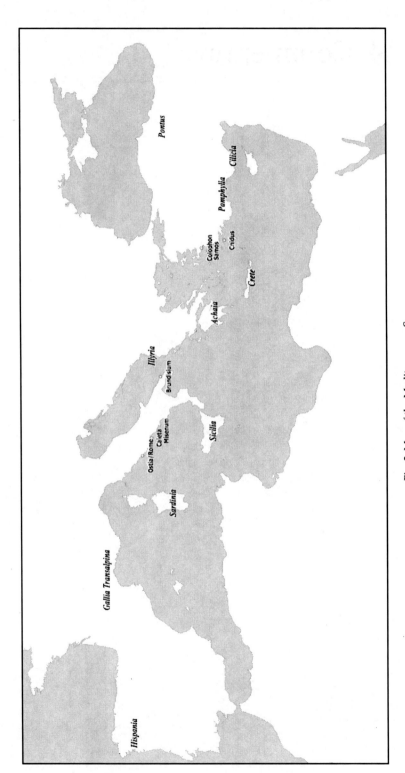

Fig. 3 Map of the Mediterranean Sea

27: THE ONLY WAY IS POMPEY

At the end of the opening section of the speech (§§ 1-6), Cicero offers his audience a blueprint of the first half (§§ 6-49), outlining the three topics he feels he ought to cover (§ 6):

> *primum videtur de genere belli, deinde de magnitudine, tum de imperatore deligendo esse dicendum.*

> ['I think it best to deal *first* with the nature of the war, *next* with its scope, and *finally* with the general to be chosen'.]

He then follows his blueprint to the letter. §§ 6-19 focus on the nature of the war (*genus belli*), §§ 20-26 on its extraordinary scale (*magnitudo belli*), and §§ 27-49 on the choice of the general. Cicero carefully marks the transitions from the first to the second topic, and then again from the second to the third (§ 20 and § 27):

> *quoniam de genere belli dixi, nunc de magnitudine pauca dicam* (§ 20).

> ['Since I have spoken on the nature of the war, I shall now say a few words on its scope'.]

> *Satis mihi multa verba fecisse videor, qua re esset hoc bellum genere ipso necessarium, magnitudine periculosum. Restat ut de imperatore ad id bellum deligendo ac tantis rebus praeficiendo dicendum esse videatur* (§ 27).

> [I think I have covered at sufficient length why this war is both inevitable given its kind and perilous given its immense scope. What remains to be covered is that one ought to speak, it seems, about the general to be chosen for this war and to be put in charge of such important matters.]

Note how the *satis multa* at the opening of § 27 harks back to the *pauca* in § 20. Likewise, just as Cicero mentioned the topic just covered in § 20 (*quoniam de genere belli dixi*) before introducing the next (*nunc de magnitudine pauca dicam*), he continues with his careful signposting in § 27: first we get a review of what has been covered in the previous *two* sections, i.e. the *genus* and the *magnitudo* of the war against Mithridates; then we get a reminder of what still remains on the agenda (*restat ut...*), i.e. the choice of general. The first two items of Cicero's tripartite structure, i.e. the nature and scope of the war, go together: both concern the war; the last item, in contrast, i.e. the general best suited for the job, is about the required personnel. The design is thus climactic.

If Cicero did his best to amplify the scope and danger of the war, he plays down any difficulty with choosing the general: there is only one! Given that Pompey lacks a plausible rival, the decision to put him in charge of this vital campaign, so Cicero claims, ought to be a no-brainer. He accordingly does not go on to weigh the relative merits of possible appointees, but offers an epideictic (and apodictic) explication of Pompey's singular suitability for the job. Consider, though: pretty much every member of Rome's ruling elite considered himself a competent commander (and would have licked his chops at the prospect of finishing off Mithridates). In this light, Cicero's assertion that there was no plausible alternative to appointing Pompey as supreme commander was not as uncontroversial or even self-evident as it may seem. Indeed, one could just have left the current commander there – for all the current difficulties, even Cicero admits Lucullus has done a remarkable job.

A key aspect of his argument in favour of Pompey is the peculiar mixture of Pompey's alleged excellences. These included not just traditional hallmarks of distinction such as courage, but also 'ethical' qualities grounded in his supposed integrity of character. Cicero will draw this distinction (and elaborate on it) in what follows. Here he sets up this vital part of his argument by slyly delimiting the number of possible candidates by means of two allegedly essential attributes of the appointee, one orthodox, the other surprising (at least from a Roman point of view). In his counterfactual wish introduced by *utinam*, he obliquely specifies that the commander to be put in charge better be *both* brave (*fortis*) *and* upright (*innocens*). To claim that Pompey was the only *brave* living Roman aristocrat would have been silly, so the decisive emphasis in the phrase *virorum fortium atque innocentium copiam tantam* lies squarely on *innocentium*. As we shall see, it is not least Cicero's insistence that bravery be combined with integrity of character that dries up the pool of possible candidates to leave exactly one: Pompey.

A pun that runs through the entire speech reinforces the link between the previous section on the scale of the war and the choice of the general: a war of this particular magnitude (*magnitudo*) calls for a general who is *Magnus*.

Satis mihi multa verba fecisse videor: good judgement of where to conclude one part of a speech and move on to the next belongs to the basic skill set of the able orator: it is never a good idea to abuse the patience of one's audience. Cicero flags up his apparent restraint at various moments in the speech. Here it comes with the qualifying dative *mihi*, which reinforces the subjective opinion expressed by *videor* ('I seem to myself...'), not least since *mihi* gains extra emphasis by causing the (minor) hyperbaton *satis ... multa* and by the alliteration *mihi multa*. The somewhat contrived phrasing allows for the possibility that (part of) the audience held a different opinion on the matter and wished Cicero to continue. He thereby combines explicit self-effacement with implicit self-aggrandizement: he courteously refrains from speaking for his audience but implies that some of those listening may well have wished for him to speak at greater length than he does, spellbound by his eloquence. (We ask you: can one *ever* get enough of Cicero's oratory?)

satis ... multa verba fecisse videor: the adverb *satis* modifies the adjective *multa*. The apparent emphasis on 'quantity of verbiage' continues the theme of 'economy of coverage' from the previous paragraph. See § 26: *multa praetereo consulto*: 'I deliberately pass over much' (with reference to the magnitude of the war that Rome is facing in the East). It is also much in evidence elsewhere in the speech. Already in § 3 Cicero introduces the theme of 'discursive limits' (*modus in dicendo*) when he programmatically announces that a speech on the excellence (*virtus*) of Pompey could continue without end, such is the abundance of material:

> dicendum est enim de Cn. Pompei singulari eximiaque virtute; huius autem orationis difficilius est exitum quam principium invenire. ita mihi non tam copia quam modus in dicendo quaerendus est.

> ['I have to speak about the unique and extraordinary excellence of Gnaeus Pompeius; and on this topic it is more difficult to find closure than to start. I therefore need to seek in my speech not so much full expression as due measure.']

The entire speech thereby emerges as an exercise in self-restraint, an attempt to keep verbal diarrhoea within reasonable limits – just like 'his' Pompey, Cicero purports to possess the qualities of *temperantia* and *continentia*, while ensuring that the job at hand gets done properly. In addition to quantity, his phrasing in § 27 suggests that his treatment of the war has not just been lengthy, but also of sufficiently high quality to address all contingencies: *satis ... fecisse* evokes the composite verb *satisfacere*, which means 'to give sufficient attention to a matter', 'to treat it to everybody's *satisfaction*'.

qua re esset hoc bellum genere ipso necessarium, magnitudine periculosum: *qua re* (an ablative of cause, literally: 'because of which thing', i.e. 'why', which then became a standard adverbial expression) introduces an indirect question (hence the subjunctive). The imperfect subjunctive *esset* expresses contemporaneity in secondary sequence (after *verba fecisse*). By pulling *esset* up front, Cicero causes the emphasis to fall squarely on the noun (*bellum*) and its attributes (*necessarium*, *periculosum*, following each other in asyndeton). The three items are linked by homoioteleuton: *bellum ... necessarium ... periculosum*.

hoc bellum genere ipso necessarium, magnitudine periculosum: *genere ipso* and *magnitudine* are ablatives of respect: they specify in what sense/respect the war is inevitable and perilous. Cicero presents the attributes in the form of an asyndetic contrast (*necessarium, ... periculosum*): the war is unavoidable, *yet* also very dangerous – potentially a toxic combination. Together, the attributes generate a sense of urgency or even coercion: the war *will* happen, and it is absolutely vital that it be managed by the most able.

restat ut de imperatore ad id bellum deligendo ac tantis rebus praeficiendo dicendum esse videatur: after the emphasis on personal judgement in the previous sentence (*mihi ... videor*), Cicero changes tack and continues with a string of *im*personal constructions: *restat, dicendum esse, videatur*. All three verbs lack a clear agent – as do *deligendo* and *praeficiendo*. Literally: 'it remains that it seems right [*to whom?*] that one [*who?*] ought to speak about the general to be selected for this particular war [*by whom?*] and put in charge of such important matters [*by whom?*].' The vagueness here arguably comes with an undertone of complicit humour: everybody knows the answers to these questions, but Cicero titillates expectations by playing coy.

de ... dicendum esse: the preposition *de* goes with *dicendum esse* (a gerundive of obligation): *dicere de* = 'to speak about'. (This sentence offers a nice opportunity to revise the gerundive: it features both a gerundive of obligation, i.e. *dicendum esse*, and two adjectival uses of the gerundive, i.e. *de imperatore deligendo ac tantis rebus praeficiendo*.)

de imperatore ad id bellum deligendo ac tantis rebus praeficiendo: *imperatore* stands in parallel to *bellum* in the previous sentence and, like *bellum*, which is modified by *necessarium* and *periculosum*, has two attributes: the gerundives (or passive verbal adjectives) *deligendo* and *praeficiendo*, which respectively govern *ad id bellum* and *tantis rebus* (a dative). The repetition of *bellum* here, together with the synonymous phrase *tantis rebus*, subsumes discussion of the war under the choice of the general, in a climactic design.

ad ... deligendo: the preposition *ad*, here indicating purpose, goes with the gerundive *deligendo* (*deligere ad* = 'to choose for').

[*Extra information*:
esse videatur: as one of the student-authors put it, who, incidentally, started Latin from scratch at Cambridge: 'I think if I were studying this as an AS-level text, and particularly as this is the first set paragraph, I'd quite like a point on the clausula of *esse videatur* in sentence 2, even if it's not something that the exam will be looking for. Something along the lines of: "This is a Ciceronian clausula, one of the key methods by which Cicero adapts the formal rules of Greek rhetoric to his Latin prose. Clausulae (etymologically related to *claudere* = 'to close') are regular rhythmic patterns that lead up to a sense break or the end of a sentence, to provide structure and add emphasis; historians such as Livy or Tacitus tend to avoid them, but Cicero often makes an effort to slot them in. The pattern seen here is a cretic, which scans 'long short long' (– u –), but with a so-called 'resolution' of the second long syllable into two short syllables, i.e. 'long short short short' (– u u u), followed by a trochee, which scans long short (– u) (though at the end of a verse/sentence the short syllable is anceps or 'ambiguous', i.e. it can be either short or long). Statistically speaking, the cretic + trochee (or + spondee, which scans long long) is one of Cicero's favourite clausulae.[1] And the phrase *esse videatur* itself occurs so frequently that this formula has come to be known as the '*esse-videatur* type'."]

Utinam, Quirites, virorum fortium atque innocentium copiam tantam haberetis, ut haec vobis deliberatio difficilis esset, quemnam potissimum tantis rebus ac tanto bello praeficiendum putaretis!: The main sentence consists of the wish-clause introduced by *utinam*. Then we have a consecutive *ut*-clause (set up by *tantam*) and an indirect question

---

1   See Wilkinson (1963) 156.

introduced by *quemnam*. The main verb *haberetis* is in the imperfect subjunctive: subjunctive, because this is the mood Latin uses to express wishes (the technical term is optative, from *opto, -are, -avi, -atum*: 'I express a wish for', 'I desire'); imperfect, because Cicero imagines the wish as unrealizable. (For *realizable* wishes, as the grammar buffs among you will know, Latin uses the present subjunctive for a situation in the present and the perfect subjunctive for a situation in the past; for *unrealizable* wishes, the imperfect subjunctive for a situation in the present and the pluperfect subjunctive for a situation in the past.)

Quirites: 'Quirites' is how speakers address the citizens of Rome in a public assembly. Etymological explanations of the term vary. Some argue that it means 'sons of Quirinus', a god worshipped by the Sabines on the Quirinal Hill (one of the seven hills of Rome). Livy 1.13 reports that the members of the civic community that emerged from the union of Sabines and Romans were called 'Quirites', after the Sabine town of Cures. He is followed by Ovid, who at *Fasti* 2.476-80 moots the further possibility that the name comes from the Sabine word for spear, i.e. *curis*. Some modern scholars derive *Quirites* from an older, reconstructed **co-viri-um*, meaning 'assembly of men'. What matters for present purposes is that 'Quirites is what the Romans called themselves when addressing each other as "citizen men," without reference to class or rank.'[2]

virorum fortium atque innocentium copiam: *fortitudo* and *innocentia* are two distinct qualities: the former, courage, refers to prowess on the battlefield; the latter, integrity, refers to good personal or civic ethics. Especially in this particular case, as Cicero goes on to argue, it is absolutely essential that the appointee has both – as Pompey does.

ut haec vobis deliberatio difficilis esset: a result clause set up by *copiam* *tantam*. As with *satis* *mihi* *multa* at the paragraph's opening, Cicero's placement of the personal pronoun *vobis* generates a minor hyperbaton: *haec ... deliberatio.*

quemnam potissimum tantis rebus ac tanto bello praeficiendum [sc. *esse*] **putaretis!**: The interrogative pronoun *quemnam* (*quis* + *nam*) introduces an indirect question (hence the subjunctive) dependent on *deliberatio*.

---

2   http://www.vroma.org/~araia/quirites.html

quemnam has a double function: it is both the accusative object of *putaretis* and the subject accusative of the indirect statement introduced by *putaretis*, i.e. *quemnam ... praeficiendum esse*: 'whom you believe ought to be put in charge of...'. Cicero here repeats the lexicon of the previous sentence: *deligendo* and *praeficiendo* return economically in *praeficiendum* [sc. *esse*]; *id bellum* and *tantis rebus* return chiastically and amplified in *tantis rebus* and *tanto bello*. The shift that *praeficere* undergoes, from passive verbal adjective (*praeficiendo*) to gerundive of obligation (*praeficiendum*), mirrors the shift in emphasis from Cicero and speaking (cf. *dicendum esse*) to the citizens and deciding.

Nunc vero – cum sit unus Cn. Pompeius, qui non modo eorum hominum qui nunc sunt gloriam, sed etiam antiquitatis memoriam virtute superarit – quae res est quae cuiusquam animum in hac causa dubium facere possit?: Cicero continues with a rhetorical question (*Nunc vero ... quae res est quae ... possit?*), interrupted by a parenthetical *cum*-clause (*cum sit unus ... superarit*). Such parentheses are a stylistic hallmark of oral discourse.[3]

Nunc vero: here introducing a fact or consideration opposed to a previous wish: '(But) as it is': see *OLD* s.v. *nunc* 11.

cum sit unus Cn. Pompeius: the *cum* here has causal force. *unus* stands in predicative position to *Cn. Pompeius*. The meaning here is *not* 'one Pompey' or 'a single Pompey', but 'Pompey alone', 'only Pompey': Cicero categorically excludes alternatives.

[*Extra information*:
The theme of singularity is a constant throughout the speech, but especially in the part under discussion here: Cicero uses *unus* in §§ 28, 29, 31, 33, 35, 44 (2x), 46, but it occurs throughout the entire speech, according to the principle that *unum esse* [sc. Pompey], *in quo summa sint omnia* (§ 13: 'there is one man who possesses in all respects the highest qualifications' [sc. for the war against Mithridates]). The attribute *singularis* has a similar function. It occurs with reference to Pompey's qualities in §§ 3 (*virtus*), 10 (*virtus*), 49 (*virtus*), 61 (*innocentia*), and 64 (*militaris virtus*). If in §§ 27-49 Cicero argues that one single individual is the supreme embodiment of the *summus imperator*, in the paragraphs that follow he goes on to counter the objection

---

3 Powell (2013) 49.

by a group of powerful *nobiles* that this particular command ought not to be given to one man only. See §§ 51-2: ... *ea omnia quae a me adhuc dicta sunt, eidem isti vera esse concedunt, – et necessarium bellum esse et magnum, et <u>in uno Cn. Pompeio</u> summa esse omnia. Quid igitur ait Hortensius? Si <u>uni</u> omnia tribuenda sint, dignissimum esse Pompeium, sed <u>ad unum</u> tamen omnia deferri non oportere*: 'These very same men concede that everything I have said so far is true – namely that the war is inevitable and important and that only Pompey possesses all the necessary qualities to the highest degree. What, then, does Hortensius [one of the powerful *nobiles* who opposed Manilius' proposal that Pompey be appointed] say? If the entire command must be given to one, Pompey is the worthiest recipient; but one shouldn't entrust the entire command to one man only.']

qui non modo eorum hominum qui nunc sunt gloriam, sed etiam antiquitatis memoriam virtute superarit: the first *qui* introduces a relative clause of characteristic (with *Cn. Pompeius* as antecedent), which explains the subjunctive *superarit* (see next note for an explication of the form). *superarit* governs two accusative objects, coordinated by *non modo ... sed etiam*: *gloriam* and *memoriam*. Each takes a genitive: *eorum hominum* [*qui nunc sunt*] depends on *gloriam* and *antiquitatis* on *memoriam*. *virtute*, an ablative of instrument or means, stands *apo koinou* with both accusative objects. By means of his excellence, Pompey surpasses both the glory obtained by any of his contemporaries and the recorded achievement of past generations. The arrangement is climactic and plays on the widespread feeling in Rome that it was difficult to measure up to the standards set in the past. Pompey, however, manages to outshine his contemporaries and to outperform the ancestors.

superarit: the syncopated form of *supera-ve-rit*:[4] third person singular perfect subjunctive active. The tense is present perfect ('has surpassed') rather than a simply past ('surpassed').

eorum hominum qui nunc sunt gloriam: the formulation picks up on *virorum fortium atque innocentium copiam tantam* from the previous sentence. Cicero has just claimed that currently there are no *viri fortes atque innocentes*

---

4   to syncopate = to shorten words by omitting syllables or letters in the middle. It derives from Greek *sun-* ('with') and *kopto* ('to cut').

at Rome fit for the job, except Pompey. It hence comes as no surprise that he should outshine his contemporaries in *virtus*.

memoria antiquitatis: a somewhat contrived synonym for *gloria*: it refers to the achievements of the Romans of old that entered into the collective memory of their families or clans (*gentes*) and the *res publica* at large – in other words, 'long-term glory'.[5] *antiquitatis* is an objective – rather than subjective – genitive: it is not the ancient times that do the remembering; rather, they are the object of remembrance.

virtute: *virtus* is the second of the four essential hallmarks of the perfect general, as Cicero goes on to remind his audience in the subsequent paragraph: *ego enim sic existimo, in summo imperatore quattuor has res inesse oportere, scientiam rei militaris, virtutem, auctoritatem, felicitatem.* From an etymological point of view, *vir-tus* is what distinguishes the *vir*.[6] Originally, *virtus* seems to have indicated martial prowess above all. But in the course of the Roman assimilation of Greek philosophical thought, the semantics of the term expanded considerably, as *virtus* became the preferred Latin term to render the Greek *arete*, which in philosophical discourse also signified ethical qualities.[7] In this process it became a generic designation for good qualities more generally. The English 'virtue', while deriving from Latin *virtus*, inevitably carries moral connotations (as in 'virtue ethics') and hence does not capture the full semantic range and distinctive emphasis of the Latin term very well. 'Excellence' or 'personal ability/quality' (*virtus*) or 'excellences' (*virtutes*) is therefore frequently the better option in translating. (Not all excellences need have a moral dimension.)

quae res est quae cuiusquam animum in hac causa dubium facere possit?: *quae res est* sets up a relative clause of characteristic (hence the subjunctive *possit*): 'what thing is there of such a kind that it could...'.

cuiusquam animum: 'the mind of anyone' – an elaborate way of saying *quemquam* ('anyone').

---

5 For a study of the memorial culture of the Roman republic see Flower (1996).
6 See esp. Cicero, *Tusculan Disputations* 2.43: *appellata est enim ex viro virtus* ('for the word for excellence [*virtus*] is derived from the word for man [*vir*]').
7 For a recent monograph on the term, see McDonnell (2006), though reviewers have argued that he unduly simplifies the evidence: see e.g. Kaster (2007).

animum ... dubium facere: *facere* coordinates the two accusatives with *dubium* in predicative position: 'to make the mind hesitant' (*not* 'to make the hesitant mind').

28: THE PERFECT GENERAL, POMPEY THE KID, AND MR. EXPERIENCE

Cicero now explicates the reasons for his judgement that Pompey has outperformed both his contemporaries and the Romans of old. To do so, he briefly switches registers: he theorizes. In the first sentence of the paragraph, he defines, in the abstract, his ideal of the consummate military leader or perfect general. His *summus imperator* has four essential attributes – *scientia rei militaris* ('knowledge of military affairs'), *virtus* ('overall excellence'), *auctoritas* ('commanding prestige' or 'authority'), and *felicitas* ('divine blessing'). These attributes serve Cicero as blueprint for the rest of §§ 28-49. He treats each one in turn. The first quality in the list, *scientia rei militaris*, which is also the least complex, receives the briefest coverage: Cicero deals with it in the rest of § 28, before moving on to *virtus* (§§ 29-42), *auctoritas* (§§ 43-46), and *felicitas* (§§ 47-48). (Note the unequal distribution: *scientia militaris* receives 1 paragraph, *virtus* 14, *auctoritas* 4, and *felicitas* 2: is there a rationale for this?) Throughout, he aims to demonstrate that it is impossible to imagine anyone possessing any of these qualities to a higher degree than Pompey – let alone all four together. Pompey thereby emerges as the living embodiment of the perfect general.

Ego enim sic existimo, in summo imperatore quattuor has res inesse oportere: scientiam rei militaris, virtutem, auctoritatem, felicitatem: the *sic* sets up the indirect statement *in summo imperatore quattuor has res inesse oportere*: see *OLD* s.v. 4b. One could say in English 'as follows', but this would be a bit cumbersome. *scientiam rei militaris, virtutem, auctoritatem, felicitatem* stand in apposition to *quattuor has res. has* is thus best translated 'the following'. *res* here means something akin to 'qualities'.

scientiam rei militaris, virtutem, auctoritatem, felicitatem: an asyndetic list that is arranged climactically. Cicero moves from knowledge based on experience (*scientia rei militaris*) to innate ability/personal qualities/overall excellence (*virtus*) to impact on/perception by others in socio-political settings (*auctoritas*) to endorsement/support from the gods (*felicitas*). After setting out his ideal, Cicero proceeds to look for it in reality. He does so from here on out by means of a systematic 'compare and contrast' that pitches

Pompey against an anonymous collective of 'everyone else'. Accordingly, watch out for comparative forms: they make a frequent appearance! In § 28 alone, there are four: *scientior*, *saepius*, *plura*, and *plures* – all designed to illustrate Pompey's unparalleled knowledge of military matters.

> **quis igitur hoc homine scientior umquam aut fuit aut esse debuit?**
> (i) **qui**
> > (*a*) **e ludo atque e pueritiae disciplinis bello maximo atque acerrimis hostibus**
> > (*b*) **ad patris exercitum atque in militiae disciplinam profectus est;**
>
> (ii) **qui**
> > (*a*) **extrema pueritia miles in exercitu fuit summi imperatoris,**
> > (*b*) **ineunte adulescentia maximi ipse exercitus imperator;**
>
> (iii) **qui**
> > (*a*) **saepius cum hoste conflixit quam quisquam cum inimico concertavit,**
> > (*b*) **plura bello gessit quam ceteri legerunt,**
> > (*c*) **plures provincias confecit quam alii concupiverunt;**
>
> (iv) **cuius adulescentia ad scientiam rei militaris**
> > (*a*) **non alienis praeceptis sed suis imperiis,**
> > (*b*) **non offensionibus belli sed victoriis,**
> > (*c*) **non stipendiis sed triumphis est erudita.**

Cicero starts by posing a rhetorical question (*quis ... debuit?*) that demands the obvious answer: 'nobody'. What follows are four climactically arranged sentences, all starting with a connecting relative (*qui, qui, qui, cuius*) that pick up *hoc homine*. (i) and (ii) sketch Pompey's rise from kindergarten to general; (iii) and (iv) step back and compare his overall achievement in (and hence empirical knowledge of) military matters to that of anyone else. The design of (i) and (ii) is essentially bipartite, here flagged up with (*a*) and (*b*) (though there is a whiff of a tricolon in (i) as well: see below): they outline Pompey's progression from *puer* to *miles* (i) and from *miles* to *imperator* (ii). The basic organizing principle of both (iii) and (iv) is the tricolon, flagged up with (*a*) (*b*) (*c*).

quis igitur hoc homine scientior umquam aut fuit aut esse debuit?: *scientior*, which picks up *scientiam rei militaris* in the previous sentence, is the comparative form, in the nominative masculine singular, of *sciens*, *scientis* ('knowledgeable'). Cicero elides the objective genitive *rei militaris* that we need to understand with *scientior*. It can easily be supplied from the previous sentence.

hoc homine: an ablative of comparison after *scientior*.

qui e ludo atque e pueritiae disciplinis bello maximo atque acerrimis hostibus ad patris exercitum atque in militiae disciplinam profectus est: between the subject (the connecting relative pronoun *qui = et hic*) at the beginning and the verb (*profectus est*) at the end, Cicero includes three well-balanced phrases that gradually increase in length, each consisting of two elements linked by *atque*:

    (i) *e ludo atque e pueritiae disciplinis* [from boy...]

    (ii) *bello maximo atque acerrimis hostibus*

    (iii) *ad patris exercitum atque in militiae disciplinam* [... to man]

(i) and (iii) correlate closely: *e ludo* sets up *ad patris exercitum*; *e pueritiae disciplinis* sets up *in militiae disciplinam*. (ii) consists of two circumstantial ablatives that specify the historical context in which Pompey made his transition from 'boy' to 'man'.

e ludo atque e pueritiae disciplinis: the meaning of *ludus* covers a wide semantic range, from 'sport, play, recreation' to 'show, entertainment, or, in the plural, public games' to 'fun, merriment, frivolity'. Here it refers to 'a place of instruction or training', more specifically, 'elementary school': *OLD* s.v. 6. *disciplinae*, in the plural, refers to different 'branches of study'. In the singular, it means 'teaching, instruction, training', but also something more akin to the English derivative 'discipline', i.e. 'orderly conduct based on moral training' or 'order maintained in a body of people under command' (*OLD* s.v. 4), which is its meaning in the phrase *in militiae disciplinam* further on in the sentence. *pueritia* means 'boyhood', which in Rome tended to come to an end between the 14th and 17th birthday, with the donning of the so-called *toga virilis* ('the toga of manhood'), which marked the beginning of *adulescentia* ('adulthood').

bello maximo atque acerrimis hostibus: the ablatives indicate the attendant circumstances in which Pompey made the transition from being a boy at school to serving in the army. The use of two superlatives (*maximo, acerrimis*) and the chiastic design (noun – adjective – adjective – noun) underscore the severity of the conflict that initiated Pompey into military life. There are two ways to construe the *atque*: it can be taken to link (i) *bello* and *hostibus* (= 'in a war of great significance and against the most bitter enemies') or (ii) *maximo* and *acerrimus hostibus*, with both phrases being predicative specifications of *bello* (= 'a war of great significance and involving the most bitter enemies'). The war in question is the Social War between Rome and her Italian allies in 91-87 BC (with the most intense fighting occurring in 90-89), which ended with Rome granting full citizenship to its 'allies-turned-enemies-turned-citizens'. The details of the conflict are irrelevant for Cicero's purposes. His main interest lies in Pompey's precocious exposure to warfare. But our sources suggest that for once his 'superlative idiom' is true to the facts: the fighting was ferocious.[8]

ad patris exercitum atque in militiae disciplinam: Pompey went straight from school (*ludus*) to military service (*exercitus*) under the command of his father Gnaeus Pompeius Strabo, one of the consuls of 89 BC, most likely as a member of his father's *consilium*. Pompey was born on 29 September 106 BC, so he must have been 17 at the time. Cicero, too, earned his military spurs under Strabo. There is no evidence to suggest, however, that he was also part of the *consilium* or that Cicero and Pompey had 'any close link'.[9]

[*Extra information*:
A *consilium* is a typically Roman institution: it was in effect a group of esteemed and experienced persons who acted in an advisory capacity, but also included well-connected young men eager to learn the ropes of public affairs; any Roman in a position of power, whether in his role as *pater familias* or as a magistrate or pro-magistrate of the Roman people, was expected to consult his *consilium* before making an important or difficult decision. We know of the presence of Pompey filius in the *consilium* of his father because of an inscription, which provides us with 'the single surviving list of a

---

8   Sources include Appian *Bellum Civile* 1.48.207ff., Velleius Paterculus 2.21.1, Florus 2.6.14.
9   Seager (2002) 194 n. 10.

commander's suite'.[10] The inscription in question is *ILLRP* (= *Inscriptiones Latinae Liberae Rei Publicae*) 515. You can access the full text and a translation (as well as a photo of the inscription) at http://www.theaterofpompey.com/pdcs_articles/rg_sp.pdf. It's worth checking out, just to get a sense of the sheer size of the *consilium*.]

qui extrema pueritia miles in exercitu fuit summi imperatoris, ineunte adulescentia maximi ipse exercitus imperator: Cicero here uses an ablative of time (*extrema pueritia*) and a temporal ablative absolute (*ineunte adulescentia*) to underscore both Pompey's precociousness and his comet-like ascent to the top: *at the very end* of his boyhood (*extrema pueritia*), he was *already* a soldier (*miles*), yet *at the beginning* of his adulthood (*ineunte adulescentia*), he was *already* a general (*imperator*). The emphasis on the end of one period in Pompey's life (*pueritia*) and the beginning of another (*adulescentia*) underscores that he rose virtually overnight from common soldier (*miles*) to commander-in-chief (*imperator*). In reality, however, several years elapsed between his entry into military life under his father in 89 and 83 BC when he put himself in command of an army that he had raised by his own initiative, relying on family networks, in the turbulent years of civil war between Sulla and the Marians. In fact, Pompey's comet-like (and unconstitutional) rise to the pinnacle of Rome's politico-military hierarchy would have been inconceivable without the chaos of suicidal infighting within Rome's ruling elite. Cicero glosses over the unsavoury enabling conditions of Pompey's stunning success (and irregular *curriculum vitae*), choosing instead to focus on the truly extraordinary speed of his ascent to the top. The chiastic arrangement *miles in exercitu summi imperatoris – maximi ... exercitûs imperator* enhances the effect: the shifts in case from the genitive *summi imperatoris* to the nominative *ipse ... imperator* and from the ablative *in exercitu* to the genitive *maximi ... exercitûs* underscore the transformation of Pompey from military novice to general, with the *ipse* emphasising that Pompey has become *imperator himself*. And even though he wasn't yet the *summus imperator* that he is at the time of Cicero's speech, the transference of the superlative from the general under which Pompey served (*summi imperatoris*) to the army he had under his command at a young age (*maximi ... exercitûs*) prefigures his own attainment of the attribute *summus* in due

10 Badian (2009) 17.

course. Cicero may here also be hinting at Pompey's nickname *Magnus* ('the Great').

[*Extra Information*:
Plutarch records the moment when Pompey was first hailed as *imperator* – by none other than Sulla. See his *Life of Pompey* 8.2; the year is 83 BC, after Pompey had won several victories over Sulla's Marian enemies:

> When Pompey learned that Sulla was near, he ordered his officers to have the forces fully armed and in complete array, that they might present a very fine and brilliant appearance to the imperator; for he expected great honours from him, and he received even greater. For when Sulla saw him advancing with an admirable army of young and vigorous soldiers elated and in high spirits because of their successes, he alighted from off his horse, and after being saluted, as was his due, with the title of Imperator, he saluted Pompey in return as Imperator. And yet no one could have expected that a young man, and one who was not yet a senator, would receive from Sulla this title.

Two years later, after a decisive rout of king Iarbas' troops in Africa, Pompey's own soldiers hailed him as *imperator* – a stepping stone towards his first triumph (for which see below).[11]]

summi imperatoris: most likely a complimentary reference to Pompey's father Strabo (who celebrated a triumph in 89 BC for the siege and sack of Asculum and thus could be said to have earned the attribute *summus*), rather than Sulla: Pompey didn't join Sulla's side until several years later, and Cicero at any rate tries to downplay the Sulla-connection whenever possible.

qui *saepius* cum hoste <u>con</u>flixit *quam* quisquam cum inimico <u>con</u>certavit, *plura* bello gessit *quam* ceteri legerunt, *plures* provincias <u>con</u>fecit *quam* alii <u>con</u>cupiverunt: Cicero here identifies three related pairs of (unequal) challenges and asserts that Pompey has mastered the (vastly) more difficult one in each pair more frequently (see the three comparatives *saepius*, *plura*, *plures*, each followed by *quam*) than anyone else has mastered the one that requires comparatively little effort. The four composite verbs *confligere*, *concertare*, *conficere*, and *concupescere* endow the sentence with an alliterative beat, further enhanced by the absence of connectives.

---

11 Plutarch, *Life of Pompey* 12.3.

saepius cum hoste conflixit quam quisquam cum inimico concertavit: to begin with, Cicero contrasts the frequency with which Pompey has defeated an enemy of Rome with the frequency with which anyone else has engaged in strife with a personal enemy. Apart from the higher number (*saepius*), there is a contrast between decisive victories on the battlefield (*conflixit*) and *in*decisive encounters in a court of law (*concertavit*) and one between an outside (military) enemy (*hostis*) and a personal-political enemy (*inimicus*).

plura bello gessit quam ceteri legerunt: the second comparison asserts that the deeds Pompey has performed in war outnumber the military deeds others have read of. We repeat here what we have already pointed out in the Introduction: depending on *the reader*, it could imply very few military feats indeed; if, on the other hand, the reader Cicero has in mind is someone like himself (who had surely perused all the major Greek and Roman historiographers and most of the minor ones as well: you can see him at it in V. Foppa's painting on page 6) the praise turns into panegyric hyperbole. The distinction between acquiring knowledge of warfare through military service as compared to reading about it in books also occurs in the speech the historian Sallust (86-c.35 BC) puts in the mouth of Marius, a *homo novus* ('new man') who held the consulship seven times, in his *Bellum Iugurthinum* 85.13: *Comparate nunc, Quirites, cum illorum superbia me hominem novum. Quae illi audire aut legere solent, eorum partem vidi, alia egomet gessi; quae illi litteris, ea ego militando didici. Nunc vos existimate, facta an dicta pluris sint* ('Compare me now, fellow citizens, a "new man", with those haughty nobles. What they know from hearsay and rʳading, I have either seen with my own eyes or done with my own hands. What they have learned from books I have learned by service in the field; think now for yourselves whether words or deeds are worth more'). We are either dealing with a topos or, possibly, with a Sallustian reworking of a Ciceronian idea.

plures provincias confecit quam alii concupiverunt: *provincia* can mean 'province', in the sense of 'a territory outside Italy under the direct administration of a governor from Rome' (*OLD* s.v. 3), but the English derivative is a 'false friend' here, where Cicero uses *provincia* in its original sense of 'special function or task assigned to a magistrate' (*OLD* s.v. 1). (The term *imperium* – see next sentence – underwent a semantic expansion analogous to *provincia*, from the 'right to command' to 'empire', i.e. the territory over which one has the right to issue orders.) The theme of

Pompey's qualities and achievements surpassing the wildest dreams of his contemporaries recurs in § 48.

cuius adulescentia ad scientiam rei militaris non alienis praeceptis sed suis imperiis, non offensionibus belli sed victoriis, non stipendiis sed triumphis est erudita: the subject of the sentence is *adulescentia*, the verb is *est erudita*. The principle of praise here is the same as in the previous sentence: Cicero identifies three pairs of (unequal) sources of the *scientia rei militaris* that Pompey acquired at the outset of his adulthood (*praecepta v. imperia*; *offensiones v. victoriae*; *stipendia v. triumphi*) and argues that his knowledge derives from the superior ones. These – *imperia, victoriae, triumphi* – constitute the core of aristocratic ambition in republican Rome: military commands (*imperia*) were meant to result in victories (*victoriae*) and ideally the victories were of such magnitude that the general in charge could celebrate a triumph (*triumphus*).

non alienis praeceptis sed suis imperiis: Pompey knows about warfare not because he was the recipient of instruction by someone else (*alienis praeceptis*), but because he was holding the right of command over Roman armies himself, and more than once (*suis imperiis*: note the plural). The contrast is twofold: *alienis* contrasts with *suis*, *praeceptis* with *imperiis*. Even though the grammatical subject of the sentence is *adulescentia*, Cicero uses the reflexive pronoun *suis*, which refers to the understood subject, i.e. Pompey.

non offensionibus belli sed victoriis: Pompey did not have to learn from his mistakes (*offensionibus belli* means something akin to the 'School of Hard Knocks', i.e. the painful education one gets via life's trials and tribulations, here specifically military defeats). Cicero implies that he always emerged from battle victoriously. This is not strictly speaking true, or at least not the whole truth: especially in his campaign against Sertorius in Spain, Pompey experienced major setbacks and outright defeats in battle before he gradually gained control of the situation. Cicero brushes over such nuances in panegyrical simplification.

non stipendiis sed triumphis: the basic meaning of *stipendium* is the cash payment soldiers received; it is also used metonymically in the sense of 'season of military service', 'campaign'. This is the meaning here: Cicero contrasts mere service in the army with the ultimate of achievement in Roman warfare, the celebration of a triumph.

triumphis: most Roman aristocrats would have been over the moon to be awarded a triumph once. By the time of the *pro lege Manilia* in 66 BC, Pompey had already triumphed twice: in 81 (?) BC for his victory in Africa over king Iarbas, in the context of the civil war between Sulla and the Marians;[12] and in 71 BC for his victory over Sertorius in Spain. He was to celebrate a third triumph in 61 BC, for his victories over the pirates and Mithridates. The highly coveted award of a triumph was supposed to follow strict regulations and was, in theory, reserved for senators who had reached at least the praetorship, which meant (again: at least) the age of 39. At the time of his first triumph, Pompey by contrast was in his twenties (!) and still only an *eques* ('knight') – the first *eques* to celebrate the ritual, against the initial resistance of Sulla and others. The people, though, took delight in the extraordinary feat. As Plutarch reports in his biography (*Life of Pompey* 14.6): 'it was a dazzling honour for him to celebrate a triumph before he was a senator. And this contributed not a little to win him the favour of the multitude; for the people were delighted to have him still classed among the knights after a triumph.'

Pompey ensured that the occasion remained memorable in other ways as well. Here is Plutarch again (*Life of Pompey* 14.4): 'When many showed displeasure and indignation at his project, Pompey, we are told, was all the more desirous of annoying them, and tried to ride into the city on a chariot drawn by four elephants; for he had brought many from Africa which he had captured from its kings. But the gate of the city was too narrow, and he therefore gave up the attempt and changed over to his horses.' Plutarch implies that Pompey and his advisors were 'geometrically challenged' when they tried to squeeze the elephants through the gates, and many a modern scholar has followed suit. Seager speaks of an 'element of farce' that 'marred the proceedings';[13] and Cole thinks that 'unfortunately, Pompey had to alter his grandiose plans when the elephants would not fit through

---

12 We know that the triumph took place on 12 March, but the year is uncertain: 81, 80, 79 BC are all possibilities. See Seager (2002) 29 for discussion; he argues for 81 BC as the most likely date.

13 Seager (2002) 28.

the gate'.[14] Surely, however, Pompey and his advisors had sufficient mathematical ability to measure up the backsides of two elephants and the size of a Roman gate. Hence it is much more likely that we are dealing with one of those carefully stage-managed instances of innovative aristocratic self-promotion that formed an essential component of the political culture of the Roman republic. We need to imagine the long triumphal procession grinding to a halt, with everybody watching Pompey attempting the impossible before conceding defeat and switching over from elephants to (conventional) horses – a spectacular and, as Plutarch proves, truly memorable scenario that both signalled his overweening ambition and his ultimate willingness to abide by tradition. The elephants, apart from evoking the African theatre of operation, also marched in the tradition of good old aristocratic emulation (recalling Lucius Metellus (c.290-221 BC), high pontiff, twice consul, dictator, chief commander of the cavalry, etc., who in his triumphal procession after the First Punic War displayed elephants in Rome for the first time) and reinforced Pompey's self-fashioning as a Roman equivalent of Alexander the Great and 'Alexander's mythical ancestors, Heracles and Dionysus, the divine conquerors of the world.'[15]

Quod denique genus esse belli potest, in quo illum non exercuerit fortuna rei publicae?: *quod* is an interrogative adjective modifying *genus*; *in quo* introduces a relative clause of characteristic (hence the perfect subjunctive *exercuerit*). After tracing Pompey's rise to military stardom, Cicero here refocuses his discourse on the issue under consideration with another rhetorical question. The phrase *genus belli* recalls the earlier discussion of the nature (*genus*) of the war against Mithridates. Cicero stresses that Pompey, in the course of his career, has successfully fought in every conceivable kind (*genus*) of war, and in doing so did well by the *res publica* – his appointment under the *lex Manilia* would thus virtually guarantee another victory.

---

14   Cole (2013) 34 n. 50.
15   Weinstock (1971) 37. For Lucius Metellus, see Pliny, *Natural History* 7.139, for Pompey and Alexander, see Sallust, *Histories* 3.84 McGushin ('From his earliest youth, Pompeius had been persuaded by the flattery of his supporters to believe that he was the equal of king Alexander. Therefore he tried to rival Alexander's achievements and plans') and Plutarch, *Life of Pompey* 2.2, for the ritual of the triumph more generally, see Beard (2007).

fortuna rei publicae: *fortuna* should arguably be capitalized (*Fortuna*) and understood as a divine quality endowed with agency: here the *Fortuna* of the *res publica* is said to have taken it upon herself to train Pompey. The Romans dedicated several temples to various manifestations of *Fortuna*: 293 BC (*Fors Fortuna*), mid-third-century BC (*Tres Fortunae*), c.204-194 BC (*Fortuna Primigenia*), 180-173 BC (*Fortuna Equestris*), 101 BC (*Fortuna Huiusque Diei*), in line with shrines and temples to other divine qualities such as *Concordia, Felicitas, Fides, Honos, Libertas, Mens, Ops, Pietas, Salus, Spes, Victoria,* or *Virtus*.[16] Cicero frequently features personified divine qualities as agents in his speeches: 'He describes victoria, for example, as witness and as judge; ... fortuna rei publicae is said to be keeping Pompey busy in all kinds of wars [= our passage here]; fortuna populi romani is described as bringing Pompey to Asia [= *Man.* 45: see below]; and fides is represented leading Cicero himself.'[17] The passage here belongs to a wider sequence of references to Pompey's special relationship to *Fortuna* or *Felicitas*: see §§ 45, 48, 49 below.

Civile, Africanum, Transalpinum, Hispaniense, servile, navale bellum, varia et diversa genera et bellorum et hostium, non solum gesta ab hoc uno, sed etiam confecta, nullam rem esse declarant in usu positam militari, quae huius viri scientiam fugere possit: the sentence has two subjects: *bellum* (prefaced by the string of attributes *Civile, Africanum, Transalpinum, Hispaniense, servile,* and *navale*) and *genera* (prefaced by the two attributes *varia* and *diversa* and governing the genitive phrase *et bellorum et hostium*). Two perfect passive participles agreeing with *genera* follow: *gesta* and *confecta*. The main verb of the sentence is *declarant*, which is placed smack in the middle of the indirect statement it introduces: *nullam rem* is the subject accusative; and the infinitive is either *esse* (as a complete predicate), which would turn *positam* into a perfect passive participle agreeing with *rem* ('... that there is/exists no thing that falls within the remit of military experience...') or *esse ... positam* ('... that no thing falls within the remit of military experience...'). By turning the string of wars in which Pompey participated into eloquent witnesses for his knowledge in military matters, Cicero anticipates the English saying that 'the facts speak for themselves'.

---

16 See the Appendix in Clark (2007) 283-86.
17 Clark (2007) 214-15.

Nevertheless, the list is a telling piece of evidence for the increasing complexity of warfare in late-republican Rome. As Robert Brown notes: '*Bellum* traditionally signified to the Romans a just war waged against non-allied external foes, whether in Italy or overseas – such at least was the ideal. The era of the Gracchi ushered in a century of internal conflict in which the notion of war became fraught with complications.'[18] And he cites our passage as a case in point, not least since *Man.* 28 is our earliest attestation for the phrase *ciuile bellum*. He elaborates: 'Undoubtedly the term was in common use by the 60s but the date of its origin is indeterminable. ... At any rate, the Ciceronian passage attests vividly to the growing complexity of the notion of war. The list presents an odd mixture of abstract and concrete terms. *Ciuile* refers to the wars of the 80s against Cinna and Carbo. The next three wars – *Africanum, Transalpinum, Hispaniense* – exhibit the traditional formula [i.e. the geographical specification of a war on foreign/hostile territory]. *Bellum seruile* ... shifts back to political categorization. *Bellum nauale*, which refers to the campaign against the pirates in 67, formally resembles *ciuile* and *seruile* but characterizes the war by mode rather than enemy. Thus three (or four) *genera belli*: *ciuile, seruile, nauale*, and perhaps in the case of the *bellum Hispaniense*, a *genus mixtum* (a hybrid of civil and foreign war) – none of which, it should be noted, corresponds to the standard type of war fought by the Romans before this era. To classify the complex wars of the late Republic there was a need for expansion and refinement of the traditional terminology.'[19]

Civile ... bellum: in the same year the Social War (91-87 BC) ended, Rome tottered into Civil War between Sulla and (initially) Marius and his supporters. A brief timeline is as follows:

> 87: Marius and the tribune Publius Sulpicius Rufus try to relieve Sulla, who was consul at the time, of his command against Mithridates and transfer it to Marius.
>
> 87: Sulla flees the city, only to march on Rome at the head of six legions he commanded in the Social War. He manages to gain control of Rome, declare Marius and several of his supporters public enemies (*hostes*) and then leave for the East to wage war against Mithridates as planned.
>
> 87: Once Sulla has left the city, renewed fighting breaks out between Sulla's supporters, including the other consul of 87, Gnaeus Octavius, and the Marian

---

18 Brown (2003) 94.
19 Brown (2003) 104.

party, including, prominently, Marius himself, who plotted his return from Africa, his son, Lucius Cornelius Cinna, and Quintus Sertorius. The Marians gain the upper hand.

86: Marius dies.

84: Cinna dies.

83: Sulla, after some initial, inconsequential victories over Mithridates, returns to Italy and defeats the Marian party, now under the leadership of Gnaeus Papirius Carbo, who flees to Africa, and Quintus Sertorius, who retreats to the Hispanic peninsula (with particular strongholds in modern-day Portugal).

In 84 BC, we find Pompey in the camp of Carbo, but soon afterwards he decided to transfer his allegiances to Sulla, raising a private legion from his client base (that is, without senatorial authorization) and presenting it to Sulla upon Sulla's return to Italy from his campaign against Mithridates. This is the moment when he was first hailed as *imperator* (see above). He then helped Sulla to crush the Marian opposition in Italy, with notable success and an ever-swelling army. Cicero acknowledges, but then quickly glosses over, this problematic chapter in Pompey's CV, re-labelling those military operations that were part of the civil conflict but did not take place on Italian soil with reference to the geographical regions where they happened. See below on *Africanum bellum*, *Transalpinum bellum* and *Hispaniense bellum* – three phrases that give the impression of warfare against external enemies. Brown points out that *ciuile bellum* is 'a contradiction in terms, inasmuch as cooperation in war against external enemies would normally be considered one of the chief duties and characteristics of a citizen. "Civil war" in English has lost the paradoxical sense it held in Rome, where the distinction between *ciues* and non-*ciues* was a crucial determinant of status, obligations, and rights.'[20]

Africanum ... bellum: Pompey proceeded to fight against the remaining supporters of Marius who had fled to Africa, but he also campaigned against the African king Iarbas, who backed the Marians. Capture of the king and his kingdom paved Pompey's path to celebrating his first triumph (see above under **triumphis**).[21] (No Roman celebrated a *civil-war* triumph until Julius Caesar.)

---

20   Brown (2003) 103.
21   Plutarch, *Life of Pompey* 12.

Transalpinum ... bellum: after some initial setbacks, Quintus Sertorius, Marius' former ally, managed to consolidate his power base in Spain and, as a renegade, engaged in prolonged warfare against the official Roman presence on the Hispanic peninsula – with notable success. In 77 BC, Pompey was sent to Spain to reinforce the war effort and, on his way, engaged in various battles with Gallic tribes. Cicero's label *Transalpinum bellum* refers to these rather inconsequential encounters.

Hispaniense ... bellum: Pompey struggled mightily against Sertorius, but eventually managed to gain the upper hand; his ultimate victory was facilitated by the assassination of Sertorius during a banquet in 72 BC.

servile bellum: with the war in Spain finished, Pompey returned to Italy, just in time to join in the tail end of Rome's suppression of the slave uprising under Spartacus in 71 BC, upstaging Crassus, who had been responsible for the heavy lifting. See further below on § 30.

navale bellum: in 67 BC, the tribune Aulus Gabinius introduced a bill that called for someone to be given an extraordinary command against the pirates. It was apparent to everybody that the command would go to Pompey (as it did), who quickly brought the pirate problem under control. The *lex Gabinia* was in many ways the blueprint for the *lex Manilia*, and Pompey's success against the pirates Cicero's greatest trump: he spends five full paragraphs of the set text (§§ 31-35) rehearsing Pompey's running of the campaign and returns to the topic throughout the rest of the speech.

varia et diversa genera et bellorum et hostium: the use of synonyms (*varia, diversa*) and polysyndeton (*et bellorum et hostium*) reinforces the point that Pompey has seen every type of warfare, every type of enemy: his *scientia rei militaris* is grounded in comprehensive experience.

non solum gesta ab hoc uno, sed etiam confecta: this is the second time in the paragraph that Cicero uses *conficere* (see above: *plures provincias confecit quam alii concupiverunt*). In each instance, the emphasis is on Pompey's talent to get things done: an important consideration, given the long drawn-out nature of Rome's struggle with Mithridates, which had been flaring up intermittently for the last two decades, and the failure of other generals to finish the job (notably Lucullus, whose ineffective endeavours Cicero recalls in the early parts of the speech).

ab hoc uno: another reminder of Pompey's singularity.

nullam rem esse declarant in usu positam militari, quae huius viri scientiam fugere possit: *quae* (referring back to *rem*) introduces a relative clause of characteristic (hence the subjunctive *possit*).

29: HIS EXCELLENCE (AND EXCELLENCES)

After fairly briskly dispatching the first of four essential attributes of his perfect general, *scientia rei militaris*, in § 28, Cicero here moves on to the second in his list, *virtus*, which receives more extensive coverage (§§ 29-42). In § 29 he introduces three decisive conceptual operations that remain crucial for how the section on *virtus* unfolds:

> (i) He fragments the singular *virtus* into a plurality of *virtutes*. These *virtutes* he defines further in two ways:
>
> (ii) By adding the attribute *imperatoriae*, he implies that there are *virtutes* specific to the general. This in turn entails that the *virtutes* specific to the general do not constitute the sum-total of *virtutes*: there are others as well.
>
> (iii) Within the subcategory of *virtutes imperatoriae*, he distinguishes between those that are *commonly* (cf. *quae vulgo existimantur*) recognized and those that are not. He goes on to list those he considers common ones right away (*labor in negotiis, fortitudo in periculis, industria in agendo, celeritas in conficiendo, consilium in providendo*), but postpones his treatment of the 'uncommon' ones until § 36, i.e. halfway through the section.

All three of these moves are of crucial importance to Cicero's agenda in the *pro lege Manilia*. And all are to some degree both unorthodox and self-serving. To begin with, the switch from the singular *virtus* to the plural *virtutes* 'de-essentializes' *virtus*. Instead of opting for one basic, 'essential' meaning of the term (such as 'martial prowess'), Cicero opens up an entire portfolio of *virtutes*, in which any one quality (such as 'martial prowess') is just one (if perhaps a privileged one) among several others that need to be taken into consideration as well. The use of the plural *virtutes* is not in itself unusual – it also occurs elsewhere in Latin literature, from Plautus and Terence onwards.[22] And yet, in this particular setting, the way in which Cicero 'pluralizes' *virtus* may well have raised the eyebrows of those who, for whatever reason, preferred to think of *virtus* as consisting primarily

---

22 Cicero's discussion of *virtus* at *de Inventione* 2.159, where he defines the term philosophically (and very much *against* Roman common sense) as *animi habitus naturae modo atque rationi consentaneus* ('a disposition of the mind in harmony with nature and reason') and posits that it is comprised of four parts, i.e. *prudentia* ('practical wisdom'), *iustitia* ('justice'), *fortitudo* ('bravery'), and *temperantia* ('moderation'), is slightly different again: it betokens an attempt to impose a Greek intellectual grid of canonical excellences on the Roman notion, but again demonstrates how malleable *virtus* was in Roman discourse, dependent on genre and occasion.

in one particular quality (such as – again – straightforward military excellence). Similarly, other Roman aristocrats might well have balked at the differentiation of *virtutes imperatoriae* into those that are commonly recognized and those that are not. They might have objected that *if* one wanted to distinguish between *virtus* and *virtutes imperatoriae* in the first place, then the *common* understanding of *virtutes imperatoriae* as consisting of *labor, fortitudo, industria, celeritas,* and *consilium* is quite comprehensive, that, in other words, there are no 'uncommon' *virtutes* that qualify for being added to the list. But what Cicero hints at here, he elaborates in detail in §§ 36-42, where he submits that in addition to the 'common ones' the perfect general is also outstanding in *innocentia, temperantia, fides, facilitas, ingenium* and *humanitas*. In contrast to 'courage', 'strategic brilliance', and 'martial prowess', these are all 'soft' virtues, which put the emphasis on ethical excellences, such as integrity of character, self-restraint, trustworthiness, and ease in social intercourse. The conceptual operations here thus ultimately enable Cicero to endow *virtus* with a range of *untraditional* or at least unorthodox meanings – a conceptual creativity that, as we shall see, is a key part not only of his promotion of Pompey, but of his self-promotion as well.

Iam vero virtuti Cn. Pompei quae potest oratio par inveniri?: Cicero begins the new section with a rhetorical question, flagging up the inability of speech (even his) to match reality. The interrogative adjective *quae* and the noun it modifies (*oratio*) are postponed, yielding proleptic pride of place to Pompey's *virtus*. The word order, with *virtus* coming first and the *oratio* about it a distant second, thus mirrors the facts. The *v*-alliteration *vero – virtuti* (cf. also *in<u>v</u>eniri*) adds rhetorical colour.

Iam vero: *iam* can be used to mark a transition to a new topic (here from Pompey's *scientia rei militaris* to his *virtus*); in this sense, it is frequently strengthened by *vero* (as here): *OLD* s.v. *iam* 8a.

inveniri: the basic meaning of *invenio* is 'to encounter, come upon, meet, find'. In rhetoric, it acquired the technical sense 'to devise arguments or topics for a speech'. *Inventio* ('invention', 'finding something to say') is the first of five canonical parts in classical rhetorical theory of how to prepare and deliver an oration. The others are *dispositio* ('the organization of the argument'), *elocutio* ('style', i.e. 'artful expression'), *memoria* ('memory', 'recall'), and *pronuntiatio* or *actio* ('delivery'). Cicero's earliest surviving piece of theoretical prose is entitled *de Inventione*. Cicero thus seems to imply that he could falter at the first task when faced with the challenge of capturing Pompey's *virtus* in discourse. Despite this (mock-)diffidence, he will of course rise to the occasion.

quid est quod quisquam aut illo dignum aut vobis novum aut cuiquam inauditum possit adferre?: The subject and the predicate of the question are *quid* and *est*. *quid* is also the antecedent of *quod*; the subject of the *quod*-clause is *quisquam*; *dignum, novum, inauditum* are predicates of *quod*. Cicero uses a polyptoton of the generalizing *quisquam* ~ *cuiquam* and a polysyndetic (*aut – aut – aut*) tricolon to underscore the futility of anyone (*quisquam*) trying to put Pompey's outstanding ability into words that would be worthy of Pompey (*illo*), novel to the Roman people (*vobis*), or unfamiliar to anyone (*cuiquam*) in the whole wide world. The rhetorical question calls for the answer 'nothing'. Cicero, of course, *will* find something to say worthy of Pompey, new to his audience, and simply unheard of – starting with the next sentence where he claims that there are *virtutes imperatoriae* not commonly thought of as such, a claim that (as we shall see) forms the basis for an interesting bipartite structure to this section. In what follows, then, the posture of modesty adopted here thus imperceptibly turns into a platform of oratorical megalomania that culminates in the assertion at the end of the section (§ 42) that outstanding public oratory features among those things worthy of a general. There is, then, plenty that is novel and unheard of in Cicero's discourse about (Pompey's) *virtus*, and in a special sense the originality of his approach also proves 'worthy' of Pompey (as well as of Cicero himself).

quid est ... quod quisquam ... possit adferre?: *quod* introduces a relative clause of characteristic (hence the subjunctive *possit*): 'what is there of such a kind that...'

Neque enim illae sunt solae virtutes imperatoriae, quae vulgo existimantur,
labor in negotiis,
fortitudo in periculis,
industria in agendo,
celeritas in conficiendo,

consilium in providendo,
quae tanta sunt in hoc uno, quanta in omnibus reliquis imperatoribus,
quos aut vidimus aut audivimus, non fuerunt: the subject of the sentence
is *illae*, which takes *solae virtutes imperatoriae* as predicate and functions as
antecedent of the relative pronoun *quae*: 'those are not the only qualities
specific to a general, which are thought of as such by the people – namely...'.

quae, a connecting relative (= *et ea*), is in the nominative *neuter* plural (cf.
tanta) as Cicero steps back and sums up the preceding qualities (which are
of indiscriminate gender).

labor in negotiis: *labor* is here used in the relatively rare sense of '*application
to work*', 'industry', 'perseverance': *OLD* s.v. 2. Most commonly, it means
'work', 'labour', 'toil', 'physical exertion', 'hardship'. Cicero uses *labor* as
a positive hallmark elsewhere, often in conjunction with another term
such as *studium* (*de Oratore* 1.260: *Atheniensem Demosthenem, in quo tantum
studium fuisse tantusque labor dicitur*: 'Demosthenes, the Athenian, in whom
there is said to have been so much enthusiasm and application to work') or
industria (*in Verrem* 3.103: *hominum summi laboris summaeque industriae*: 'men
of the greatest industry and diligence'). More frequently, *labor* is not itself a
virtus, but the context in which excellence manifests itself. See e.g. *Tusculan
Disputations* 1.2: *in laboribus et periculis fortitudo* ('courage in hardships and
dangers'). The willingness to undergo physical toil and bear hardship is a
key feature of Roman-aristocratic self-promotion.

As for *neg-otium*: as the negation of *otium* ('free time', 'leisure'), it refers
to the fact of being occupied, i.e. 'work' or 'business' and, in particular,
'public or official business', both in the singular and (as here) plural, with
or without the attribute *publicus*.

fortitudo in periculis: *fortitudo* means 'courage' and 'courage' only (unlike
virtus, which can mean 'courage' but also has a wide range of other
meanings). Quintessentially, it captures facing up to danger, in particular
on the battlefield. In § 28, Cicero implicitly divided the qualities that
characterize the perfect military commander into 'hard' and 'soft' ones,
when he lamented the absence of a large pool of *viri fortes atque innocentes*
to choose from (*utinam, Quirites, virorum fortium atque innocentium copiam
tantam haberetis...!*). His supreme commander needs to be brave (*fortis*) first
and foremost, but also show integrity of character (*innocens*) – one of the
'uncommon' qualities Cicero will return to in § 36.

[*Extra information*:

The adjective *fortis* is very common, the noun *fortitudo* less so. Cicero uses it a lot in his philosophical works to translate the Greek term for 'manliness' and courage, i.e. *andreia* (from *anêr*, meaning 'man') since he employs *virtus* (in terms of etymology, the closest equivalent to *andreia*) to translate the Greek term for ethical excellence, i.e. *aretê*.[23] In the speeches, in contrast, *fortitudo* occurs only nine times.]

industria in agendo: *industria* means 'diligence', 'application', 'industry', referring to the careful and purposeful pursuit and execution of tasks, not least in military matters.

celeritas in conficiendo: Given that the war against Mithridates had been dragging on for more than two decades, Pompey's track-record of bringing conflicts to a quick and decisive conclusion (proven not least in his campaign against the pirates: a point that Cicero will hammer home in §§ 32-35, with repeated references to 'speed') is particularly pertinent.

consilium in providendo: *consilium* has a range of meanings, from 'advice/counsel' to 'advisory body/council'. Here it refers to the 'exercise of judgement' or 'discernment' in matters of military strategy or more generally 'strategic intelligence'.

quae tanta sunt ..., quanta ... non fuerunt: *tanta* modifies *quae* in predicative position and correlates with *quanta* ('these are present to such a degree, as...').

in hoc uno ... in omnibus reliquis imperatoribus: an antithesis that contrasts this one specific individual with all the rest. It is reinforced by the chiasmus of (a) *hoc* (b) *uno* :: (b) *in omnibus* (a) *reliquis*.

quos aut vidimus aut audivimus: the antecedent of *quos* is *imperatoribus*. With *vidimus* and *audivimus* Cicero harks back to the end of § 27, where he argued that Pompey outshines in excellence both the glory of his contemporaries (*eorum hominum, qui nunc sunt, gloriam*) and the memory of historical

---

23 McDonnell (2006) 334.

superstars (*memoriam antiquitatis*): *vidimus* refers to individuals within living memory (whether still alive or dead: *vidimus* is in the perfect) and *audivimus* to generals more distant in time or culture. The ancient world produced its share of military geniuses, and Cicero's formulation evokes the spectre of one figure in particular: Alexander the Great. He was widely considered the best and the most successful military leader there ever was, and Pompey, from early on, modelled himself on the Macedonian prince in a spirit of imitation and emulation, starting with his adoption of the epithet '*Magnus*'.

30: WITNESSES TO THE TRUTH!

Cicero now calls on witnesses that can testify to Pompey's nonpareil *virtutes imperatoriae*, thus drawing the language of forensic oratory into the political domain. Mere humans will not do: he gives us a parade of personified countries: Italy, Sicily, Africa, Gaul, Spain, and again Italy, in a powerful sweep across the entire Western Mediterranean, are called upon to vouch for Pompey's excellence in warfare. When Cicero says *Testis est Italia, Sicilia, Africa*, etc., there is no suggestion that he is referring to the Italian, Sicilian, African etc. people. The regions called for testimony are foreshadowed by the list in § 28 about the breadth of Pompey's military experience: *civile, Africanum, Transalpinum, Hispaniense, servile, navale bellum, varia et diversa genera et bellorum et hostium.*

The drum of '*testis est* + country + relative clause' in asyndetic sequence is relentless:

(i) **Testis est Italia**, *quam* ille ipse victor L. Sulla huius virtute et subsidio confessus est *liberatam*.

(ii) **Testis est Sicilia**, *quam* multis undique *cinctam* periculis non terrore belli, sed consilii celeritate explicavit.

(iii) **Testis est Africa**, *quae* magnis *oppressa* hostium copiis eorum ipsorum sanguine redundavit.

(iv) **Testis est Gallia**, *per quam* legionibus nostris iter in Hispaniam Gallorum internecione patefactum est.

(v) **Testis est Hispania**, *quae* saepissime plurimos hostes ab hoc superatos prostratosque conspexit.

(vi) **Testis est iterum et saepius Italia**, *quae* cum servili bello taetro periculosoque premeretur, ab hoc auxilium absente expetivit, quod bellum exspectatione eius attenuatum atque imminutum est, adventu sublatum ac sepultum.

In terms of overall design, Cicero uses ring-composition, starting and ending with Italy, together with a massive rhetorical climax. On his return to Italy (vi), he breaks the established pattern in various ways. First, he adds the adverbs (themselves arranged climactically) *iterum et saepius* in the main clause. Second, he integrates a further construction (the *cum*-clause *cum ... premeretur*) within the relative clause. And third, he continues his account of this particular campaign by means of a connecting relative (or another relative clause) (*quod*). The sense of climax is further enhanced by the way in which Cicero gradually amplifies the degree of agency granted to his geographical personifications in the relative clauses.

- In the first two instances (*Italia, quam...*; *Sicilia, quam...*), they are accusative objects (though the first *quam* is also the subject accusative of the indirect statement introduced by *confessus est*). The subjects are Sulla (*confessus est*) and Pompey (*explicavit*).

- In the third (*Africa, quae...*) and fourth (*Gallia, per quam...*) instances, Cicero does without a human agent, and the regions gain in prominence as the (passive) targets of military or strategic actions.

- And in the final two instances (*Hispania, quae...*; *Italia, quae...*) the regions are the subjects of verbs that presuppose active agency (*conspexit; expetivit*).

One of the effects of personification is to suggest a special relationship of Pompey to the divine sphere – compare the idea of the river(-god) Tiber in the *Aeneid*, who is on speaking terms with Virgil's hero. This adds to the claim, which in fact permeates the speech, that Pompey is favoured by the gods. See further § 48 (discussed below), where Pompey emerges as having special powers over the forces of nature.

Testis est Italia, quam ille ipse victor L. Sulla huius virtute et subsidio confessus est liberatam (sc. *esse*): the relative pronoun *quam* has a double function: it is the accusative object of *confessus est* and the subject accusative of the indirect statement dependent on *confessus est*: *quam ... liberatam* (supply: *esse*). Cicero here refers to Pompey's contribution to Sulla's victory over the Marians in 84-83 BC, specifically his raising of a private army in 84 BC for Sulla's cause. He glosses over the awkward fact that Romans here fought against Romans, leaving it unspecified whom Pompey liberated Italy *from* – an effect reinforced by the passive construction and obfuscated agency – instead of saying, forcefully, 'Pompey liberated Italy', Cicero fudges: 'Italy was liberated by means of Pompey's excellence and help'.

ille ipse victor L. Sulla: Cicero here invokes Sulla as the ultimate winner. It is quite difficult to render the emphasis achieved through *ille ipse* in English: 'that paragon of a victor, Lucius Sulla himself'. The sense is that there is no greater authority on the subject than the former dictator.

confessus est: the verb captures the fact that every Roman aristocrat was keen to claim credit for military achievement: Cicero insists that even the general in charge overall, Sulla, acknowledged Pompey's outstanding contribution to the campaign – even though he will have done so grudgingly.

liberatam: the use of the verb *liberare* ('to free') is striking, especially when compared to other sources. Valerius Maximus (5.2.9), Plutarch (*Life of Pompey* 8), and Appian (*Bellum Civile* 1.80) note that Pompey tapped into the social networks of his father to raise an army for Sulla's cause; and they recognize his contribution to the Sullan victory over the Marians in Italy. But their accounts fall far short of Cicero's claim (attributed to Sulla) that 'Pompey freed Italy', which in comparison emerges as a massive hyperbole.

[*Extra information*:
The verb *liberare* (and the noun *libertas*) carried a powerful, if diffuse ideological charge in the political thought of the late Roman republic. For those with a popular bent, *libertas* referred first and foremost to the sovereignty of the people, which they saw under threat from an in-group of powerful *nobiles*. For the senatorial oligarchy, *libertas* essentially consisted in the preservation of oligarchic equality in access to positions of power (i.e. the absence of an autocrat or tyrant and the maintenance of the status quo).[24] For this reason, they systematically objected to every 'extraordinary command' – such as the one Manilius and Cicero wanted to give to Pompey – as constituting a threat to *libertas*. By associating Pompey with the freeing of Italy from hostile oppression Cicero obliquely appropriates the notion of *libertas* for his cause.]

huius virtute et subsidio: *huius* (the genitive singular of *hic*) refers to Pompey; *virtute* and *subsidio* are ablatives of means.

Testis est Sicilia, quam multis undique cinctam periculis non terrore belli, sed consilii celeritate explicavit: after Sulla and his supporters had vanquished the Marian forces in Italy, high-ranking Marian officers, notably the consul of 82, Carbo, fled South to Africa and Sicily. The senate, by now controlled by Sulla, invested Pompey with praetorian *imperium* and sent him in pursuit. Cicero gives a more precise account of events in §

---

24 See further Arena (2013).

61, in the context of the paradoxical argument that in the case of Pompey, the unprecedented has tradition:

> Quid tam novum quam adulescentulum privatum exercitum difficili rei publicae tempore conficere? confecit. huic praeesse? praefuit. rem optime ductu suo gerere? gessit. quid tam praeter consuetudinem quam homini peradulescenti, cuius aetas a senatorio gradu longe abesset, imperium atque exercitum dari, Siciliam permitti atque Africam bellumque in ea provincia administrandum? fuit in his provinciis singulari innocentia, gravitate, virtute: bellum in Africa maximum confecit, victorem exercitum deportavit. quid vero tam inauditum quam equitem Romanum triumphare? at eam quoque rem populus Romanus non modo vidit, sed omnium etiam studio visendam et concelebrandam putavit.

> [What is so novel as that a mere youth, holding no office, should raise an army at a time of crisis in the commonwealth? Yet he did raise one. Or that he should command it? Yet he did command it. Or that he should achieve a great success under his own direction? Yet he did achieve it. What so contrary to custom as that one who was little more than a youth and far too young to hold senatorial rank should be given a military command and be entrusted with the province of Sicily and Africa and the conduct of a campaign there? He displayed in the performance of these duties remarkable integrity, dignity and capacity: the campaign in Africa, a very serious one, he brought to an end and led his army home victorious. What, indeed, so unheard of as that a Roman knight should hold a triumph? Yet even that the Roman People not merely witnessed but thought fit to attend, and to join in celebrating it with universal enthusiasm.]

Plutarch (*Life of Pompey* 10) reports that Pompey took over Sicily with ease and showed generally great kindness to the indigenous population (no doubt in part with a view to extending his networks of loyal supporters), but that he deliberately humiliated the captured Carbo before having him executed. Cicero again suppresses the civil-war dimension of Pompey's operations in Sicily (gently hinted at in the phrase *multis ... periculis*), choosing to focus on the positive consequences of his arrival for the island (and Roman province) and his ability to establish control through swift strategic planning (*consilii celeritate*) rather than the application of violence or the threat of arms (*terrore belli*).

multis undique cinctam periculis: *multis* and *periculis* go together. The word order is iconic: *multis* and *periculis* encircle (*cingere*) the other words that belong to the participle construction (*undique cinctam*).

non terrore belli, sed consilii celeritate: the word order is chiastic: ablative of means (*terrore*) + genitive (*belli*) :: genitive (*consilii*) + ablative of means (*celeritate*).

Testis est Africa, quae magnis oppressa hostium copiis eorum ipsorum sanguine redundavit: in Africa, Pompey fought both against the Marians and their African allies. This enables Cicero to use the straightforward term for 'external enemy', i.e. *hostis*. Slaughtering *hostes* was unproblematic from a Roman point of view. In fact, the rules for celebrating a triumph required a significant amount of carnage (several thousand enemy soldiers killed). Pompey met the requirement in his victory over the African king Iarbas (which earned him his first triumph), a fact reflected in Cicero's emphasis on bloodshed.

Testis est Gallia, per quam legionibus nostris iter in Hispaniam Gallorum internecione patefactum est: the subject of the relative clause is *iter*. Cicero continues the rhetoric of gore, evoking the notion of a 'road paved with corpses'. He is referring to Pompey's mass-slaughter of Gauls on his way to his appointment in Spain. (*Gallorum* is an objective genitive dependent on *internecione*.)

Testis est Hispania, quae saepissime plurimos hostes ab hoc superatos prostratosque conspexit: if Cicero could present Pompey's slaughter of Africans and Gauls as an uncontroversial achievement, matters become messy again with Spain, where Pompey fought against the Roman renegade Sertorius (a former supporter of Marius, who had established an 'alternative' republic in Spain) as well as indigenous foes. Cicero retains the emphasis on external enemies (*hostes*), but scales back his rhetoric of gore. (Interestingly, in the list of wars in § 28, some manuscripts gloss *Hispaniense* [sc. *bellum*] with *mixtum ex civilibus atque ex bellicosissimis nationibus*: 'consisting of engagements with both citizens and the most ferocious nations'.)

Testis est iterum et saepius Italia, quae cum servili bello taetro periculosoque premeretur, ab hoc auxilium absente expetivit, quod bellum exspectatione eius attenuatum atque imminutum est, adventu sublatum ac sepultum: *servile bellum* refers to the slave revolt orchestrated by Spartacus, which started near Capua (in the vicinity of Naples). The uprising, which began in 73 BC, when Pompey was still fighting in Spain, was initially successful and spread quickly through Southern Italy. The senate eventually put Crassus in charge of eight legions to suppress the rebellion, and he soon re-established Rome's military dominance, winning a decisive victory in 71 BC. By this time, Pompey had returned with his legions from Spain and joined in the mop-up operations. Afterwards, he claimed that the credit for the defeat of the slaves belonged primarily to him, rather than Crassus. See Plutarch, *Life of Crassus* 11. In passing over Crassus in silence, Cicero perpetuates Pompeian spin.

iterum et saepius: literally 'again and more often', in idiomatic English 'over and over again': *saepius* is the comparative form of the adverb *saepe*.

cum: *not* the preposition + ablative (*despite the fact* that an ablative follows!), but the conjunction + subjunctive. *premeretur* is in the imperfect subjunctive to indicate contemporaneous action in secondary sequence.

servili bello taetro periculosoque: Cicero first identifies this war with *servili* and then glosses it with two further attributes that stress the monstrosity of a war against slaves (*taetro*) and the degree of danger that was involved (*periculoso*), not least since it happened very close to home.

ab hoc ... absente: Cicero again uses the demonstrative pronoun to refer to Pompey. *absente* stands in predicative position to *hoc* and may have concessive force, with an oblique dig at Crassus: Italy sought help from Pompey, *even though* he was far away (and other generals in the country). The alliteration *auxilium absente* heightens the apparent paradox; and the hyperbaton generated by the insertion of *auxilium* in-between *hoc* and *absente* puts further emphasis on *absente*. *absente* is the first of three ablatives in this sentence that position Pompey in space and bring him ever closer: first he is absent (*absente*); then he is expected to arrive (*expectatione*); and finally he is there (*adventu*). The design builds up a powerful sense of anticipation and endows his arrival with semi-divine connotations, akin to an epiphany.

quod bellum exspectatione eius attenuatum atque imminutum est, adventu sublatum ac sepultum [sc. *est*]: the *quod*-clause is a syntactically and thematically awkward appendix. It conspicuously breaks the pattern of the previous sentences: *testis est* + region + relative clause, with the region as antecedent of the relative pronoun. There are two ways to construe the *quod*: (i) as a relative pronoun that contains its antecedent (*bellum*) within the relative clause: '… a war, which was …'; (ii) as a connecting relative (= *et id*): 'and this war was…' The second solution is arguably more elegant. The powerful, virtually synonymous pairs of verbs *attenuatum atque imminutum* and *sublatum ac sepultum* obfuscate the fact that Pompey's contribution to the victory was hardly decisive. In fact, the weakening and diminishing of the war in anticipation of Pompey's arrival captures not so much the actual military situation in Southern Italy as the psychology of the inhabitants of Rome, for whom the return of Pompey (further) defused the threat posed by Spartacus.

adventu sublatum ac sepultum [sc. *est*]: the ablative *adventu* is studiously ambiguous. We can take it in a temporal sense ('upon his arrival, the war was finished'); but Cicero invites his audience to spot a causal relation as well: *because of* Pompey's arrival, the war was dead and buried. Either way, the formulation deftly sidesteps the awkward fact that Pompey's military contribution to the war effort was rather inconsequential.

This is not the first passage in which Cicero endows an arrival of Pompey with military significance. Early on in the speech, he claimed that Pompey's mere appearance in the Greek East on his mission against the pirates checked the advance of Mithridates and Tigranes (§ 13):

> cuius adventu ipso atque nomine, tametsi ille ad maritimum bellum venerit, tamen impetus hostium repressos esse intellegunt ac retardatos.

> [They recognize that his very arrival and name, even though he only came for the war against the pirates, nevertheless checked and delayed the attack of the enemy.]

The idiom (in particular the noun *adventus*) and the scenario suggest a god at work and liken the manifestation of the general to an epiphany, i.e. divine power rendered visible. Cicero reinforces this impression at the end of § 13, again in an idiom that recurs in our passage here:

> hunc audiebant antea, nunc praesentem vident tanta temperantia, tanta mansuetudine, tanta humanitate, ut ii beatissimi esse videantur, apud quos ille diutissime commoretur.

[They heard of him; now they see him face to face in such self-control, such gentleness, such human kindness that those seemed to be most blessed with whom he spent the most time.]

The term *praesens*, which in religious contexts is used to refer to the efficacious presence of a god, and Pompey's impact on those around him (profound bliss: *beatissimi*) are symptomatic of divine force. Cicero here links his assimilation of Pompey to the divine sphere with his 'soft qualities' (*temperantia, mansuetudo, humanitas*), on which he will elaborate in detail in § 36.

31: PACIFYING THE POND, OR: POMPEY AND THE PIRATES

With his last 'geographical witness', which is the entire Mediterranean coastline and every city located on it, Cicero has reached a new topic on which he will dwell for several paragraphs (§§ 31-35): Pompey's war against the pirates in the previous year (67 BC). Pirates had bugged Rome for decades and were an endemic danger to seafaring in the Mediterranean. Plutarch has the following graphic account of their doings (*Life of Pompey* 24.1-6):

> The power of the pirates had its seat in Cilicia at first, and at the outset it was venturesome and elusive; but it took on confidence and boldness during the Mithridatic war, because it lent itself to the king's service. Then, while the Romans were embroiled in civil wars at the gates of Rome, the sea was left unguarded, and gradually drew and enticed them on until they no longer attacked navigators only, but also laid waste islands and maritime cities. And presently men whose wealth gave them power, and those whose lineage was illustrious, and those who laid claim to superior intelligence, began to embark on piratical craft and share their enterprises, feeling that the occupation brought them a certain reputation and distinction. There were also fortified roadsteads and signal-stations for piratical craft in many places, and fleets put in here which were not merely furnished for their peculiar work with sturdy crews, skilful pilots, and light and speedy ships; nay, more annoying than the fear which they inspired was the odious extravagance of their equipment, with their gilded sails, and purple awnings, and silvered oars, as if they rioted in their iniquity and plumed themselves upon it. Their flutes and stringed instruments and drinking bouts along every coast, their seizures of persons in high command, and their ransomings of captured cities, were a disgrace to the Roman supremacy. For, you see, the ships of the pirates numbered more than a thousand, and the cities captured by them four hundred. Besides, they attacked and plundered places of refuge and sanctuaries hitherto inviolate, such as those of Claros, Didyma, and Samothrace; the temple of Chthonian Earth at Hermione; that of Asclepius in Epidaurus; those of Poseidon at the Isthmus, at Taenarum, and at Calauria; those of Apollo at Actium and Leucas; and those of Hera at Samos, at Argos, and at Lacinium. They also offered strange sacrifices of their own at Olympus, and celebrated there certain secret rites, among which those of Mithras continue to the present time, having been first instituted by them. But they heaped most insults upon the Romans, even going up from the sea along their roads and plundering there, and sacking the neighbouring villas. Once, too, they seized two praetors, Sextilius and Bellinus, in their purple-edged robes, and carried them away, together with their attendants and lictors. They also captured a daughter of Antonius, a man who had celebrated a triumph, as she was going into the country, and exacted a large ransom for her.

And so does Cassius Dio, as part of his account of Pompey's career (36.20-21):

> Pirates always used to harass those who sailed the sea, even as brigands
> did those who dwelt on land. There was never a time when these practices
> were unknown, nor will they ever cease probably so long as human nature
> remains the same. But formerly freebooting was limited to certain localities
> and small bands operating only during the summer on sea and on land;
> whereas at this time, ever since war had been carried on continuously in
> many different places at once, and many cities had been overthrown, while
> sentences hung over the heads of all the fugitives, and there was no freedom
> from fear for anyone anywhere, large numbers had turned to plundering.
> Now the operations of the bandits on land, being in better view of the
> towns, which could thus perceive the injury close at hand and capture the
> perpetrators with no great difficulty, would be broken up with a fair degree
> of ease; but those on the sea had grown to the greatest proportions. For
> while the Romans were busy with their antagonists, the pirates had gained
> great headway, sailing about to many quarters, and adding to their band all
> of like condition, to such an extent that some of them, after the manner of
> allies, assisted many others. Indeed, I have already related how much they
> accomplished in connection with others. When those wars had been ended,
> the pirates, instead of desisting, did much serious injury alone by themselves
> both to the Romans and to their allies. They no longer sailed in small force,
> but in great fleets; and they had generals, so that they had acquired a great
> reputation. First and foremost they robbed and pillaged those sailing the sea,
> no longer permitting them any safety even during the winter season, since
> as the result of their daring, practice, and success they made voyages in
> security even then; and next they despoiled even those in the harbours. For if
> any one ventured to put out against them, he would usually be defeated and
> perish; but even if he conquered, he would be unable to capture any of the
> enemy by reason of the speed of their ships. Accordingly, they would return
> after a little, as if victors, and would ravage and set in flames not only farms
> and fields, but also whole cities; some places, however, they conciliated, so
> as to gain naval stations and winter quarters in a friendly land as it were.

Cicero's audience, the Roman people, had much at stake in the attempt to
bring the problem under control. Already at this time, the city of Rome relied
to a significant degree on imported corn to feed its growing population,
and the pirates posed a serious threat to the supply lines from Sicily and
elsewhere. The pirates had their basis in the Eastern Mediterranean and
subduing them was thus tied up with the other main military challenges
in the region, i.e. the drawn-out war against Mithridates (the topic of the
lex Manilia and Cicero's speech). One of Cicero's key talking points is the
speed with which Pompey managed to dispatch the pirates. He hints at it
in the last sentence of this paragraph and returns to it in detail in § 35.

Testes [sc. sunt] nunc vero iam <u>omnes</u> orae atque <u>omnes</u> exterae gentes ac nationes, denique maria <u>omnia</u>, cum universa, tum in singulis oris <u>omnes</u> sinus ac portus: the main verb [= *sunt*] has to be supplied. The dissolution of the formula *testis est X*, foreshadowed by the extension of the formula in the preceding sentence (*testis est <u>iterum et saepius</u> Italia...*), indicates a slight change in tone and topic. Instead of calling upon specific countries, Cicero here invokes a plurality of subjects as witnesses – the entire coastline of the Mediterranean Sea, all neighbouring peoples, every bay and harbour – to capture Pompey's truly astounding success against the pirates. In various ways, the design of the sentence reinforces the impression that Cicero's witnesses are innumerable: (i) *omnes orae*, (ii) *omnes exterae gentes ac nationes*, and (iii) *maria omnia* constitute a 'classic' tricolon, even though at first it appears that Cicero has here violated 'the law of successively growing cola' – *maria omnia* is much shorter than *omnes exterae gentes ac nationes*. But this apparent anti-climax in fact sets up the final piece of rhetorical gushing, which throws the entire tricolon out of sync: *cum universa, tum in singulis oris omnes sinus ac portus*. *denique* suggests that *maria omnia* will be the final item, but Cicero then proceeds to explore it in ways that produce deliberate inconcinnities, both in terms of syntax and theme. Only the *cum*-part (the attribute *universa*) fits grammatically with *maria*; in the *tum*-part, Cicero introduces the new subjects *sinus* and *portus*, which stand on their own – a fact further reinforced by yet another instance of *omnis*, which thereby figures four times in one tricolon (i.e. one time too often). Likewise, the *tum*-part, through inclusion of the phrase *in singulis oris*, points back to the first item (*omnes orae*), bringing the sentence full circle: it is as if Cicero, in the way he has designed the sentence, is tracing the entire (irregular) coastline of the Mediterranean Sea. The attributes *omnes – omnes – omnia – universa – singulis* all add to the impression of comprehensiveness.

nunc vero iam: the words recall the *iam vero* of § 29. Each one can be used on its own to mark a transition to a new topic or item or to set up a rhetorical climax. English has a wide range of similar words – 'further', 'moreover', 'now', 'indeed' – but combining them would produce clumsy prose.

omnes exterae gentes ac nationes: the word *gens* has two basic meanings: it can refer to a Roman clan or group of families sharing the same *nomen* and the same supposed ancestors (for example: *gens Iulia*, alleged to derive from Aeneas' son Ascanius renamed Iulus); or it can refer (as here) to a non-Roman nation, people, or ethnicity. In those cases, Roman authors often add the attribute '*exter, -era, -erum*' ('foreign') to eliminate ambiguity.[25] *gens* is etymologically related to *gigno* ('to bring into being, to create'), just as *natio* comes from *nascor* ('to be born'): the two terms are virtual synonyms. The pleonasm adds to the rhetoric of comprehensiveness and generates a parallel design that has *maria, cum universa* at its centre:

omnes orae	~	*in singulis oris*
	maria, cum universa	
omnes exterae gentes ac nationes	~	*omnes sinus ac portus*

sinus atque portus: both are fourth declension nouns in the nominative plural. Like most fourth-declension nouns, they are both masculine. (The two most important exceptions are *manus, -us,* and *domus, -us,* which are feminine.)

cum ... tum...: *cum* is a nasty little word because it can mean all sorts of things. It can be either a preposition with the ablative or a conjunction, introducing a range of subordinate clauses in either the indicative or the subjunctive. But it also has some other uses. Followed by *tum*, for instance, it is used to co-ordinate (and rank) two related circumstances. So whenever you encounter the word, it is a good idea to take a step back and consider what kind of *cum* you are dealing with. Here, the word that follows *cum*, i.e. *universa*, could be in the ablative (suggesting, falsely, that we are dealing with the preposition). It *isn't*, of course! If one tries this option out, insurmountable difficulties soon arise: 'with universal...' doesn't make a whole lot of sense, and a noun that would complete the phrase is of course nowhere to be found – *universa* is in the neuter nominative plural agreeing with *maria*. Perhaps, then, we are dealing with the conjunction? But no finite verb form, in either the indicative or the subjunctive, is coming up! So on to the third option, which requires a *tum* – and lo and behold, here it is![26]

---

25 Note that the masculine nominative singular is *exter* and not (as some vocabulary lists have it) *exterus*.

26 Note that the meaning of *cum* you need here is overlooked in some vocabulary lists, including those approved by OCR.

quis enim toto mari locus per hos annos aut tam firmum habuit praesidium, ut tutus esset, aut tam fuit abditus, ut lateret? The subject of the rhetorical question, which requires the answer 'none', is *quis ... locus*, which takes two verbs coordinated by *aut – aut*: *habuit* (which governs the accusative object *firmum ... praesidium*) and *fuit*. The two *ut*-clauses are both consecutive, each set up by a *tam*. Cicero specifies two possibilities by which places might have remained unaffected from the pirates: either they had such a powerful garrison that the pirates would not have dared to attack or they were so well hidden that the pirates would have been unable to locate them. But the way Cicero phrases the question implies that such places did not exist: the entire Mediterranean (cf. *toto mari*) was under threat from piracy during these years.

quis ... locus: *quis* is an interrogative adjective modifying *locus*.

toto mari: an ablative of place. This is a neat phrase to revise some difficult declensions. *mare, maris,* n. is a pure, third-declension i-stem noun, which means that the dative and the ablative look identical:

	Singular	Plural
Nominative	mare	maria
Genitive	maris	marium
Dative	marī	marībus
Accusative	mare	maria
Ablative	marī	marībus
Vocative	mare	maria

totus, on the other hand, belongs to a group of adjectives that mix the 2nd and the 3rd declension. This means that, unlike straight 2nd declension adjectives, it *is* possible to distinguish between the neuter *dative* singular (*toti*) and the neuter *ablative* singular (*toto*):

	Singular			Plural		
	Masculine	Feminine	Neuter	Masculine	Feminine	Neuter
Nominative	tōtus	tōta	tōtum	tōtī	tōtae	tōta
Genitive	tōtīus	tōtīus	tōtīus	tōtōrum	tōtārum	tōtōrum
Dative	tōtī	tōtī	tōtī	tōtīs	tōtīs	tōtīs
Accusative	tōtum	tōtam	tōtum	tōtōs	tōtās	tōta
Ablative	tōtō	tōtā	tōtō	tōtīs	tōtīs	tōtīs
Vocative	tōte	tōta	tōtum	tōtī	tōtae	tōta

The following little rhyme from George Lord may help you remember the irregular genitive and dative singular endings of *totus* and related adjectives:

> *unus, solus, totus, ullus,*
> *uter, alter, neuter, nullus*
> The ending that these words will give
> is -*ius* in the genitive.
> For dative endings, don't be wrong,
> Like *alius* the -*i* is long.

ut tutus esset ... ut lateret: two result clauses in secondary or historic sequence. The main verbs (*habuit* and *fuit*) are 'perfects without have' (as Morwood calls them) or 'aorists':[27] they refer to a past state of affairs that does not continue in the present (as opposed to present perfects or 'perfects with have'). In historic sequence, the imperfect subjunctive in subordinate clauses (like the result clauses here) refers to the same time as (or a later time than) the verb of the main clause.

quis navigavit, qui non se aut mortis aut servitutis periculo committeret, cum aut hieme aut referto praedonum mari navigaret? In this second rhetorical question, Cicero shifts the focus from (stationary) locations around the Mediterranean to travellers. Just as with the locations, he uses *aut – aut* (this time two pairs) to sketch out the dire condition of sea-faring before Pompey took care of the pirates. If the previous sentence focused on *geographical* ubiquity (*quis ... locus*, i.e. none), here the stress is on the absence of *temporal* respite from danger: people had the choice of sailing either in winter-time when storms would threaten their lives, or during the proper sailing season (which extended from March to October), when pirates would threaten their liberty. (Though one should perhaps not insist on too strict a match between the two pairs of *aut*: while *mortis ... periculo* maps up principally with *hieme* and *servitutis ... periculo* with *referto praedonum mari*, the pirates clearly posed a threat to both liberty *and* life.)

quis navigavit, qui non se aut mortis aut servitutis periculo committeret: unlike the *quis* of the previous sentence, which is an interrogative *adjective*

---

27 Morwood (1999) 86.

(modifying *locus*), the *quis* here stands on its own, as a proud interrogative *pronoun*. *navigavit* is another 'perfect without have' (see note above). The verb in the relative clause introduced by *qui* is in the imperfect subjunctive – imperfect to indicate contemporaneous action in historic sequence; subjunctive because the sense is consecutive/resultative: 'who set sail *without the consequence/result* of putting his life or liberty in danger?' *committeret* governs both a direct object (the reflexive pronoun *se*) and an indirect object (the dative *periculo*). The English equivalent is: 'to expose someone to something'. The two genitives *mortis* and *servitutis* both depend on *periculo*.

hoc tantum bellum, tam turpe, tam vetus, tam late divisum atque dispersum quis umquam arbitraretur aut ab omnibus imperatoribus uno anno aut omnibus annis ab uno imperatore confici posse? Cicero adds yet another rhetorical question but significantly delays the interrogative pronoun (*quis*), which is the subject of the sentence. The main verb is *arbitraretur*, which introduces an indirect statement: *hoc tantum bellum, tam turpe, tam vetus, tam late divisum atque dispersum* is the sprawling subject accusative, *posse* the verb. The present passive *confici* goes with *posse*. As in the two previous rhetorical questions, Cicero uses *aut – aut* to construct an either/or alternative. *uno anno* and *omnibus annis* are 'ablatives of time within which'.

hoc tantum bellum, tam turpe, tam vetus, tam late divisum atque dispersum: the noun here is *bellum*, which Cicero pads out with a string of modifiers: *tantum* refers to the size, *turpe* to the ethics (Rome being bullied by pirates is 'shameful' or 'dishonourable'), *vetus* to the duration, and *late divisum atque dispersum* to the complex geography (it was spread across the entire Mediterranean).

quis umquam arbitraretur: *arbitraretur* is in the imperfect subjunctive. The subjunctive here has *potential* force: Cicero's rhetorical question demands 'no-one' as an answer and he uses the potential subjunctive to present it as an unlikely possibility that anyone would ever have believed feasible what Pompey then actually went on to do.

ab omnibus imperatoribus uno anno aut omnibus annis ab uno imperatore: Cicero neatly correlates extremes (both in the sense of minima and maxima) in duration of time and in the number of available generals: countless generals, but only one year; countless years, but only one general. The design is chiastic: ablative of agency (*ab omnibus imperatoribus*) + ablative of time (*uno anno*) :: ablative of time (*omnibus annis*) + ablative of agency (*ab uno imperatore*). Put differently, from the point of view of military strategy he identifies two pairs that each consists of one positive and one negative aspects: many generals, but very short period of time; all the time in the world, but only one general. Neither scenario, he implies, anyone would have considered a recipe for success. This serves him as foil for Pompey's achievement, who managed to get the job done despite combining *the respective negatives*: only one general + very limited amount of time.

32: THE PIRATES OF THE MEDITERRANEAN

Cicero continues with his onslaught of rhetorical questions, but now gives them a special edge: they all involve his audience, the Roman people, whom he holds to account at least partially for the dire state of affairs caused by the pirates. On the face of it, the tactic of collective shaming is curiously negative, but it generates room for the special relationship between Pompey and the people that Cicero will bring into play in subsequent paragraphs, while also reminding them that technically they are in charge of the far-flung empire that Rome has become. This comes with certain responsibilities, not the least of which is appointing generals capable of dealing effectively with military challenges.

The paragraph falls into three parts. We begin with a string of rhetorical questions (all calling for a negative answer) that put the spotlight on Cicero's audience, the Roman people:

(i) *quam provinciam ... tenuistis...*?

(ii) *quod vectigal vobis tutum fuit*?

(iii) *quem socium defendistis*?

(iv) *cui praesidio ... fuistis*?

(v) *quam multas existimatis insulas esse desertas...*?

He then addresses a rhetorical question to himself:

(vi) *sed quid ego longinqua commemoro*?

After the one sentence that is not a rhetorical question in this paragraph (*fuit hoc quondam ... non sua tecta defendere*), Cicero returns to interrogative mode with three further rhetorical questions that all follow the same pattern: they are introduced by a verb in the deliberative subjunctive, which sets up an indirect statement, followed by a circumstantial *cum*-clause (note, though, that the *cum*-clauses do *not* belong into the indirect statements):

(vii) *... ego ... mare ... clausum fuisse dicam,* **cum***...*

(viii) *... [eos] captos [esse] querar,* **cum***...*

(ix) *... tutum mare non fuisse dicam,* **cum***...*

The pattern continues in the following paragraph (see below). In those last three rhetorical questions Cicero contrasts the ill-fortune that the pirates inflicted on non-Roman citizens (allies, envoys sent to Rome, merchants) with that suffered by Roman armies or official representatives of the Roman people (*exercitus vestri, legati populi Romani, secures,* i.e. axes here symbolic of praetors and their magisterial power).

Quam provinciam tenuistis a praedonibus liberam per hosce annos?: *quam* is an interrogative adjective modifying *provinciam* ('which province'). *tenuistis* governs the direct object *provinciam*; the adjective *liberam* stands in *predicative* position to *provinciam*: NOT 'which *free* province did you keep' (because then you are stuck with *a praedonibus*, which you can't properly fit in), BUT 'which province did you keep *free*' (and then *a praedonibus* fits in very nicely: 'free from pirates'). For *tenuere*, see *OLD* 20: 'to cause to remain, keep, maintain (in a given condition)'.

per hosce annos: *hosce* is the combination of the accusative masculine plural form of *hic, haec, hoc* (*hos*) and the enclitic particle *-ce*, which can be added to demonstratives to strengthen their force: 'throughout *these particular* years'.

quod vectigal vobis tutum fuit?: *quod* is an interrogative adjective modifying *vectigal* ('what revenue'). As *liberam*, *tutum* stands in *predicative* position. NOT: 'what *safe* revenue was there?' BUT: 'What revenue was *safe*?' *vobis* is a dative of advantage, producing an elegant alliteration with *vectigal*.

quem socium defendistis?: Whereas *provincia* and *vectigal* refer to matters of direct concern to the Roman people, the case is less clear-cut with a *socius* ('ally' – more commonly in the plural: *socii*).[28] Still, Cicero implies that it is a matter of *fides* to protect allies.

cui praesidio classibus vestris fuistis?: *cui* may look like yet another interrogative adjective this time in the dative (after the *quam*, the *quod*, and the *quem* of the previous sentences); indeed, it could be one in form, *but it is not* – despite the irritating, since potentially misleading, fact that it is followed by a noun in the same case (dative), i.e. *praesidio*. The facts of the matter are that *cui* is an interrogative pronoun and that *cui* and *praesidio* are two *different* kinds of dative co-ordinated by the verb *fuistis*. *cui* is a dative of advantage ('for whom?'), *praesidio* is a dative of means (*finalis*) answering to the question 'what for?' and standing in predicative position *to the subject* of the sentence (which here is embedded in *fuistis*): 'for whom were *you a bulwark*?' or 'whom did *you* serve *as a bulwark*?'

---

28 On Rome's allies (or, rather, 'slaves to Rome') see the recent monograph by Myles Lavan (2013).

classibus vestris: an ablative of instrument.

quam multas existimatis insulas esse desertas, quam multas aut metu relictas aut a praedonibus captas urbes esse sociorum?: After several interrogative *adjectives* (*quam, quod, quem*) and an interrogative *pronoun* (*cui*), we now get an interrogative *adverb*: *quam* could be an interrogative adjective in the accusative feminine singular, but the fact that it is followed by *multas* makes it clear that it is the adverb meaning 'how'. The main verb of the sentence is *existimatis*, which introduces an indirect statement. The subject accusatives are *multas ... insulas* and *multas ... urbes* and the infinitives are *esse desertas, relictas* (sc. *esse*), and *captas ... esse*.

metu: an ablative of cause.

Sed quid ego longinqua commemoro?: *quid* is here used adverbially, meaning 'why?'

longinqua: the adjective is in the neuter accusative plural and stands in for a noun: 'matters that are remote'.

Fuit hoc quondam, fuit proprium populi Romani, longe a domo bellare, et propugnaculis imperii sociorum fortunas, non sua tecta defendere: Cicero feels outrage, which is reflected in his syntax. Instead of the straightforward *fuit hoc quondam proprium populi Romani* ('this was once characteristic of the Roman people'), he restarts his sentence with a repetition of *fuit* (literally: 'this was once, it was characteristic of the Roman people'). The two infinitive phrases (i) *longe a domo bellare,* and (ii) *propugnaculis imperii sociorum fortunas, non sua tecta defendere* stand in apposition to the demonstrative pronoun *hoc* (in the nominative neuter singular). (Like any other noun, the substantial infinitive can stand in apposition to a noun or (in this case) pronoun.) Such so-called 'appositional infinitives' are best translated by adding a 'namely': 'this was once the case, it was characteristic of the Roman people, namely to wage war...'. As Gregory Hutchinson (2013) points out, the construction resembles (and recalls) a passage in one of the speeches that the Athenian orator Demosthenes delivered against the Macedonian king Philip II, the father of Alexander the Great (*Phil.* 3.36: 'There was, there was something then, Athenians...'). For Athens, Demosthenes laments, 'unbroken victory, empire, and altruistic enterprise belong (hitherto) only in the past' (272). Both Cicero and his Athenian counterpart thus claim that their state has been shamefully letting down its proud tradition of asserting its own proud traditions! (We owe this reference to John Henderson.)

fuit proprium populi Romani: *proprium* (in the nominative) stands in predicative position to the subject of the sentence (embedded in *fuit*) and governs the possessive genitive *populi Romani*.

longe a domo: Macdonald has the following note on the preposition *a*, Cicero's use of which here some of you may find surprising: 'It is Cicero's practice to use the accusative and ablative cases without prepositions to indicate motion to or from a point when that point is indicated by the name of a town or small island, or by the words *domus, rus*, and *humus*. The preposition, however, is used in certain circumstances and is regularly found in conjunction with *longe*.'[29]

Sociis ego nostris mare per hos annos clausum fuisse dicam, cum exercitus vestri numquam a Brundisio nisi hieme summa transmiserint?: This is the *first* of three rhetorical questions (demanding the answer 'no') that are *not* introduced by an interrogative adjective or pronoun but acquire their status as questions from the deliberative subjunctive of the main verb (here *dicam*: 'am I to say...?'). *dicam* introduces an indirect statement, with *mare* as subject accusative and *clausum fuisse* as infinitive. *sociis ... nostris* is a dative of (dis)advantage.

Sociis ego nostris ... exercitus vestri: Cicero here plays with personal pronouns and possessive adjectives to position himself polemically vis-à-vis his audience. He uses an inclusive *nostris* with reference to the allies ('our' – i.e. yours and mine), but uses a differentiating *vestris* with reference to the armies ('your').

cum exercitus vestri numquam Brundisio nisi hieme summa transmiserint: the subject of the *cum*-clause is *exercitus vestri* (nominative plural – the forms of the genitive singular are identical, so don't get confused!). *transmiserint* is perfect subjunctive.

---

29 Macdonald (1986) 65.

Brundisio: an ablative of separation. Brundisium (modern Brindisi) was a major port on the Adriatic coast of Italy, offering the shortest route to Greece. But because of the pirates, Cicero claims, even full-scale armies didn't dare to embark except outside the regular sailing season.

hieme summa: an ablative of time: 'in the middle of winter'.

Qui ad vos ab exteris nationibus venirent captos querar, cum legati populi Romani redempti sint?: This is the *second* of three rhetorical questions (demanding the answer 'no') that acquire their status as questions from the deliberative subjunctive of the main verb (here *querar*: 'am I to lament...?'). *querar* introduces an indirect statement with an – elided! – *eos* as subject accusative (and antecedent of the relative pronoun *qui*) and *captos* (sc. *esse*) as infinitive.

cum legati populi Romani redempti sint: *legati* is nominative plural, *populi Romani* genitive singular. Cicero here refers to the piratical habit of kidnapping Roman officials and collecting ransom in return for their release.

Mercatoribus tutum mare non fuisse dicam, cum duodecim secures in praedonum potestatem pervenerint?: This is the *third* of three rhetorical questions (demanding the answer 'no') that acquire their status as questions from the deliberative subjunctive of the main verb (here *dicam*: 'am I to say...?'). *dicam* introduces an indirect statement with *mare* as subject accusative and *fuisse* as infinitive; *tutum* despite its position in front of *mare* is predicative: NOT 'the safe sea was not' BUT: 'the sea was not safe'. *mercatoribus* is a dative of (dis)advantage.

cum duodecim secures in praedonum potestatem pervenerint: high magistrates of the Roman republic went about their business with an entourage of lictors, who carried the *fasces*: a bound bundle of wooden rods that included an axe (*securis*) when they left the city. The *fasces* were a symbol of magisterial power, with the axe in particular signifying jurisdiction over life and death. Outside Rome, consuls had twelve, praetors six lictors. Cicero here refers to an incident that involved the capture of two praetors (hence 2 x 6 = 12 axes). We know their names (Sextilius and Bellinus) from Plutarch's *Life of Pompey* 24, but nothing else.

33: PIRATES *ANTE PORTAS!*

This section sees a continuation of the onslaught of questions Cicero began in § 31. They serve to illustrate how great the threat the pirates presented was and therefore how great Pompey must be as a general to have successfully defeated them. In the course of his geopolitical sweep, Cicero brings the enemy ever closer to home. He begins in the Eastern Mediterranean (Cnidus, Colophon, and Samos are located in Asia Minor and the Aegean Sea); then he moves to the West Coast of Southern Italy (Caieta and Misenum, both located south of Rome); and finally – and climactically – arrives at the mouth of the Tiber, the city of Ostia, and the harbour of Rome, a mere 15 miles from the capital. Other touches contribute to the (increasing) sense of danger. When he mentions Greek (and anonymous other) locations, Cicero makes no reference to eyewitnesses, but leaves no doubt that even distant places are of vital concern to Roman interests since they help to secure the supply of corn to the capital on which the populace depended for their daily bread (eloquently evoked by Cicero in the relative clause *quibus vitam et spiritum ducitis*). The sack of Caieta, however, occurred within sight of a Roman official (*inspectante praetore*) and the outrageous assault on Ostia virtually within eyeshot of the Roman people (*prope inspectantibus vobis*). These instances of enforced spectatorship find resolution in the final sentence, with the exclamation *pro di immortales!* functioning as pivot between tragedy and triumph. Cicero recalls once more the appearance of the pirates at Ostia, but only as foil for this conclusion that since then Pompey has dealt with the problem so thoroughly that now there is not even any hearsay of pirate activity anywhere in the Mediterranean. The phrase *Oceani ostium* refers to the straits of Gibraltar: in a sense, then, we traverse the entire Mediterranean from East to West in the course of this paragraph, in parallel with the concluding claim that Pompey has rid the entire Sea of pirates.

However, although Cicero is right to argue that Pompey had significant and considerable success against the pirates compared to many of his predecessors, he did not crush them entirely. Rather, he decided to resettle them at Soli in Cilicia (from then on called Pompeiopolis = 'the city of Pompey'), where they were able to build up their strength again during the civil wars. Cicero later seems critical of Pompey's decision not to punish the pirates harshly instead; in his *de Officiis*, written in 44 BC, he criticises the subjugation of morality to expediency in contemporary Rome (in contrast to the righteousness of their ancestors) by saying 'we give immunity to pirates and make our allies pay tribute' (3.49). It was not until Augustus held power long term that the threat of the pirates was completely removed.

Cnidum aut Colophonem aut Samum, nobilissimas urbes, innumerabilesque alias captas esse commemorem, cum vestros portus atque eos portus, quibus vitam et spiritum ducitis, in praedonum fuisse potestate sciatis?: The sentence continues and concludes the sequence of rhetorical questions that began in the previous paragraph and followed the pattern of a verb in the deliberative subjunctive (here: *commemorem*) setting up an indirect statement (*Cnidum ... captas esse*) followed by a circumstantial *cum*-clause (*cum vestros portus ... sciatis*). The rhetorical design of the sentence is the same as that of the three preceding ones: Cicero contrasts the ill-fortune that the pirates inflicted on non-Roman citizens (in this case famous, and not so famous, Greek cities) with that suffered by Romans in what amounts to an '*a fortiori praeteritio*'. The fact that the pirates had been encroaching upon Rome itself trumps their abuse of allies and others: there is no reason why Cicero should treat the latter in any detail, given that the former is so much more shocking. But he tweaks the syntax of the *cum*-clause slightly, thereby achieving an elegant transition to his approach in the subsequent sentences. In the previous three *cum*-clauses, he stated the outrage committed on Romans as a matter of fact: *cum ... transmiserint; cum ... redempti sint; cum ... pervenerint.* He could have continued this pattern by writing: *cum vestri portus atque ei portus, quibus vitam et spiritum ducitis, in praedonum fuerint potestate.* Instead, he uses the second person plural of a verb of knowing (*sciatis*), which governs the indirect statement *vestros portus atque eos portus* [= subject accusative] ... *in praedonum fuisse* [= infinitive] *potestate*. This direct address to the audience continues in the next sentence: *an vero ignoratis*...?

commemorem: deliberative subjunctive introducing an indirect statement: the accusatives are Cnidus, Colophon, Samos, as well as innumerable other cities Cicero does not name, and the infinitive is *captas esse*. Like many of the verbs in this section, *captas esse* is passive; the agents are of course the pirates, so we need to understand an implied *a praedonibus*.

Cnidum aut Colophonem aut Samum, nobilissimas urbes, innumerabilesque alias: Plutarch, *Life of Pompey* 24, recounts the indiscriminate plundering of the pirates in the Eastern Mediterranean, mentioning Samos (but not Cnidus or Colophon): 'Besides, they attacked and plundered places of refuge and sanctuaries hitherto inviolate, such as those of Claros, Didyma, and Samothrace; the temple of Chthonian Earth at Hermione; that of Asclepius in Epidaurus; those of Poseidon at the Isthmus, at Taenarum, and at Calauria; those of Apollo at Actium and Leucas; and those of Hera at *Samos*, at Argos, and at Lacinium.'

cum vestros portus atque eos portus ... in praedonum fuisse potestate sciatis?: *sciatis* is in the subjunctive in a circumstantial *cum*-clause. It introduces another indirect statement: *vestros portus* and *eos portus* are the subject accusatives, and *fuisse* the infinitive. Cicero distinguishes between the harbours that were (or ought to have been) under direct control of the Roman people (*vestros portus*) and those from which shipments of corn were sent to Rome (*eos portus*). The pirates managed to bring each type into their power, at least temporarily.

quibus vitam et spiritum ducitis: *quibus* is either an ablative of origin or an instrumental ablative; the indicative *ducitis* signals that the relative clause is not part of the indirect statement (otherwise the verb would be in the subjunctive): Cicero is stating a fact. The phrase *vita et spiritus* refers, literally, to 'breath as the concomitant of life or consciousness' (*OLD* s.v. *spiritus* 3); here Cicero uses it metaphorically to refer to Rome's corn supply, which the pirates put under threat.

in praedonum fuisse potestate: there is both a prepositional hyperbaton (the preposition *in* is not immediately followed by *potestate*, the noun it governs) and verbal hyperbaton (*fuisse* breaks up the phrase *praedonum potestate*) here. These smaller rhetorical flourishes do not compromise the audience's understanding of Cicero's sentences or force it to wait until the end of the sentence for key information as a periodic sentence does, but add some spice and make the syntax a little more exciting. The unusual word order could also mirror the disruption the pirates caused to Roman systems.

An vero ignoratis portum Caietae celeberrimum ac plenissimum navium inspectante praetore a praedonibus esse direptum? ex Miseno autem eius ipsius liberos, qui cum praedonibus antea bellum gesserat, a praedonibus esse sublatos?: *ignoratis* introduces two further indirect statements:

(i) *portum* (subject accusative) ... *esse direptum* (infinitive)

(ii) *liberos* (subject accusative) ... *esse sublatos* (infinitive)

Unlike the main verb in the previous sentence, *commemorem*, or the three at the end of § 32 (*dicam, querar, dicam*), Cicero does not use a deliberative subjunctive or the first person singular to ask this question. Instead, he addresses his audience directly with *ignoratis*, a second person *plural* present indicative active. Why does he alternate? Perhaps he wanted to add some variety, perhaps he wanted to ensure he held the people's attention by putting them on the spot, perhaps he wanted to obfuscate his less than precise 'recall' of events (for which see below). (The rhetorical question presupposes 'no, we do know' as an answer, whether it is actually true or not...). With *querar* in the subsequent sentence, Cicero switches back to the deliberative subjunctive.

an: the particle *an* introduces a direct question that includes a notion of surprise or indignation and/or expects a negative answer (as here).

portum Caietae: a harbour, situated on the coast of Latium south-west of Formiae (a town north of Naples). Cicero here surprisingly uses a genitive of definition ('the harbour *of Caieta*'); usually in classical Latin geographical specifications stand in apposition to the general noun: *urbs Roma* (rather than *urbs Romae*). (English, in contrast, prefers the genitive of definition: 'the city of Rome'.)

celeberrimum ac plenissimum navium: *navium* is genitive plural and stands *apo koinou* with *celeberrimum* and *plenissimum*. The superlatives rhetorically pad out the facts.

inspectante praetore: an ablative absolute. If this phrase is translated with concessive force ('*even though* a praetor was watching'), it gives the impression that not even the presence of Roman authority-figures sufficed to stop the pirates. The indifference of pirates to the presence of a Roman magistrate with normal *imperium* seems implicitly to justify giving extraordinary powers to Pompey. There is also a neat contrast between Pompey's ability to subdue enemies while still far away (cf. the end of § 30: while still absent from Italy, he nevertheless managed to have a significant impact on the suppression of the revolting slaves) and the inability of an ordinary magistrate to thwart the pirates running riot in his sphere of command. Listing the sufferings and misfortunes of senators, who were at the top of the Roman pecking order, at the hands of the pirates also suggests that the average Roman citizen was vulnerable and would be entirely powerless against them. This impression is furthered through the parallel between the phrases *inspectante praetore* and *inspectantibus vobis* two sentences later. They are both ablative absolutes with the verb *inspecto* and so suggest the Roman people are just as helpless as the praetor at Caieta. It is not entirely clear who the praetor actually was – and given his pathetic inability to deal with the pirates the suppression of his name is probably a deliberate act of rhetorical mercy on Cicero's part. One promising candidate is M. Antonius Creticus, one of the praetors of 74 BC, who was in charge of a fleet located at Misenum, the place where the alleged abduction of his children occurred.

ex Miseno autem eius ipsius liberos, qui cum praedonibus antea bellum gesserat, a praedonibus esse sublatos?: Intuitively, one is tempted to relate *eius ipsius* back to the 'watching praetor' of the previous sentence; but this is not a requirement. The pronouns, which are the antecedent of the relative pronoun *qui*, could simply look forward to a different individual – i.e. the person who *had* waged war against the pirates *some time ago*. And indeed, commentators link this reference to a piece of information in Plutarch's *Life of Pompey*, who reports that the pirates abducted the daughter (singular!) of M. Antonius, the *father* (!) of M. Antonius Creticus, off the coast of Italy; then they go on to argue that Cicero here uses 'a rhetorical plural' instead of the accurate singular. However, for the plural to register *as* 'rhetorical', the audience would have to have their facts straight. Yet how many citizens present at the delivery of the speech would have been able to grasp on the spot that Cicero is referring to two different Antonii and two events separate in time, and, moreover, is using a rhetorical plural? Our guess is: not too many (especially since he keeps matters anonymous). For the inattentive listener, Cicero conjures up a praetor who had fought the pirates unsuccessfully and had his children abducted on top of it. Why does he do it? Arguably, because in terms of both simplicity and drama, his potted version of events is rhetorically superior to one that is painstakingly accurate (but boring in its details). It deserves emphasis, though, that Cicero always treads very carefully when he distorts history: M. Antonius had commanded a fleet against the pirates back in 102 BC, and with the pluperfect *gesserat* and the adverb *antea* he seems to acknowledge, however obliquely, that the Antonius at issue is not the praetor, but his father, without troubling the audience by elaborating on this point explicitly.

gesserat: although this verb is in a subordinate clause in indirect speech (introduced by *ignoratis*), it is in the indicative because Cicero accepts this as fact, not simply as something reported which he does not wish to verify.

Nam quid ego Ostiense incommodum atque illam labem atque ignominiam rei publicae querar, cum prope inspectantibus vobis classis ea, cui consul populi Romani praepositus esset, a praedonibus capta atque oppressa est?: Cicero reverts to the deliberate subjunctive. *querar,* however, does not introduce an indirect statement but takes a series of direct objects linked by *atque*: (i) *Ostiense incommodum,* (ii) *illam labem,* (iii) *ignominiam rei publicae,* all of them referring to the same event. What follows is not, as previously, a *cum*-clause in the subjunctive, but a *cum*-clause in the indicative (*cum classis ea ... capta atque oppressa est*) – an unexpected shift in mood that underscores Cicero's indignation at arguably the greatest outrage committed by the pirates against the Roman people, the attack on the harbour of Ostia, reported also in Cassius Dio (36.23): 'As these operations of theirs met with success it became customary for the pirates to go into the interior, and they inflicted many injuries on those even who had nothing to do with the sea. This is the way they treated not only the distant allies of Rome, but even Italy itself. For, believing that they would obtain greater gains in that quarter and also that they would terrify all the others still more if they did not keep their hands off that country, they sailed into the very harbour of Ostia as well as other cities in Italy, burning the ships and pillaging everything.'

Ostiense incommodum: the adjective *Ostiense* is here used to indicate location: 'the set-back at Ostia'. Ostia, Rome's seaport, comes from the Latin word for 'the mouth of a river', i.e. *ostium*, which in turn derives from the Latin word for mouth, i.e. *os*. It is the place where the river Tiber flows into the Mediterranean.

illam labem: the demonstrative pronoun or (as here) adjective *ille, illa, illud* often carries the notion of 'common knowledge', 'fame', or (as here) 'notoriety': 'that disaster (which you are all familiar with)'.

ignominiam rei publicae: *rei publicae* could be either a possessive genitive ('disgrace of the commonwealth') or a dative of disadvantage ('disgrace for the commonwealth').

prope inspectantibus vobis: an ablative absolute. *prope* ('almost') renders the hyperbole acceptable: Ostia was located about 30 kilometers from the city.

classis ea, cui consul populi Romani praepositus esset: the antecedent of *cui* is *classis ea*, with the demonstrative adjective *ea* (in unusual postpositive position) setting up the consecutive relative clause – hence the (pluperfect passive) subjunctive *praepositus esset*. The consecutive force underscores the fact that the pirates didn't just sink any old fleet, but a fleet of such importance that it was under the command of a consul of the Roman people. Who that consul was we do not know.

capta atque oppressa est: although these are verbs in a *cum*-clause, it is a temporal *cum*-clause and so is followed by the indicative, not the subjunctive. With the relevant vowels elided (final 'a' in *capta*, 'e' in *atque*, 'e' in *est*) this phrase scans entirely spondaic. The spondaic rhythm adds to the grave tone and feeling of disaster Cicero's has built up across this and the preceding sections.

pro di immortales!: Cicero uses the interjection *pro* followed by the vocative *di immortales* as pivot from highlighting, via a long string of rhetorical questions, what threat the pirates posed to the Roman people, to Pompey's quick and resounding victory over them in the previous year. The invocation of the immortal gods at this point is thematically appropriate insofar as Cicero goes on to position Pompey vis-à-vis the divine sphere in the following sentence in two countervailing ways: by referring to him as a 'human being' (cf. *hominis*), he emphasizes the distinction between 'mortals' and 'immortals' and leaves no doubt that Pompey belongs to the former, yet by means of the phrases *divina virtus* and *tantam ... lucem adferre rei publicae* he subtly assimilates him to the gods.

tantamne unius hominis incredibilis ac divina virtus tam brevi tempore lucem adferre rei publicae potuit, ut vos, qui modo ante ostium Tiberinum classem hostium videbatis, nunc nullam intra Oceani ostium praedonum navem esse audiatis? The final sentence of the section is yet another rhetorical question. However, this time, Cicero uses the device to marvel at Pompey's remarkable skill in ridding the Mediterranean of the pirates so effectively and so quickly. *adferre* governs both an accusative object (*tantam ... lucem*: note the massive hyperbaton) and a dative (*rei publicae*). *tantam* and *tam* set up the result clause *ut ... audiatis*. *audiatis* governs an indirect statement with *nullam ... navem* (another massive hyperbaton) as subject accusative and *esse* as infinitive. Within the *ut*-clause, Cicero highlights the fantastic turn-around achieved by Pompey by means of the antithesis of *modo* ('just recently') and *nunc* ('now') and a geographical contrast: if a little while ago the pirates ran riot at the mouth of the Tiber (*ante ostium Tiberinum*), now none of their ships can be found anywhere within the entire Mediterranean (*intra Oceani ostium*). The danger has receded from sight (*videbatis*) to the absence of any rumour (*audiatis*). Set out schematically, the *ut*-clause and the relative clause therein compare and contrast as follows:

modo	~	*nunc*
ante	~	*intra*
ostium Tiberinum	~	*Oceani ostium*
classem hostium	~	*nullam ... praedonum navem*
videbatis	~	*audiatis*

Cicero introduces a touch of (chiastic) variation into his otherwise parallel design by playing with the position of attributes and genitives: (a) *ostium* (b) *Tiberinum* – (b) *Oceani* (a) *ostium*; (a) *classem* (b) *hostium* – (b) *praedonum* (a) *navem*.

tantamne ... lucem: *-ne* is an interrogative particle used in direct questions; it tends to attach itself to emphatic words (such as *tantam* here).

incredibilis ac divina virtus: Cicero endows this aspect of Pompey's *virtus* with two elevating attributes: *divina* ('divine' or 'god-like') and *incredibilis* ('defying belief').

In the political culture of the Roman republic 'godlikeness' was not an unproblematic form of praise:[30] to elevate a specific individual above the rest of humanity was at variance with the principle of oligarchic equality that underwrote the senatorial regime of republican government. At the same time, many outstanding individuals – from Scipio Africanus Maior to Sulla and the young Caesar – staked claims to a special relationship with the gods, and Cicero's panegyric of Pompey would have been flat if he had not explored Pompey's relationship with the divine sphere. He does so most explicitly in the paragraphs on *felicitas* (§§ 47-48: see below), but also elsewhere in the speech, not least by strategically deploying the attribute *divinus*. Cicero ascribes Pompey's success over Sertorius to his *divinum consilium ac singularis virtus* (§ 10) and the term recurs as attribute of his *virtus* both here and in § 36 (discussed below).[31] It is not easy to determine how Cicero wanted the attribute to be understood in each individual instance. The semantics of *divinus* range from the literal (pertaining to the divine sphere) to the metaphorical. In the latter sense *divinus* loses its association with the divine and becomes synonymous with more mundane markers of distinction such as *praeclarus*, *eximius*, or *mirabilis*. In some instances, it is obvious whether the usage is literal or metaphorical. In § 42, for instance, Cicero claims that Pompey was born *divino quodam consilio* to end all wars, clearly referring to some supernatural charter (to be discussed in more detail below). From an ideological point of view, such a passage is fairly unproblematic. While Pompey appears to be acting in accordance with the will of the gods, this kind of religious privilege stays short of the claim that he himself possesses supernatural powers. Suggestive ambiguities arise, however, when the adjective is made to refer not to the gods, but to human beings or their capacities, as is the case with Pompey's *divinum consilium* and *divina virtus*. In those instances it remains unclear whether the literal or the metaphorical meaning of the attribute is in force. Whether Pompey's exercise of judgement or his courage are truly divine, a gift from the gods, or merely outstanding is impossible to decide – and Cicero exploits this ambiguity for a panegyric that plays with fire while trying to avoid a

---

30 This paragraph is based on Gildenhard (2011) 266-67.
31 Contrast § 20, where Cicero praises the *virtus*, *assiduitas* and *consilium* of Lucullus; unlike Pompey's qualities, those of Lucullus' come without distinguishing attributes.

conflagration: he nudges Pompey skywards without explicitly claiming divinity for him.

tam brevi tempore: Pompey cleared the Western Mediterranean of pirates in just 40 days and the Eastern Mediterranean in 49 days in the course of the summer of 67 BC.

lucem adferre rei publicae: The phrase receives discussion by Kathryn Welch, in her study of light metaphors used in Roman public discourse: 'The phrase *lucem adferre* is not a common one in Cicero. It is used on only one other occasion [*Philippics* 13.44] and there it serves to indicate the depths to which the *res publica* has sunk. ... In both cases, the emphasis is on *virtus* placed at the disposal of the community for its greater good.'[32]

ante Oceani ostium: *ante* here is the preposition + accusative; *Oceani ostium* (literally: 'the mouth of the Ocean') refers to the strait of Gibraltar.

---

32 Welch (2005) 326.

34: POMPEY'S CRUISE CONTROL (I): 'I HAVE A FLEET – AND NEED FOR SPEED'

This and the next paragraph elaborate on Pompey's campaign against the pirates, putting the emphasis on the speed with which he completed the task of sweeping the Mediterranean clean, thus securing the corn-supply for the capital (heavily dependent on overseas imports) and expanding Rome's imperial control in the process. The repetition of the phrase *tam brevi tempore* ('in such a short period of time') underscores the continuity to what has come before; and Cicero again puts the emphasis on Pompey's ability to get things done: *celeritas in conficiendo* (§ 29) continues to be his major theme in this paragraph as well (cf. *celeritate, celeriter, conficere*). Seemingly inconspicuous words (*tam, tot, tanti, umquam, nondum*) serve to enhance the sense of wonder at Pompey's achievement.

Atque haec qua celeritate gesta sint, quamquam videtis, tamen a me in dicendo praetereunda non sunt: translating literally, one would get: 'And even though you see (sc. for yourselves) with what speed (*qua celeritate*) these things (*haec*) were accomplished, they nevertheless ought not to be passed over by me in my speech.' This, of course, produces nonsense: Cicero has just spoken about 'these things' (*haec*), so he can't possibly be disinclined to mention them now. Rather, what he doesn't want to pass over without comment is the *speed* with which Pompey accomplished his task of eliminating the pirates. So why doesn't the Latin say this? As it happens, *haec*, which belongs into the indirect question introduced by *qua*, has been pulled up front (into a so-called proleptic position) to facilitate the transition, with the awkward, further consequence that it has 'bullied' the gerundive *praetereunda non sunt* into agreeing with it grammatically though not in sense. There is another oddity involved in the gerundive construction: unusually, Cicero opts for an ablative of agency (*a me*) to go with it rather than a dative of agency (*mihi*). (It is difficult to know why he opted for the ablative – perhaps he liked the assonance of (*t-*)*a-me-*(*n*) *a me*?) If one were to iron out every wrinkle, the sentence would run: *atque quamquam videtis qua celeritate haec gesta sint, tamen mihi in dicendo praetereundum non est.* Possibly, the grammatical incongruities enact the theme of the sentence: surpassing speed, manifesting itself in somewhat rough-and-ready prose. For another instance of this, see below on *quam celeriter*.

qua: an interrogative adjective in agreement with *celeritate*; it introduces an indirect question, dependent on *videtis*, hence the subjunctive *gesta sint*. The tense is perfect for past action in primary sequence.

in dicendo: a gerund, so literally 'in speaking'.

Quis enim umquam aut obeundi negotii aut consequendi quaestus studio tam brevi tempore tot loca adire, tantos cursus conficere potuit, quam celeriter Cn. Pompeio duce tanti belli impetus navigavit?: The demonstrative adverb *tam* ('in *so* little time') sets up the relative adverb *quam* ('as'), which is followed by another adverb (*celeriter*). This is a bit awkward. If one construes *quam* with *tam* as well as *celeriter* and translates literally one would get: 'who in their zeal for attending to business or making profit, was ever able to visit so many places, to complete such long journeys *in as little time as quickly as* it took for the charge of such a massive military operation to sweep across the sea under the leadership of Gnaeus Pompeius?' This isn't good English. Intelligibility improves if one construes *celeriter* as a free-standing adverb with *navigavit*: 'in so little time ... as it took Pompey's force to sail *speedily*...'. The point that Cicero is making, reinforced by the pleonastic *celeriter*, is that no-one on his business travels could have visited as many places in as short a time as it took Pompey to sweep across the entire Mediterranean on his military campaign.

aut obeundi negotii aut consequendi quaestus studio: *studio* is an ablative of cause or modus that governs two adjectival gerundive phrases in the genitive singular coordinated by *aut – aut*: *obeundi negotii* and *consequendi quaestus*. The *aut – aut* here clearly does not set up logically *exclusive* alternatives, but rather 'emphasizes the necessity of one alternative, without excluding the possibility of the other simultaneously' (*OLD* s.v. *aut* 2b).

quam celeriter Cn. Pompeio duce tanti belli impetus navigavit?: The subject of the *quam*-clause is *impetus*, which basically means 'aggressive movement', 'onslaught', and therefore is a rather peculiar choice of diction: Cicero seems to abstract from Pompey's fleet (which did the actual sailing) and put the emphasis entirely on the decisive quality of speed. The genitive attribute *tanti belli* enhances the oddity: how can the 'movement of so great a war' sail? It is Cicero's way of saying that Pompey moved the war quickly across the Mediterranean, and as he tries to capture the speed of operation in words, his prose waxes poetical: *impetus* is (as it were) the personification of Pompey's military prowess.

Cn. Pompeio duce: *Cn.* = *Gnaeo.* The phrase is an ablative absolute consisting of two nouns, but lacking a participle (which one could think of as being the – non-existent – present participle of *sum*): 'with Gnaeus Pompeius being the leader' = 'with Gnaeus Pompeius as leader'. (Julius Caesar spotted this gap in the Latin language and in the *de Analogia,* his treatise on grammar and style, proposed *ens, entis* as a present participle form of *sum*, on the analogy of *potens, potentis* (the present participle of *posse*). It didn't catch on until much later.)

qui nondum tempestivo ad navigandum mari Siciliam adiit, Africam exploravit; in Sardiniam cum classe venit, atque haec tria frumentaria subsidia rei publicae firmissimis praesidiis classibusque munivit: sailing on the Mediterranean in winter was a risky business in light of the frequent storms at that time of the year, but Pompey considered securing the corn-supply from overseas (Sicily, Africa, Sardinia) a matter of utmost urgency that countenanced no delay, whatever the dangers. The message here is that he acted in the interest of the Roman people with no regard for personal safety.

qui: a connecting relative (= *et is*).

nondum tempestivo ad navigandum mari: the entire phrase is an ablative of location. The central word is the noun *mari* ('on a sea'), which is modified by the adjective *tempestivo* in *predicative* position (NOT 'a seasonable sea...', BUT 'a sea seasonable to...'). *tempestivo* is in turn modified by the adverb *nondum* ('not yet') and governs the preposition *ad* + accusative which here expresses purpose and governs the gerund ('verbal noun') *navigandum* ('a sea not yet seasonable for sailing'). Given the meaning of 'tempest' and 'tempestuous' in English, the Latin *tempestivus*, which agrees with *mari*, may be a 'false friend'. It comes from the noun *tempestas*, which can mean 'bad or stormy weather' or more generally 'violent disturbance', but its basic meaning is 'period', 'season', 'weather'. The adjective *tempestivus* refers to something 'ready', 'in season', 'suitable or opportune for a specific season or time'.

... Siciliam adiit, Africam exploravit, in Sardiniam ... venit, atque haec tria frumentaria subsidia ... munivit: the sentence features four main verbs. The first three – referring to Pompey's operations in the Western Mediterranean – follow upon each other asyndetically, in line with Pompey's 'breathless speed'. Cicero uses a connective (*atque*) to link the third and the fourth item, which sums up the previous three by giving the reason for Pompey's visits to Sicily, Africa, and Sardinia, i.e. securing the corn supply.

35: POMPEY'S CRUISE CONTROL (II): 'I HAVE A FLEET – AND NEED FOR SPEED'

Cicero continues his account of Pompey's war against the pirates. After securing the corn supply through quick visits to Sicily, Africa, and Sardinia, Pompey undertook a systematic sweep of the entire Mediterranean, from West to East, starting in Spain and ending in Asia Minor, more specifically Cilicia, the traditional stronghold of the pirates, which he 'pacified' and brought under permanent Roman control. The paragraph falls into three main parts. The first sentence (*Inde cum ... Ciliciam adiunxit*) retraces the various stages of the campaign with a broad brush, before Cicero focuses in on various details (*omnes ... imperavit*). He then pithily sums up Pompey's main achievement: taking care of the seemingly intractable pirate problem within one single campaigning season (*Ita tantum bellum ... confecit*). Apart from Pompey's supreme military achievement, Cicero begins to highlight the 'soft' qualities that characterize his approach to campaigning, in preparation for the next paragraph. Thus he stresses that Pompey did not simply kill all and sundry but accepted surrender and was in general willing to negotiate with enemies to reach a diplomatic solution to conflict. What Cicero fails to mention is the strategic rationale behind Pompey's preference for quick-fix diplomacy over prolonged warfare in solving the pirate problem. Pompey tried to avoid at all costs getting bogged down in a protracted military campaign that might have ruled him out of consideration for the looming war against Mithridates – a much more appealing prospect than chasing after pirates and storming their strongholds. As it happened, Metellus, the Roman general in charge of military operations in Crete at the time, pushed for a complete military victory over the local communities, which resulted in the embassy to Pompey: the Cretans hoped to receive more favourable terms of surrender from him.

Inde cum se in Italiam recepisset, duabus Hispaniis et Gallia Transalpina praesidiis ac navibus confirmata, missis item in oram Illyrici maris et in Achaiam omnemque Graeciam navibus Italiae duo maria maximis classibus firmissimisque praesidiis adornavit, ipse autem, ut Brundisio profectus est, undequinquagesimo die totam ad imperium populi Romani Ciliciam adiunxit: this is a long sentence, which is best broken down into its constituent parts:

(i) We begin with a *cum*-clause: **Inde cum se in Italiam recepisset...**

(ii) then we get an ablative absolute: ...**duabus Hispaniis et Gallia Transalpina praesidiis ac navibus confirmata...**

(iii) ... and another ablative absolute: ...**missis item in oram Illyrici maris et in Achaiam omnemque Graeciam navibus...**

(iv) ...before we reach the main clause. It falls into two halves:

> (a) **Italiae duo maria maximis classibus firmissimisque praesidiis <u>adornavit</u>;**

> (b) **ipse autem ... undequinquagesimo die totam ad imperium populi Romani Ciliciam <u>adiunxit</u>**

(v) the final piece is a temporal *ut*-clause, inserted into the second half of the main clause: **ut Brundisio profectus est.**

Before looking at each part in turn, it is worth pondering the organizing principles of the sentence as a whole. The importance of Italy and Rome (and the Roman people) stands out. Italy is the only region mentioned twice – in <u>Italiam</u>; <u>Italiae</u> *duo maria* – and Cicero concludes the sentence with a reference to the (now extended) empire of the Roman people (*ad imperium populi Romani*), which thereby emerge at the centre of Pompey's thoughts and actions. Grammar reinforces the point. First, Pompey is the (implied) subject of all the clauses that contain references to Italy, places therein (Brundisium), or the Roman people: (i) *recepisset*; (iv) *adornavit, adiunxit*; (v) *profectus est*. In contrast, Cicero packs Pompey's actions in Spain, Gaul, and Greece into two (passive) ablative absolutes: (ii) and (iii). And second, whereas the two Spains and Gaul were furnished *praesidiis ac navibus*, Pompey secured the two seas and coastlines of Italy in the superlative: <u>maximis</u> *classibus* <u>firmissimis</u>que *praesidiis*.

Inde cum se in Italiam recepisset: *inde* is pulled up front to provide a transition but belongs into the temporal *cum*-clause (with subjunctive; the tense is pluperfect to indicate a time prior to that of the main verb *adornavit*, which is in the perfect).

duabus Hispaniis et Gallia Transalpina praesidiis ac navibus confirmata: the plethora of ablatives may be confusing. The noun-phrases that make up the ablative absolute are the chiastically arranged *duabus Hispaniis* (the reference is to *Hispania Citerior*, i.e. 'Nearer Spain', and *Hispania Ulterior*, i.e. 'Further Spain', of course from the point of view of Italy) and *Gallia*

Transalpina. confirmata (perfect passive participle in the ablative singular) agrees with the nearest one in case, number, and gender, i.e. *Gallia Transalpina*, but pertains to *duabus Hispaniis* as well. *praesidiis ac navibus* are ablatives of means or instrument. All three regions had been Roman provinces for some time. Hispania Citerior and Hispania Ulterior were set up in 197 BC; Gallia Transalpina in Southern France, perhaps better known under the alternative name Gallia Narbonensis, in 120 BC. (The first Roman province was Sicily, established in the wake of the first Punic war in 240 BC.)

missis item in oram Illyrici maris et in Achaiam omnemque Graeciam navibus: in the previous ablative absolute, Cicero began with the nouns (*Hispaniis et Gallia*) and ended with the participle (*confirmata*); here he inverts the pattern, beginning with the participle (*missis*) and ending with the noun (*navibus*). The focus is on Greece, which Cicero brings out in a climactic tricolon: we start on the West coast of the Greek peninsula (*in oram Illyrici*), move on to a major province (*in Achaiam*), and end with the comprehensive *omnem Graeciam* (also modified by the preposition *in* + accusative, indicating direction).

Italiae duo maria maximis classibus firmissimisque praesidiis adornavit: *Italiae* is a possessive genitive dependent on *duo maria*, which is the accusative object of *adornavit*. The subject is Pompey (implied). The *duo maria* of Italy are the *Mare Hadriaticum/Superum* (today's Adriatic Sea, separating the Italian from the Balkan Peninsula) and the *Mare Tyrrhenum/ Inferum* (today's Tyrrhenian Sea).

ipse autem ... undequinquagesimo die totam ad imperium populi Romani Ciliciam adiunxit: *undequinquagesimus* is put together from *unus* + *de* + *quinquagesimus*, i.e. 1 (*unus*) taken off (*de*) the 50th (*quinquagesimus*) = 49th. The word for '50' is *quinquaginta* [*quinque* + *ginta*]. *undequinquagesimo die* is an ablative of time. *totam* agrees with *Ciliciam* and is emphasized through the hyperbaton.

ut Brundisio profectus est: *ut* (with the indicative) here has the temporal sense 'from the time when'. *Brundisio* is an ablative of separation. Latin does not use a preposition with cities and smaller islands, but if you were to depart from (say) Sardinia, the idiomatic phrase would be *ex Sardinia proficisci*.

omnes, qui ubique praedones fuerunt, partim capti interfectique sunt, partim unius huius se imperio ac potestati dediderunt: one could suppose that *praedones* is the antecedent of *qui* and has been attracted into the relative clause ('all pirates, anywhere/wherever they were...'); alternatively, one could take *praedones* predicatively ('all those, who were pirates anywhere...'). The word order is designed to bring out the antithesis between *omnes* and *unius huius* (sc. Pompey).

unius huius ... imperio ac potestati: *imperium* refers to the right to issue commands attached to the high magistracies of the Roman commonwealth; *potestas* refers to the legal power associated with a specific role in Roman society, here Pompey's extraordinary command as defined by the *lex Gabinia*. *unius huius* is a possessive genitive.

Idem Cretensibus, cum ad eum usque in Pamphyliam legatos deprecatoresque misissent, spem deditionis non ademit obsidesque imperavit: *idem* (nominative masculine singular of the pronoun *idem, eadem, idem*) is the subject of the sentence referring to Pompey. *ademit* ('to take *something* away from *somebody*') governs an accusative object (*spem deditionis*) and a dative (*Cretensibus*). It is a dative of disadvantage, which is here negated by the *non*. The *-que* after *obsides*, which links *ademit* and *imperavit*, has a slightly adversative force: 'but/rather'.

obsidesque imperavit: *imperavit* here governs an accusative object of the thing Pompey demanded, i.e. hostages. (If Cicero wanted to say that Pompey gave orders *to* the hostages, *obsides* would be in the dative: to command somebody to do something is *imperare* + dative + *ut/ne* with subjunctive.)

Ita tantum bellum, tam diuturnum, tam longe lateque dispersum, quo bello omnes gentes ac nationes premebantur, Cn. Pompeius extrema hieme apparavit, ineunte vere suscepit, media aestate confecit: Cicero here returns to § 31, especially the beginning (*Testes nunc vero iam omnes orae atque omnes exterae gentes ac nationes*) and the end (*hoc tantum bellum,* *tam turpe, tam vetus, tam late divisum atque dispersum quis umquam arbitraretur aut ab omnibus imperatoribus uno anno aut omnibus annis ab uno imperatore confici posse?*) Note the repetitions (with variation), which achieve a sense of closure of Cicero's treatment of the war against the pirates:

§ 31	§ 35
omnes exterae gentes ac nationes	*omnes gentes ac nationes*
tantum bellum	*tantum bellum*
tam vetus	*tam diuturnum*
tam late divisum atque dispersum	*tam longe lateque dispersum*
confici posse	*confecit*

quo bello omnes gentes ac nationes premebantur: *bello*, a reiteration of *bellum* and the antecedent of *quo*, has been attracted into the relative clause: 'a war, by which...'

Cn. Pompeius extrema hieme apparavit, ineunte vere suscepit, media aestate confecit: an elegant, asyndetic (and hence 'speedy') tricolon, with a touch of variation in the ablatives: *extrema hieme* and *media aestate* are ablatives of time, *ineunte vere* is a temporal ablative absolute.

36: 'THOU ART MORE LOVELY AND MORE TEMPERATE': POMPEY'S SOFT SIDES

Cicero now moves on from hailing Pompey's martial prowess and his stunning success as a general to a consideration of his other qualities. Already in § 13, he differentiated between Pompey's impact on (Eastern) provincials and that of other generals on the grounds of Pompey's special character traits – *temperantia, mansuetudo, humanitas*:

> His vos, quoniam libere loqui non licet, tacite rogant, ut se quoque, sicut ceterarum provinciarum socios, dignos existimetis, quorum salutem tali viro commendetis; atque hoc etiam magis, quod ceteros in provinciam eius modi homines cum imperio mittimus, ut etiam si ab hoste defendant, tamen ipsorum adventus in urbis sociorum non multum ab hostili expugnatione differant. Hunc audiebant antea, nunc praesentem vident, tanta temperantia, tanta mansuetudine, tanta humanitate, ut ei beatissimi esse videantur, apud quos ille diutissime commoratur.

> [Since they [sc. the Eastern allies of Rome] are not allowed to speak their mind, they beseech you silently that, just like the allies of the other provinces, you consider them, too, worthy so as to entrust their safety to such a man – especially given that with the other men we send with a command into a province of this kind, even if they ward off the enemy, their arrivals in the cities of the allies do not differ much from a hostile takeover. Previously they were hearing, now, with him present, they see that this man is of such self-control, of such gentleness, of such human kindness that those seem to be most blessed amongst whom he remains for the longest period of time.]

The relative clause *quas paulo ante commemorare coeperam* harks back to the beginning of his discussion of *virtus* in § 29, where he insisted that *virtus* comprises not just martial prowess and military genius, but also moral qualities and talent for diplomacy: *Neque enim illae sunt solae virtutes imperatoriae, quae vulgo existimantur, labor in negotiis, fortitudo in periculis, industria in agendo, celeritas in conficiendo, consilium in providendo.* Cicero covered the 'orthodox' *virtutes imperatoriae* in §§ 29-35. What follows now is a discussion of *virtutes imperatoriae* (or *artes*, as he goes on to call them: see next note), which are *not* commonly recognized as such: *innocentia, temperantia, fides, facilitas, ingenium, humanitas.*

Est haec divina atque incredibilis virtus imperatoris: *haec* is retrospective in force and sums up Cicero's discussion of Pompey's 'military prowess' or *virtus,* in the strict sense of enabling success in battle. He has already used the two elevating attributes *divina* and *incredibilis* of Pompey's *virtus* in § 33, though in inverse order: *unius hominis incredibilis ac divina virtus.*

quid?: the neuter form of the interrogative pronoun *quis, quid* occurs here elliptically to mark the transition to a further item. See *OLD* s.v. *quis*[1] 12 b.

ceterae [sc. *virtutes*], **quas paulo ante commemorare coeperam, quantae atque quam multae sunt!**: Note the word order: as is regular after *quid?,* Cicero continues with the word he wishes to stress: <u>*ceterae*</u> ... *quantae atque quam multae sunt!* (And not: *quantae atque quam multae sunt ceterae!*).

paulo: an ablative of the measure of difference.

Non enim bellandi virtus solum in summo ac perfecto imperatore quaerenda est, sed multae sunt artes eximiae huius administrae comitesque virtutis: Cicero continues his work on the meaning of *virtus.* As he has done previously, subtle touches underwrite his conceptual creativity. By attaching the gerund *bellandi* (placed before the noun it depends on, for emphasis) to *virtus*, he reiterates his earlier point that 'martial excellence' is only one aspect of a composite phenomenon. His *summus ac perfectus imperator* has others as well.

quaerenda est: a gerundive of obligation.

multae sunt artes eximiae huius administrae comitesque virtutis: the *multae ... artes* are identical to the *ceterae* [*virtutes*] of the previous sentence. Cicero thus uses *artes* and *virtutes* here as synonyms. Macdonald proposes that 'this word [sc. *artes*] means something not very different from *virtutes* but implies their practical operation', but this distinction is difficult to uphold.[33] *virtus bellandi* is a pointless quality if not applied in practice; and at *de Re Publica* 1.3 Cicero even draws a contrast between *ars*, in the sense of 'skill' that does not require constant application, and *virtus*, which 'resides entirely in its application' (*virtus in usu sui tota posita est*).

---

33 Macdonald (1986) 69.

eximiae could be either feminine nominative plural (and would then modify *artes* or *administrae comitesque*) or feminine genitive singular (going with *huius* and *virtutis*). The latter is the case: Cicero grants that martial excellence of *virtus bellandi*, to which he gestures back with the demonstrative pronoun *huius*, is *eximia*, i.e. the most important of all *artes/virtutes*; but goes on to argue that this particular excellence has many important 'handmaidens' (*administrae*) and 'companions' (*comites*).

Ac primum quanta innocentia debent esse imperatores! quanta deinde in omnibus rebus temperantia [sc. *debent esse imperatores*]**! quanta fide, quanta facilitate, quanto ingenio, quanta humanitate** [sc. *debent esse imperatores*]**!**: The subject throughout is *imperatores*, the verb is *debent*, which governs the infinitive *esse*. The elision puts the emphasis squarely on *quanta innocentia, quanta ... temperantia, quanta fide, quanta facilitate, quanto ingenio,* and *quanta humanitate*, which are all ablatives of quality or description with *esse*. Note the relentless anaphora of the pronominal adjective *quantus, -a, -um*. In terms of rhetorical registers, Cicero here again pauses (*Ac primum*) for a theoretical observation of normative force (cf. *debent*).

primum ... deinde: Cicero singles out *innocentia* and *temperantia* by using adverbs of enumeration ('first...', 'then...'), before adding the remaining qualities in a simple list.

innocentia: *innocentia* means something akin to 'integrity of character', 'moral uprightness'. It is a quality of someone not liable to become corrupted by opportunities of wealth and power, and hence rather precious in public figures, not least in the context of imperial administration/exploitation. The noun here harks back to the very opening of the section on the ideal general (and the set text). See § 27: *Utinam, Quirites, virorum fortium atque innocentium copiam tantam haberetis...*

temperantia: Cicero had already praised Pompey for his *temperantia* in § 13: see above. The term refers to 'self-control', 'moderation', or 'restraint', and in particular someone's ability to keep violent emotions (also known as 'passions') in check. At *de Inventione* 2.164, a treatise on rhetoric and the earliest surviving work of Cicero, conventionally dated to 91 BC, he defines it as follows: *temperantia est rationis in libidinem atque in alios non rectos* *impetus animi firma et moderata dominatio. eius partes continentia, clementia, modestia* ('Temperance is a firm and well-considered control exercised by the reason over lust and other improper impulses of the mind. Its parts are continence, clemency, and modesty'). At *in Catilinam* 2.25, *temperantia* functions as the antithesis of *luxuria* ('luxury'). The term went on to play a significant role in Cicero's late philosophical writings, such as the *de Finibus* (see 1.47 and 2.60) and, above all, the *de Officiis*, where it is one of the four cardinal virtues (see 1.15).

fide: *fides* is a key concept in how the Romans thought about social relations, and dictionary entries ('confidence', 'loyalty', 'trustworthiness', 'credibility') convey only a limited sense of the full semantic range and force of the qualities at issue: *fides* underwrites socio-economic exchanges, defines political interactions, and justifies Roman rule. In relationships that were both reciprocal (with each party rendering some, but not necessarily the same, kind of service to the other) and asymmetrical (with one party being much more powerful than the other), a commitment to *fides* on both sides operated as a (partial) counterweight to steep inequalities in power.[34]

facilitate: *facilitas* is an abstract noun, related to *facio* ('I do') and *facilis* ('easy to do') and refers to 'ease/aptitude in doing something', here specifically 'ease in interpersonal relations', 'affability'. *facilitas* greases 'friendship' (*amicitia*), or good social relations more generally, also between unequal parties, as Cicero makes clear in § 41: *ut is, qui dignitate principibus excellit, facilitate infimis par esse videatur.* Even though Pompey outclasses everybody within Rome's highly competitive aristocracy, when he interacts with those of a lower social rank his *facilitas* renders differences in rank and standing inconspicuous. At *pro Murena* 66, Cicero draws an illuminating contrast between *comitas et facilitas* and *gravitas severitasque*, which brings out the positive aspects of *facilitas*, but at the same time underscores that too much *facilitas* may well turn into a vice. In measure, *gravitas* and *severitas* are also 'good' qualities in the Roman system of values. See, for instance, Terence, *Hecyra* 248: *Phidippe, etsi ego meis me omnibus scio esse apprime obsequentem,* | *sed non adeo ut mea facilitas corrumpet illorum animos* ('Phidippus, I know that I am extremely indulgent to all my family, but not to the extent that my affability corrupts their characters'). *Facilitas* in this sense refers to an

---

34 Hölkeskamp (2004).

indulgent disposition willing to overlook or forgive faults in others and is frequently used synonymously with *clementia, indulgentia,* and *comitas*.

ingenio: *ingenium* is *prima facie* an odd item in the list. Most basically, it refers to 'natural disposition' and then to 'inherent quality or character', or, with a greater emphasis on talent, 'natural abilities', especially of the mental/intellectual kind: it can specifically refer to being gifted with words, whether in rhetoric or poetry. In rhetorical theory, *ingenium* is a key technical term (innate talent complementing *ars,* or 'exercise', in constituting the perfect orator, the *summus orator*). But in the sense of 'talent' it refers to inherent potential rather than inherent moral excellence, and in some of his later philosophical writings Cicero laments that some of the greatest talents (*ingenia*) in Roman history, such as Caesar, became corrupted through the desire for power (see *de Officiis* 1.23). In our passage, though, *ingenium* means something akin to 'soundness in character' – but arguably also gestures obliquely to specifically *oratorical* talent, as emerges in § 42 (see our commentary below).

humanitate: *humanitas* is one of Cicero's pet-words and has a range of meanings. Five basic senses can be identified:[35]

> **1**: *Humanitas* aids in the recognition of a universal human nature as the basis of sympathy or compassion towards others, especially on the part of someone in a position of power vis-à-vis an inferior; classic relationships of this kind are judge and defendant in a court of law or victor and defeated enemy in war.
>
> **2**: *Humanitas* constitutes a human quality that can be personified and resides, or ought to reside, in each human being but does so to different degrees; it may articulate itself as a force of conscience that governs and guides behaviour (or ought to do so) to make it conform to standards of universal ethics.
>
> **3**: *Humanitas* represents standards of civilization, which only certain periods or cultures have attained; this scenario may involve a diachronic differentiation between two stages of historical development within a single culture or an ethnographic differentiation between cultures.

---

35 The following is based on Gildenhard (2011) 202-03.

4: As a reflexive version of **3**, *humanitas* demarcates the synchronic distinction between civilization and barbarity *within* Roman culture in Cicero's here and now, thereby introducing a dividing line that cuts across the Roman citizen body.

5: *Humanitas* refers to, or is identical with, a high level of civilized manners, cultural refinement and literary education that only select individuals within a specific culture ever reach, who thereby constitute this culture's 'true' nobility.

The different meanings of course shade into one another and it is not always easy to pin down precisely which sense takes precedent; in the passage under consideration here it is arguably **1** and **2** (just as in § 13, cited above).

[*Extra information*: *Ciceroniani sumus*
Cicero's creative investment in *humanitas* has yielded extraordinary dividends in terms of his intellectual legacy. In the Renaissance, Sense **5** got reactivated in the phrase of *studia humanitatis*, out of which our 'Humanities' evolved. In that sense all of us students of the humanities are Ciceronians.]

quae breviter qualia sint in Cn. Pompeio consideremus: *quae* is a connecting relative (= *et ea*) in the accusative neuter plural, referring back to all of the enumerated qualities. It is the accusative object of *consideremus* (in the hortative subjunctive), which also governs the indirect question (hence the subjunctive *sint*) *qualia sint in Cn. Pompeio*. The subject of the indirect question are again the collective qualities. Literally: 'Let us consider these briefly, of what kind they are in Gnaeus Pompeius.' *qualia* is the nominative neuter plural of the interrogative pronoun *qualis*.

summa enim omnia sunt, Quirites, sed ea magis ex aliorum contentione quam ipsa per sese cognosci atque intellegi possunt: Cicero claims that Pompey (*in Cn. Pompeio* has to be understood with *summa enim omnia sunt* from the previous sentence) possesses all (*omnia*) of these qualities to the highest possible degree (*summa*). But in order to fully appreciate Pompey's outstanding excellence, Cicero goes on to argue, the best method is to compare and contrast (cf. *ex aliorum* <u>*contentione*</u>) his qualities (*ea*, just like *omnia*, is a generic neuter plural in the nominative, referring back to the catalogue of *artes/virtutes*; it is the subject of *possunt*) with those of other generals rather than to look at them in isolation (*ipsa per sese*). Cicero's insistence on the heuristic value of comparing and contrasting feeds right into his agenda of singling out Pompey as the only possible candidate for the job: throughout the speech, he not only promotes Pompey, but also demotes, if often obliquely, anyone else who might have taken on the command. This strategy defines the opening section of the speech in particular, where he damns Lucullus, hitherto in charge of the war against Mithridates, with faint praise and explains why Pompey would succeed where Lucullus failed.

Quirites: the citizens of Rome. See note on § 27.

cognosci atque intellegi: the two present passive infinitives are virtual synonyms, with *cognoscere* perhaps placing the emphasis more on the first encounter ('to get to know') and *intellegere* on the outcome ('to understand').

37: SPQR CONFIDENTIAL

This follows on from Cicero's announcement at the end of the previous paragraph that Pompey's 'soft qualities' stand out with particular clarity when compared to the behaviour of others in similar positions of power. Without naming names (*ego autem nomino neminem*), he goes on to imply that corruption is rife among Rome's military leaders, who use public resources for despicable private ends: personal advancement or enrichment. Such illegal activities violate public trust and have their roots, so Cicero suggests, in an unwholesome character. Ambition and greed, he implies, run rampant in Rome's ruling elite. The consequences are not just felt at Rome, with the embezzlement of public funds, but also in the provinces – wherever Roman armies go, they descend upon the local population (regardless whether it consists of Roman citizens or allies) like a swarm of locusts. The argument here feeds into Cicero's promotion of Pompey: he has the qualities needed to win the hearts and minds of provincials, which is a key asset in Rome's war against Mithridates.

In a sense, Cicero here continues the theme that was at the centre of his prosecution of Gaius Verres in 70 BC for misconduct in provincial administration, as recorded (with a considerable dose of artistic license) in his *Verrine Orations*. And it is tempting to read the *de imperio* as part of the story of Cicero, Scourge of Bad Provincial Governance or General Corruption. The problem with this is that after securing Verres' exile, he went on to *defend* several people accused of provincial exploitation (Marcus Fonteius in 69, for example). The response might be that *those* people (unlike Verres) were innocent, but it seems more likely that Cicero was playing by the rules of the game, whereby you defend whoever asks for your help (especially if they are politically/socially prominent people), whatever you think of their personal innocence.

Still, the alleged corruption of Rome's provincial government and the ruthless exploitation of the allies remain leitmotifs of Cicero's argument right to the very end of the speech. He even uses the vices of his contemporaries to put Pompey's greatness into perspective, most explicitly in § 67: *quasi vero Cn. Pompeium non cum suis virtutibus, tum etiam alienis vitiis magnum esse videamus* ('as though indeed it were not obvious that Pompeius owes his greatness not to his own merits alone but also to the demerits of other men'). This 'comparative levelling' of Pompey's 'absolute' excellence also informs the section here, and comes out most notably in § 40 when Cicero revisits the reasons for Pompey's seemingly extraordinary speed – he implies there that the speed wasn't extraordinary at all: Pompey simply refuses to let himself get sidetracked by the temptations that routinely slow down all the others.

Quem enim imperatorem possumus ullo in numero putare, cuius in exercitu centuriatus veneant atque venierint?: The main verb of the sentence is *possumus*, which takes the object infinitive *putare*. *putare* governs the accusatives *Quem ... imperatorem*. *Quem* is either an interrogative adjective ('which general can we believe to be of any esteem...?') or an interrogative pronoun, with *imperatorem* in predicative position ('whom can we believe to be a general of any esteem...?')

ullo in numero: the phrasing of (*in*) *numero* with a pronominal adjective (in this case *ullus*) is idiomatic: OLD s.v. *numerus* 11a. *in aliquo* (*nullo*) *numero* (*haberi*) means '(to be held) of some (no) account/esteem'. Cicero's question here is rhetorical: one cannot consider a general who sells posts in his army to be 'of any account/esteem' – that is, he is no general at all.

cuius in exercitu centuriatus veneant atque venierint?: *cuius* is a possessive genitive in the masculine singular of the relative pronoun, dependent on *exercitu* and referring back to *imperatorem*: 'in whose army...' The subject of the relative clause is *centuriatus* (a 4th-declension noun here in the nominative masculine plural). The verbs are *veneant* (3rd person plural present subjunctive active [in form, but passive in meaning]) and *venierint* (3rd person plural perfect subjunctive active [in form, but passive in meaning]), from *veneo, -ire, -ii* (*-itum*), which functions as the passive to *vendo* ('to sell') – 'to be sold'. *veneo* is easily confused with *venio, venire, veni, ventum* ('to come'). In the perfect active subjunctive the forms of the two verbs are indeed identical, but the 3rd person plural present subjunctive active of *venio* would be *veniant*. *veneant atque venierint* are in the subjunctive because the relative clause is one of characteristic: 'a general of the sort who...'.

centuriatus: the nominative masculine plural of the 4th-declension noun *centuriatus, -us*, i.e. 'office of the centurion' – a relatively well remunerated position in the Roman army.

quid hunc hominem magnum aut amplum de re publica cogitare, qui pecuniam ex aerario depromptam ad bellum administrandum aut propter cupiditatem provinciae magistratibus diviserit aut propter avaritiam Romae in quaestu reliquerit?: The main verb (*possumus*) and its object infinitive (*putare*) need to be supplied from the previous sentence. *putare* introduces an indirect statement with *hunc hominem* as subject accusative and *cogitare* as infinitive. *magnum aut amplum* agree with *quid*: 'What [matter] grand and edifying can we believe this man to be thinking about the state, who...'

qui introduces another relative clause of characteristic, which explains the subjunctives *diviserit* and *reliquerit*. They are in the perfect: Cicero is referring to apparently well-known incidences in the past. *pecuniam* is the accusative object of both *diviserit* and *reliquerit*, coordinated by *aut – aut*. At issue are two forms of corrupting passion – *cupiditas* ('desire for power and glory') and *avaritia* ('greed, i.e. desire for wealth') – that lead to illegal use of public funds: bribery and embezzlement. What makes the clause difficult to take in is the participle *depromptam*, which agrees with *pecuniam* and governs the phrases *ex aerario* and *ad bellum administrandum*:

> *qui*
>
> > *pecuniam [ex aerario depromptam ad bellum administrandum]*
> >
> > > *aut propter cupiditatem provinciae magistratibus*
> > >
> > > > *diviserit*
> > >
> > > *aut propter avaritiam Romae in quaestu*
> > >
> > > > *reliquerit?*

qui pecuniam ... magistratibus diviserit: the construction of *dividere* here is 'to distribute an accusative object (*pecuniam*) among recipients in the dative (*magistratibus*)'.

pecuniam ex aerario depromptam ad bellum administrandum: *depromptam* is the perfect passive participle of *depromere* in the accusative feminine singular agreeing with *pecuniam*. It governs the prepositional phrases *ex aerario* and *ad bellum administrandum*. The preposition *ad* here expresses *purpose*: '*for* war to-be-waged', '*in order to* wage war'.

ex aerario: an *aerarius* is someone who works in copper or other precious metals (*aes, aeris,* n.). The adjective *aerarius* refers to something that pertains to, or is made of copper, bronze, etc. Hence the Latin phrase for treasury, i.e. *aerarium stabulum* – 'a dwelling/stable (*stabulum*) pertaining to precious metal'. *stabulum* was considered redundant, hence the freestanding *aerarium*, i.e. 'a place where precious metal is kept' – or, specifically, the place in the temple of Saturn at Rome, where the state treasury was located, or, simply, 'the treasury'. In the late republic, the urban quaestors were in charge of its administration, overseen by the senate. They would provide funds for magistrates or pro-magistrates to finance their military operations, on the understanding that such funds would be invested in the best public interest, rather than for illegal private benefits.

propter cupiditatem provinciae: *provinciae* is an objective genitive dependent on *propter cupiditatem*. As Macdonald points out, 'this must mean "ambition to retain his province" rather than "obtain a province".'[36]

Romae: a locative ('in Rome').

Vestra admurmuratio facit, Quirites, ut agnoscere videamini, qui haec fecerint: literally, Cicero says: 'your murmuring of disapproval, citizens, makes it that you seem to recognize [those], who have done these things'. 'makes it', of course, is awkward English – 'shows' or 'demonstrates' is much more elegant. Cicero elides the accusative object of *agnoscere* (*eos*), which is also the antecedent of the relative pronoun *qui*. *qui haec fecerint* is an indirect question dependent on *agnoscere*: hence the subjunctive. Note that Cicero treads very carefully here, by means of one of his favourite hedges: the use of *videor*. He does not say, factually and brutally, *ut agnoscatis* ('that you recognize') but *ut agnoscere videamini* ('that you seem to recognize').

Vestra admurmuratio facit, Quirites: Cicero here makes it out that he is reacting spontaneously to the audience. Instances such as these raise the question of the relationship between three different versions of the same speech: (a) what Cicero prepared beforehand (though he would have spoken freely, rather than read from a script); (b) what he said during

---

36   Macdonald (1986) 69.

the oral delivery of the speech; (c) the version disseminated in writing afterwards. Did Cicero anticipate an *admurmuratio* from the audience at this moment already in the planning phase? Did the *admurmuratio* arise spontaneously and Cicero captured the moment in the written version? Was there perhaps no *admurmuratio* during the delivery at all, but Cicero kept, or added it, in the published version to convey a sense of 'life delivery' and interactivity for those who encountered the speech in writing? We simply do not know.[37]

ego autem nomino neminem; quare irasci mihi nemo poterit, nisi qui ante de se voluerit confiteri: Cicero here introduces a comment on his own behalf, which almost sounds like a parenthesis.

ego autem nomino neminem: Cicero implies that his audience knows very well whom he is referring to, but still refrains from naming names. The *autem*, then, has adversative force: *despite the fact* that everyone knows whom I am talking about, Cicero is saying, I (notice the emphatic use of the personal pronoun *ego*), for my part, keep my hands clean and will abstain from explicit mudslinging. *nomino neminem* constitutes a deft paronomasia, which partly makes up for the anti-climactic *neminem*. Imagine Cicero to pause ever so slightly after *nomino* – raising the expectation that he is about to crucify rhetorically a corrupt aristocrat; perhaps some members in the audience are beginning to sweat nervously at this point – only to let the air out with the categorical *neminem*.

quare irasci mihi nemo poterit, nisi qui ante de se voluerit confiteri: *poterit* is future, *voluerit* future perfect. Cicero argues that since he has not named anyone, nobody will be able to be angry with him unless that person 'will have wanted' to out himself as guilty beforehand. *nisi* does not introduce a conditional clause; it has a limiting function – 'except he, who...'. The antecedent of the relative pronoun (*is*) is elided.

ante: used adverbially: 'beforehand'.

---

37 For a more detailed discussion of written *v.* spoken versions of Cicero's speeches see Gildenhard (2011) 14-15, with further bibliography.

Itaque propter hanc avaritiam imperatorum quantas calamitates ... nostri exercitus ferant, quis ignorat?: The main clause is the question *quis ignorat*, which governs the indirect question introduced by the interrogative adjective *quantas*: hence the subjunctive of *ferant*. *propter hanc avaritiam imperatorum* belongs into the indirect question, but is pulled up-front for emphasis.

Itaque: the connective *itaque* ('hence', 'therefore') introduces a sentence or thought that emerges from, and stands in some sort of causal relation to, what comes before. Here, though, the link is not with the immediately preceding (*ego autem nomino neminem; quare irasci mihi nemo poterit, nisi qui ante de se voluerit confiteri*) but the prior *vestra admurmuratio facit, Quirites, ut agnoscere videamini, qui haec fecerint*. It thus reinforces the sense of *ego ... confiteri* as a parenthetical aside.

quocumque ventum est: only verbs that take an accusative object in their active forms have a complete passive (they are so-called 'transitive verbs'). Verbs that are 'intransitive', i.e. don't take an accusative object, only form an *impersonal* passive in the *third* person *singular*. *venio, venire, veni, ventum* ('to come') is intransitive, and *ventum est* is its impersonal perfect passive. Its use here stresses the action and obfuscates agency: Cicero could have said *quocumque venerunt* [sc. *nostri exercitus*]. Another nuance to note is the indicative (*ventum est*): given that the indefinite relative clause is part of the indirect question, Cicero could have used the subjunctive by assimilation; but he retains the indicative to enhance the graphic nature of his rhetoric: the disgraceful conduct of Roman armies is an indisputable matter of fact.

38: OF LOCUSTS AND LEECHES

In this paragraph Cicero considers the impact the presence of an army has on the wider population, both within Italy and beyond. In his effort to rouse sympathy with the plight of allies and external nations affected by warfare or, more specifically, undisciplined or marauding troops owing to a lack of leadership, he encourages his audience to draw on recent personal experiences. We get the following three scenarios:

    (i) Roman armies on the march *through Italy* (*itinera*)
    (ii) Roman armies attacking *enemy* cities (*hostium urbes*)
    (iii) Roman armies camping in their winter quarters (*hiberna*, sc. *castra*) among *allied nations* (*sociorum civitates*)

In what is *prima facie* a highly counterintuitive argument (phrased carefully, to be sure, in the form of a rhetorical question), Cicero implies that (i) and (iii) have caused greater havoc than (ii). The 'collateral damage' caused by troop movement *within* Italy (cf. *in Italia*) serves as basis for his suggestion that *outside* Italy (cf. *apud exteras nationes*) the destructive impact on *allied* nations (*sociorum civitates*) by Roman *winter quarters* exceeds the harm done to *enemies* (cf. *hostium*) by Roman soldiers *sacking their cities*. This is baffling – and prepares for the explanatory punch-line set up by *enim*. The reason for this unfortunate paradox is that soldiers tend to plunder their host community into ruin unless their general checks their marauding; but only a general who exercises self-control (a rare creature indeed, so Cicero implies) is able to control his army.

Itinera, quae per hosce annos in Italia per agros atque oppida civium Romanorum nostri imperatores fecerint, recordamini: *Itinera* is pulled up front for emphasis. Opinions on how to interpret the subjunctive *fecerint* in the *quae*-clause vary: some think that we are dealing with a generic relative clause ('Recall *the kind of* marches that our generals made...');[38] others that it is an indirect question dependent on *recordamini*, with *quae* being interrogative rather than relative ('Recall the marches which/which marches our generals made...').[39] The latter seems more attractive, not least since it continues the pattern from the end of the previous paragraph: *quantas calamitates ... ferant, quis ignorat? Itinera, quae .... fecerint, recordamini!*

38 Radice and Steel (2014) 70.
39 Macdonald (1986) 70.

per hosce annos: it is unclear how far back Cicero wants his audience to think: does *per hosce annos* refer as far back as the Social War? The civil wars between Sulla and the Marians? Or just the suppression of the revolt of Spartacus? The vague chronology ensures that the identity of *nostri imperatores* remains equally vague. The sentence by itself does not imply misbehaviour on the part of the generals: Pompey, after all, was one of the *imperatores* that would have come to mind; the emphasis is rather on the burden of ordinary troop movement on the civilian population. But in the light of how the paragraph ends, one could wonder whether Roman generals and their armies always maintained impeccable discipline while travelling through Italy.

tum facilius statuetis, quid apud exteras nationes fieri existimetis: *statuetis* (3rd conjugation) is future active indicative, *existimetis* (1st conjugation) is present active subjunctive in the indirect question introduced by the interrogative pronoun *quid*, which has a double function: it is the accusative object of *existimetis* and the subject accusative of the indirect statement governed by *existimetis* (*fieri* being the infinitive).

facilius: the comparative form of the adverb *facile*.

Utrum plures arbitramini per hosce annos militum vestrorum armis hostium urbes an hibernis sociorum civitates esse deletas?: Cicero continues to address his audience directly: the main verb of the rhetorical question is *arbitramini*. It introduces an indirect statement consisting of two subject accusatives, each with a genitive attribute, coordinated by *utrum* (*hostium urbes*) ... *an* (*sociorum civitates*), and one infinitive: *esse deletas*. The emphatically placed attribute *plures* modifies both *urbes* and *civitates*. Likewise, the possessive genitive *militum vestrorum* modifies both *armis* and *hibernis*. So Cicero begins and ends with elements 'shared' by the *utrum-* and the *an*-part: *plures, per hosce annos, militum vestrorum, esse deletas*; in between we get the disjunctive contrasts: *armis* as compared to *hibernis* (ablatives of instrument); *hostium* as compared to *sociorum* (possessive genitives); *urbes* as compared to *civitates* (subject accusatives).

Utrum... an...: introduces a disjunctive question that offers more than one alternative. Cicero strongly suggests that the (*prima facie* counterintuitive) second alternative is the right one: to say that the opposite is the case would hardly be worth the effort, but to argue that winter-quarters are more pernicious for the indigenous population than the wholesale destruction of cities through armed violence baffles and intrigues. It calls for explication, which Cicero delivers in the subsequent sentence (cf. *enim*).

hibernis: allies were expected to support Roman armies that set up winter quarters in their territory. Depending on the demands made by the general on the local population and the discipline he imposed on his soldiers, the presence of a camp during the winter months could turn into a destructive imposition.

Neque enim potest exercitum is continere imperator, qui se ipse non continet, neque severus esse in iudicando, qui alios in se severos esse iudices non vult: the main sentence falls into two parts coordinated by *neque... neque...* The subject (*imperator*) and the verb (*potest*, which governs both *continere* and *esse*) remain the same.

In §§ 37-38 Cicero offers a critique of Roman generals and armies, whom he conceives as operating in the service of the Roman people (and its magistrates): cf. his repeated reference to *imperator(es)*, armies (*exercitus*), and soldiers (*milites*), and his use of the possessive adjectives *noster* and *vester*. § 37: *quem enim imperatorem...; propter hanc avaritiam imperatorum; nostri exercitus*; § 38: *nostri imperatores; militum vestrorum (armis)*. Throughout it is fairly clear that Cicero blames the generals first and foremost, rather than their troops, and the final sentence hammers the point home in no uncertain terms: an army is an extension of the will and the ethics of its leader. The principle 'there are no bad soldiers, only bad leaders' will have resonated well with Cicero's primary audience, the Roman people, many of whom will have served time as citizen-soldiers. It is also a principle he endorses elsewhere, at times with reference to Plato, who argued the same in the *Republic*. Is it true, though?

severus: fans of J. K. Rowling's Harry Potter series won't have problems with the meaning of this adjective: just think Snape.

in iudicando ... iudices: an instance of *figura etymologica*.

qui alios in se severos esse iudices non vult: *non vult* introduces an indirect statement with *alios* as subject accusative and *esse* as infinitive. *severos* agrees with *iudices* (in attributive position) and the entire phrase stands in predicative position to *alios*. The reflexive pronoun *se* (accusative singular) refers to the subject of the *qui*-clause, i.e. the general.

39: POMPEY THE PEACEFUL, OR: IMPERIALISM WITH GLOVES

In this section, Cicero moves on from describing the faults of other commanders to building up a picture of the excellent conduct of Pompey when he brought his army into Asia. At the time of the speech, Pompey was still in quarters in Asia and visiting cities in the region, to shore up his campaign against the pirates and prepare for the war against Mithridates, which he hoped would be coming his way.[40] Cicero stresses how even during the winter, when other commanders would have exploited allies, Pompey took great care not to inflict harm on anyone or abuse the goodwill of the locals. The contrast between Pompey's actions with those of other generals destroying the allied territory, as mentioned in § 37, throws the discipline of Pompey's forces (and by implication his self-control and 'imperial ethics') into proper relief.

Hic miramur hunc hominem tantum excellere ceteris, cuius legiones sic in Asiam pervenerint, ut non modo manus tanti exercitus, sed ne vestigium quidem cuiquam pacato nocuisse dicatur?: The main verb of the direct question is *miramur*, which introduces an indirect statement, with *hunc hominem* as subject accusative and *excellere* as infinitive. A relative clause follows (*cuius... pervenerint*: the verb is in the subjunctive because it is a subordinate clause within indirect speech). The *sic* therein sets up the consecutive *ut*-clause.

ut non modo manus tanti exercitus, sed ne vestigium quidem cuiquam pacato nocuisse dicatur?: The verb of the *ut*-clause is the impersonal *dicatur* (in the present subjunctive), which governs a 'nominative + infinitive construction': the subjects are *manus* and *vestigium*, the verb is *nocuisse*. Negatives are a bit of an issue here, caused by a slight adjustment to the *non modo ... sed etiam ...* ('not only... but also...') formula. Cicero here wants to say 'not only not, but not even', but does not add the required second negative to the '*non-modo*' part; rather, he uses the 'local negation' *ne ... quidem*, which in the first instance negates the word in-between, i.e. *vestigium*, to negate the entire sentence. Put differently, Cicero is saying literally: 'that not only a hand, but not even a footprint, of such a great army is said to have harmed anybody peaceful' – which makes little sense.

---

40 Plutarch, *Life of Pompey* 30.1.

What he means, however, is 'that not only *no* hand, but not even a footprint, of such a great army is said to have harmed anybody peaceful.'

hic: the adverb, rather than the demonstrative pronoun, which can be translated along the lines of 'here' or 'in these circumstances'.

hunc hominem: Pompey.

manus: in form, *manus* could be either nominative singular ('hand') or nominative plural ('band'). The verb (*dicatur*) does not help us to decide: when a verb governs two subjects, it regularly agrees with the closest one, in this case *vestigium*, which is singular. So *manus* could still be plural. The question then becomes one of interpretation.

ceteris: in the dative plural because the verb *excellere* (meaning 'to surpass' or 'to excel') takes the dative. *imperatoribus* is implied.

tantum: used adverbially here: 'so much' or 'so greatly'.

cuiquam pacato: this is dative, and acts as the object of *nocuisse*. *cuiquam* comes from *quisquam* ('anyone'); *pacato* is either the adjective *pacatus, -a, -um* (derived from *paco*), meaning 'disposed to peace, peaceable' or the perfect passive participle of *paco, -are, -avi, -atum*, meaning 'to impose a settlement on, bring under control, subdue'. The choice between 'anyone peaceful' and 'anyone who had (already) accepted the terms of Roman peace after having been subdued' involves a fine, but important distinction: were those that didn't suffer harm peaceful to begin with or is Cicero referring to communities that were once hostile but are now 'pacified' the Roman way? He comes back to Roman notions of peace and provincial exploitation with a sarcastic witticism at the end of the speech (§ 67): *ecquam putatis civitatem pacatam fuisse, quae locuples sit, ecquam esse locupletem, quae istis pacata esse videatur?* ('Do you imagine that any state has been "pacified" and still remains wealthy, that any state is wealthy and seems to these men [= greedy members of Rome's ruling elite] "pacified"?') Put differently, Cicero suggests that Roman 'pacification' proceeded until a province had been stripped of its wealth...

Iam vero quem ad modum milites hibernent cotidie sermones ac litterae perferuntur: the subject of the sentence are *sermones ac litterae*, referring to oral reports or hearsay (*sermones*) and written missives (*litterae*) that, so Cicero implies, reach Rome on a daily basis (*cotidie*) and bring news on how Pompey's soldiers comport themselves in their winter quarters. *iam vero* ('moreover') gives an emphatic beginning to what follows as if there is still much more to say about Pompey's self-control. It highlights how Pompey not only avoided damaging the areas through which he led his army, but also made sure that no-one in these areas was forced to spend money on his troops during a time when many other generals plundered the provinces to increase their own wealth.

quem ad modum milites hibernent: an indirect question (hence the present subjunctive of *hibernent*) notionally dependent on *sermones ac litterae* and introduced by *quem ad modum*.

cotidie: the adverb suggests a constant stream of news from Asia to Rome, implying in turn that Pompey was building up a high degree of goodwill with Rome's allies. (The idea of the allies preferring Pompey to be Rome's general came up already in § 13 and recurs in § 41.)

Non modo ut sumptum faciat in militem nemini vis adfertur, sed ne cupienti quidem cuiquam permittitur: this sentence summarizes the contents of the oral and written reports that reached Rome, so one could have expected Cicero to present this intelligence in indirect speech. He doesn't, thereby enhancing the vividness of his discourse. The word order serves the same purpose: by placing the consecutive *ut*-clause *ut sumptum faciat in militem*, which specifies the results of the two main clauses, i.e. *nemini vis adfertur* and *ne cupienti quidem cuiquam permittitur*, up front, Cicero raises the expectation that he is about to detail a form of financial abuse or extortion – only to cancel out this expectation instantly with <u>nemini</u> *vis adfertur*. *vis* is the subject of *adfertur*: it refers to the illegitimate use of physical force or violence. The second main clause generates a similar moment of surprise. If Cicero first stresses that no one was forced to support Pompey's soldiers against their will, he now ups the ante by arguing that, with Pompey in charge, no provincial is allowed to incur expenses on behalf of the Romans *even if he wanted to do so!*

ne cupienti quidem cuiquam permittitur: as above, the negative in *ne...
quidem* covers the entire sentence. *cupienti* is the present active participle
in the dative of *cupio* agreeing with *cuiquam*: it was *not* permitted to *anyone*,
even if he so *desired*.

**Hiemis enim, non avaritiae perfugium maiores nostri in sociorum atque
amicorum tectis esse voluerunt**: the subject is *maiores nostri*, the main verb
voluerunt, which introduces an indirect statement with *perfugium* as subject
accusative and *esse* the verb (here used as a full verb): 'the ancestors wished
there to be a shelter from ... in the houses of ...' (If Cicero had written *tecta*
instead of *in ... tectis*, *esse* would be a copula, i.e. a verb that 'links' the
subject and its predicate: 'the ancestors wished the houses of ... *to be* a
shelter from...'.)

Hiemis ..., non avaritiae perfugium: *hiemis* is an objective genitive, *avaritiae*
is a subjective genitive: in the phrase *hiemis perfugium*, someone else is
seeking shelter from 'the object' winter; in the phrase *avaritiae perfugium*,
it is 'the subject' greed that is seeking shelter. Or, put differently, *hiemis* is
the object against which the verbal action implied in *perfugium* is directed,
whereas *avaritiae* is the subject understood to carry out the verbal action
implied in *perfugium*. The fact that these two words are both in the genitive
and depend on the same noun serves to highlight the contrast between
these two diametrically opposed ways of treating the houses of the allies.

maiores nostri: with his invocation of the ancestors, Cicero implies that
Pompey has lived up to the high standards supposedly upheld in the
past, further reinforcing the idea that he was a fair and self-disciplined
commander. (Cicero mentions the glory or actions of their ancestors to spur
on the Roman people to defeat Mithridates in §§ 6, 11 and 14 of this speech.)

in sociorum atque amicorum tectis: the hyperbaton *in ... tectis* generates a
closed word order.

tectis: this is ablative plural to go with the word *in*, and literally means
'roofs'. Here this word is used to refer to the whole building (a rhetorical
device called 'synecdoche'), and therefore can be translated as 'houses'.

40: NO SIGHT-SEEING OR SOUVENIRS FOR THE PERFECT GENERAL

Cicero now argues that Pompey's outstanding character not only ensures compliance with ethical standards in military operations set by the ancestors; it also has significant strategic advantages. The very speed of movement Cicero has singled out earlier as a hallmark of Pompey's approach to warfare is ultimately grounded in his personal qualities. This is an interesting argument, not least since it runs counter to his earlier assertion that the most important manifestation of *virtus* is martial prowess, whereas the 'soft' qualities are mere handmaidens. Consider: in § 29, Cicero identified *celeritas in conficiendo* as one of the *virtutes imperatoriae*, which everybody recognizes as such; in contrast, *temperantia* is one of those seemingly 'secondary' qualities that Cicero introduces as *administrae comitesque* to *virtus bellandi* in § 36. Now it emerges that *temperantia* is in fact the enabling condition of *celeritas in conficiendo* – far from being secondary, it is foundational for Pompey's success (and hence an essential element of Cicero's conception of the *summus imperator*). Cicero does not spell any of this out explicitly. But those able to read between the lines will realize that his initial endorsement of *virtus bellandi* as the most important manifestation of aristocratic excellence is little more than a concession to Roman common sense that he himself does not share. Through the unorthodox validation of other, ethical qualities, and the (frankly astonishing) argument that they are of fundamental importance not just for winning over the hearts and minds of locals but for successful warfare, Cicero's discussion of *virtus* in the *pro lege Manilia* offers at least a partial critique and subversion of this common sense – and a redefinition of *virtus* in a distinctly Ciceronian key.

As in the previous paragraph, Cicero makes his case by means of comparison (cf. § 36: *ea magis ex aliorum contentione quam ipsa per sese cognosci atque intellegi possunt*). Unlike other generals, Pompey is immune to temptations and desires that routinely slow down members of Rome's ruling elite when on campaign in the Greek East, with its manifold attractions and opportunities for enrichment and pleasure. Whereas his peers get sidetracked, Pompey's moderation enables single-minded dedication to the task at hand. Cicero here concedes that many Roman aristocrats considered the Eastern Mediterranean as one large museum from which they could help themselves to statues, paintings, and other artworks for display back in Rome. But greed and plunder, as he has already argued in earlier sections of the speech, slow down military progress and incite hostility among the indigenous people. It is one of the main reasons why Lucullus had not been able to finish off Mithridates after defeating him in battle (§ 22):

> Primum ex suo regno sic Mithridates profugit, ut ex eodem Ponto Medea illa quondam profugisse dicitur, quam praedicant in fuga fratris sui membra in eis locis, qua se parens persequeretur, dissipavisse, ut eorum collectio dispersa, maerorque patrius, *celeritatem* persequendi *retardaret*. Sic Mithridates fugiens maximam vim auri atque argenti pulcherrimarumque rerum omnium, quas et a maioribus acceperat et ipse bello superiore ex tota Asia direptas in suum regnum congesserat, in Ponto omnem reliquit. Haec dum nostri colligunt omnia diligentius, rex ipse e manibus effugit. Ita illum in persequendi studio maeror, hos laetitia *tardavit*.

> [At first Mithridates fled from his kingdom, as Medea is formerly said to have fled from the same region of Pontus; for they say that she, in her flight, strewed about the limbs of her brother in those places along which her father was likely to pursue her, in order that the collection of them, dispersed as they were, and the grief which would afflict his father, might delay the speed of his pursuit. Mithridates, flying in the same manner, left in Pontus the whole of the vast quantity of gold and silver, and of beautiful things which he had inherited from his ancestors, and which he himself had collected and brought into his own kingdom, having obtained them by plunder in the former war from all Asia. While our men were diligently occupied in collecting all this, the king himself escaped out of their hands. And so grief retarded the father of Medea in his pursuit, but delight delayed our men.]

And, as Cicero goes on to say, the reputation of L. Lucullus' army that it would despoil even the most sacred shrines struck fear into the hearts and minds of the local population, so that they rose up in arms against the Romans and afforded protection to Mithridates (§ 23).

Age vero ceteris in rebus qua ille sit temperantia, considerate: the singular imperative of *ago*, i.e. *age*, could be used idiomatically as a transitional particle, irrespective of the how many people were in the audience – hence the seemingly weird situation that the sentence begins with a singular imperative and ends with one in the plural (*considerate*). *considerate* governs an indirect question (hence the subjunctive *sit*) introduced by the interrogative adjective *qua*, which agrees with *temperantia*. *qua ... temperantia* is an ablative of quality. *ceteris in rebus* belongs into the *qua*-clause, put is pulled up-front for emphasis. Translate in the following order: *Age vero, considerate qua temperantia ille sit in ceteris rebus*.

ceteris in rebus: the preposition that governs the ablative phrase comes second; the normal word order would be *in ceteris rebus*. The phenomenon is called 'anastrophe'.

Unde illam tantam celeritatem et tam incredibilem cursum inventum putatis?: The main verb of the question is *putatis*, which introduces an indirect statement, with *illam tantam celeritatem* and *tam incredibilem cursum* as subject accusatives and *inventum* (sc. *esse*) as (passive) infinitive. *inventum* agrees in case, number, and gender with the closest of the two subject accusatives, i.e. *cursum*. It may seem curious that Cicero here opts for a passive construction and, further, that he doesn't even specify an agent by means of an ablative of agency (e.g. *ab illo*). The reason could be that the question is designed as a 'red herring': as Cicero goes on to suggest counterintuitively, Pompey's speed wasn't extraordinary at all – all he did was not to get sidetracked because of character flaws, like all the other generals.[41]

Non enim illum eximia vis remigum aut ars inaudita quaedam gubernandi aut venti aliqui novi tam celeriter in ultimas terras pertulerunt, sed eae res, quae ceteros [sc. *imperatores*] **remorari solent, non retardarunt**: the sentence has two (negated) main verbs, linked by *sed*: *non ... pertulerunt*; *non retardarunt*. *illum* is the accusative object of both. *pertulerunt* goes with three subjects, presented as excluded alternatives coordinated by *aut – aut*: (i) *eximia vis remigum*; (ii) *ars inaudita quaedam gubernandi*; (iii) *venti aliqui novi*.

retardarunt: the syncopated form of the 3rd person plural perfect indicative active of *retarda-ve-runt*.

non avaritia ab instituto cursu ad praedam aliquam devocavit, non libido [*ab instituto cursu*] **ad voluptatem** [*devocavit*], **non amoenitas** [*ab instituto cursu*] **ad delectationem** [*devocavit*], **non nobilitas urbis** [*ab instituto cursu*] **ad cognitionem** [*devocavit*], **non denique labor ipse** [*ab instituto cursu*] **ad quietem** [*devocavit*]; a long, paratactic string of main clauses in asyndeton,

---

41   Caesar, too, built up a reputation for *celeritas*: *veni, vidi, vici*, and all that! Cf. Goldsworthy (1998), who argues that Caesar portrays himself as distilled essence of a Roman general, i.e. that *celeritas* is actually a desirable trait in a Roman general. The noteworthy point about the *celeritas* of both Pompey and Caesar then is not so much that they show *celeritas* as the superlative nature of their *celeritas*.

each starting with the negation *non*. The ablative phrase *ab instituto cursu* and the main verb *devocavit* are systematically elided after the first one.

non..., non..., non..., non..., non...: a powerful anaphora, reinforced by the asyndeton, the elisions, and Cicero's economy in the use of attributes: none of the accusative phrases except the first (*ad praedam aliquam*) has a modifier.

(i) avaritia ... ad praedam, (ii) libido ad voluptatem, (iii) amoenitas ad delectationem, (iv) nobilitas urbis ad cognitionem: the first four clauses yield an intricate chiastic design: (i) *avaritia* and (ii) *libido* designate personal characteristics; (iii) *amoenitas* and (iv) *nobilitas urbis* refer to the characteristics of specific locations. Yet (i) correlates with (iv) and (ii) with (iii): greed for plunder entails the inspection of famous cities; and lust for pleasure motivates 'wellness stops'.

non denique labor ipse ad quietem: the climactic fifth item in the list is different in nature: it refers to a positive quality of Pompey, i.e. his seemingly superhuman ability to do without rest. *ipse*, which agrees with *labor*, is here used to emphasize something regarded as exceptional or extreme: see *OLD* s.v. *ipse* 9.

postremo signa et tabulas ceteraque ornamenta Graecorum oppidorum, quae ceteri tollenda esse arbitrantur, ea sibi ille ne visenda quidem existimavit: the subject of the sentence is *ille* (referring to Pompey), the main verb *existimavit*. It introduces an indirect statement, with the polysyndetic tricolon *signa et tabulas ceteraque ornamenta* as subject accusative and *visenda* (sc. *esse*) as infinitive. *ea* sums up *signa et tabulas ceteraque ornamenta* for additional emphasis. The pronoun *sibi* is a dative of agency with the gerundive ('by him'). Cicero construes the relative clause and the second half of the main clause in parallel:

quae	~	*ea*
ceteri	~	*(sibi) ille*
tollenda esse	~	*ne visenda [sc. esse] quidem*
arbitrantur	~	*existimavit*

The parallel design heightens the contrast between Pompey and all the others (*ceteri*). It also underscores how widespread and prolific the practice of taking sculpture from Greece to Rome was and hence how admirable Pompey was to resist it. (A significant proportion of original Greek bronzes survive because the ships carrying them from Greece capsized en route to Italy.)

signa et tabulas ceteraque ornamenta: *signa* are statues, *tabulae* are paintings, and *ornamenta* refers to any other kind of civic artwork on display in the public spaces of cities that could be removed and taken to Rome.

quae ceteri tollenda esse arbitrantur: the relative pronoun *quae* has a double function: it is the accusative object of *arbitrantur* and it is the subject accusative of the indirect statement introduces by *arbitrantur* (with the gerundive *tollenda esse* as infinitive).

41: SAINT POMPEY

The paragraph consists of five sentences, with the first four focusing on Pompey's *temperantia vel continentia* (the two terms are virtual synonyms) and the final sentence moving on to Pompey's *facilitas*:

> (i) Itaque *omnes* **nunc** *in iis locis* Cn. Pompeium sicut aliquem non ex hac urbe missum, sed de caelo delapsum *intuentur*;
>
> (ii) **nunc** denique *incipiunt credere*, fuisse homines Romanos hac quondam continentia, quod iam nationibus exteris incredibile ac falso memoriae proditum videbatur;
>
> (iii) **nunc** imperii vestri *splendor* illis gentibus lucem *adferre coepit*;
>
> (iv) **nunc** *intellegunt* non sine causa maiores suos tum, cum ea temperantia magistratus habebamus, servire populo Romano quam imperare aliis maluisse.
>
> (v) **Iam vero** ita *faciles aditus* ad eum privatorum, ita *liberae querimoniae* de aliorum iniuriis *esse dicuntur*, ut is qui dignitate principibus excellit, facilitate infimis par esse videatur.

(i) – (iv) elevate Pompey; (v) emphasizes that despite his elevated status Pompey has remained humble. Grammar, syntax, and style reinforce the point. Cicero sets up (i) – (iv) as a thematic unit by means of the anaphora of *nunc*; the *iam vero* of (v) marks a new section in the argument: the two particles *iam* and *vero* will continue to provide 'transitional kit' in the following paragraph (see below). A similar effect is achieved by the subjects and the verbs. (i) – (iv) present matters from the perspective of the Eastern provincials, which Cicero introduces in (i) with the formulation *omnes in iis locis* ('everybody in this part of the world'). *omnes in iis locis* is also the implied subject of (ii) *incipiunt credere* and (iv) *intellegunt*. (iii) also maintains the provincial perspective but with an element of variation. If (i) *intuentur*, (ii) *incipiunt credere*, and (iv) *intellegunt* put the emphasis on the *perception* of *provincials*, (iii), which is the central sentence of this section, foregrounds *facts* from a *Roman* point of view (see *imperii vestri splendor*), even though the focus remains on the impact of Rome on provincial peoples: *illis gentibus* is synonymous with *omnes in iis locis*. In contrast, (v) again breaks with this pattern: we get the impersonal passive verb *dicuntur*, which carries no implication that what is being said about Pompey's accessibility and ease in interpersonal interaction is a matter of provincial perception: it holds true anywhere.

The anaphora of *nunc* endows this paragraph with special urgency: opinions in the East are (again) swinging in favour of Rome because of Pompey's presence and the way in which he has conducted his military operations so far. The Roman people, so Cicero implies, ought not to miss this opportunity and build on the momentum Pompey has generated, not least since they are the beneficiaries of Pompey's efforts on behalf of the *res publica*. In the course of the paragraph, Cicero transforms the respect, indeed worship, that Pompey commands in the East into the imperial glory of the Roman people: *nunc imperii <u>vestri</u> splendor illis gentibus lucem adferre coepit*. Now it is the 'glory of *your* empire', rather than just Pompey's personal success. Thus Pompey's temperance results in a view of the Roman empire itself as being above human, bringing 'light' to the people of the East. (The notion of the Roman people as a civilising force would have been welcome to Cicero's audience, but we should not take his word for it that the provincial people really saw Rome in this way.) Cicero even implies that the moral standards of ancestral Rome justified her empire, as demonstrated by the fact that some gave up their independence voluntarily, arguing (on the basis of no evidence) that the reason for this voluntary submission to Roman rule was the self-restraint of Roman officials at the time – the same self-restraint for which Pompey, too, is famous.

Cicero is here most likely alluding to the decision of King Attalus III of Pergamum, who died without heir in 133 BC, to leave his kingdom to the Roman people. The reasons will have had more to do with a pragmatic sense of power-politics in the region than appreciation of the outstanding morals of Roman officials – and the decision proved at any rate controversial. It was Tiberius Gracchus who decided to accept the legacy (before he got killed, that is), via the people, as a way to fund his land redistribution. (As someone who enjoyed an inherited guestfriendship with Eumenes he received the news ahead of everyone else.) Some in the senate were pretty cross with him for jumping the gun, especially when a revolt broke out, led by Aristonicus, a son of Attalus's predecessor Eumenes. It took two years to quell the uprising and another two years to set up the province of Asia. Put differently, Cicero is playing fast and loose with the historical truth.

Itaque omnes nunc in iis locis Cn. Pompeium sicut aliquem non ex hac urbe missum, sed de caelo delapsum intuentur: *intuentur* is here construed with a double accusative (*Cn. Pompeium* and *aliquem*) coordinated by *sicut*. The two participles *missum* and *delapsum* agree with *aliquem*: 'they looked upon Gnaeus Pompeius as someone who was not sent from this city, but who descended from the sky.'

delapsum: This idea of a serene descent from on high spells *epiphany*, picking up on the theme of Pompey's almost divine *virtus* which runs through the speech, elevating him above ordinary men. It is important to note, though, that Cicero here distinguishes sharply between an Eastern and a Roman point of view. Pompey's divinity is in the eyes of the beholder: the subjects of *intuentur* are Eastern provincials. For Cicero's *Roman* audience, Pompey remains *ex hac urbe missus*, i.e. a properly appointed magistrate of the senate and the people of Rome, who derived his position and powers from constitutional procedures.[42] This use of 'divergent focalization' presupposes, and taps into, the Roman prejudice about the Greek East as a hotbed of superstitious beliefs, including the elevation of humans to divine status. Cicero, in other words, nowhere asserts that Pompey *is* a god; he merely reports that, in the East, he was *perceived* as one. By making the issue one of psychology ('Pompey *seems* divine', i.e. to those who don't know better), rather than ontology ('Pompey *is* divine') he manages to portray Pompey as god-like, without subverting important principles of Rome's political culture, which had no room for the worship of human beings as gods.

Even though Cicero presents the impression of Pompey as quasi-divine as the delusion of foreign communities, he suggests that this delusion is real in its consequences insofar as it can be exploited to strategic advantage. To begin with, the quasi-religious adulation Pompey commands stands in striking contrast to the religious outrage caused by Lucullus, which Cicero reported in the opening parts of the speech. The nature of the enemy (a king) and the theatre of operation (Asia), so he suggests, call for a general who can rival his opponent in religious charisma. Pompey's ability to appear god-like thus emerges as a crucial military asset. As the recipient of the same sort of 'irrational' devotion Mithridates enjoys, Pompey will be able to fight fire with fire.[43] Cicero thus makes tactical use of a foreign

---

42   Classen (1963) 332, with reference to Cicero, *Letters to Atticus* 2.21.4. At *Man.* 13, Pompey ironically appears divine to Rome's allies in part because of his outstanding *humanitas*!

43   This is a leitmotif throughout the speech; at *Man.* 24, for instance, Cicero makes the paradoxical point that kings afflicted by misfortune can count on the sympathy of those, *qui aut reges sunt aut vivunt in regno, ut iis nomen regale magnum et sanctum esse videatur* ('who are either kings themselves or the dwellers in a kingdom, as the name of king seems to them grandiose and venerable'). Rome needs a general with the same attributes, and Pompeius *Magnus* is an obvious choice: Gruber (1988) 24. In fact, simply

system of belief, meant to encourage the Roman people to put Pompey in charge of the war.

But wasn't this technique potentially dangerous? By making the Eastern point of view part of his discourse, did Cicero not willy-nilly endow Pompey with a divine aura of sorts? How many members in the audience would have picked up on the 'divergent focalization'? Isn't Cicero violating important principles of oligarchic equality on which the senatorial tradition of republican government rested by hailing Pompey as god-like? On the other hand (and depending on how we define the context of the speech), it is equally possible to argue that the focalized deification of Pompey is a profoundly conservative form of praise in that it limits the validity (and hence the virulence) of Greek ideas about divine human beings to the Eastern Mediterranean. As we have pointed out in the Introduction, ever since Roman aristocrats became aware of the Greek practice to grant (semi-)divine status to outstanding individuals, some of them toyed with the notion of integrating this unique form of exaltation into their own public image. Cicero's strategy of geographic focalization, on the other hand, reduces the Greek concept of 'human godlikeness' to a localized, psychological phenomenon, thus radically confining its scope and implicitly denying its relevance and applicability at Rome. The fact that other cultures are more prone to turn humans into gods, so Cicero seems to be saying, may be exploited for strategic purposes in the context of imperial expansion but does (or should) not necessarily affect Pompey's domestic identity. There is, then, a dialectic of panegyric excess and republican moderation in place here that is fiendishly difficult to pin down: what do *you* think Cicero was up to?[44]

nunc denique incipiunt credere, fuisse homines Romanos hac quondam continentia, quod iam nationibus exteris incredibile ac falso memoriae proditum videbatur: *credere* introduces an indirect statement, with *homines Romanos* as subject accusative and *fuisse* as infinitive, followed by a substantive *quod*-clause, which explicates the indirect statement: '... a fact that...'. *quod* is the subject of *videbatur* and agrees with *incredibile* and *proditum*: '... a fact that ... appeared unbelievable and wrongly transmitted

---

by an inversion of *regale* and *magnum* in the cited Latin – *ut iis nomen magnum regale et sanctum esse videatur* = 'as the name of Pompey (= *Magnus*) seems to them royal and venerable' – Pompey turns into a divinely anointed king!

44 This note is based on Gildenhard (2011) 264-65.

to memory'. The striking emphasis on 'now' (*nunc*) and 'beginning' (*incipiunt, coepit*) divides Roman history for present purposes into three distinct phases: (i) an early time of moral excellence that currently is nothing but an indistinct (provincial) memory or, worse, has started to look like a mere invention; (ii) an intermediary time of decline and corruption that has rendered the alleged quality of the previous period look 'too good to be true'; (iii) the present, defined and dominated by Pompey, in whom ancestral excellence has re-emerged – and with it belief and confidence in the historical existence and continued possibility of impeccable conduct on the part of Roman magistrates. Cicero here taps into a long-standing Roman discourse that configured 'the ancestors' as benchmarks of excellence. It is important to realize that this sweeping conception of history, with its vague caesuras (Cicero doesn't explain when and why the decline kicked in or why and how Pompey has managed to buck the trend), is as much a figment of Cicero's imagination as it is tailor-made for his rhetorical aim of elevating Pompey above his contemporaries.

hac ... continentia: an ablative of quality.

quondam ... iam: the two adverbs mark a temporal contrast: given the conduct of contemporary Roman generals, by now (*iam*) the notion that once (*quondam*) there were Romans of outstanding self-restraint had lost any credibility (cf. *incredibile*) – a credibility now gradually restored by Pompey (cf. *incipiunt credere*).

falso memoriae proditum: *falso* is an adverb; despite the fact that it may look like a dative it does *not* – and cannot: *memoria* is feminine – agree with *memoriae*, which is a dative governed by *proditum*: 'falsely transmitted *to* memory'.

nunc imperii vestri splendor illis gentibus lucem adferre coepit: with the strategically placed *vestri*, Cicero has his audience partake in Pompey's supernatural aura and in turn ensures that the supernatural aura of Pompey appears as a force acting on behalf of the Roman people. The imagery continues the divine connotations of *de caelo delapsum*: the metaphorical invocation of brightness and light in *splendor* and *lucem adferre* suggests the supernatural and the salvific and reinforces the importance of just governance as the ultimate foundation of Rome's imperial rule: 'The depredations causing the light to be dimmed were the fault not only of the pirates but of greedy and unjust governors ... and a man of *singularis virtus* is needed to bring it back to those areas of the world in need of it, Rome included. This theme of Rome's problems being caused by lack of moderation in Rome's own leaders who bring about a break in *fides* between Rome and its provinces is closely linked to similar expressions in both Cicero's *De Officiis* and Sallust's *Bellum Catilinae*. In the theme of light lost and light returning we should understand that Cicero's thinking allows that Rome's claim to leadership is not intrinsic, nor is it an inalienable birthright. It will last only as long as Rome deserves it, that is, while her *imperium* is based on justice. In the same way that Rome's *lumina* cannot rely on their ancestors for their status but must face the *iudicium publicum* which will confirm their *dignitas*, so the position of Rome as the *lux orbis terrarum*, and thus the claims of the *populus Romanus* to *maiestas*, or 'greaterness', are valid only if such claims rest on the just practices of the centre and its representatives.'[45]

nunc intellegunt non sine causa maiores suos tum, cum ea temperantia magistratus habebamus, servire populo Romano quam imperare aliis maluisse: the subject continues to be *omnes* (*in iis locis*). The verb *intellegunt* introduces an indirect statement with *maiores suos* as subject accusative and *maluisse* as infinitive, which in turn governs the antithetical infinitives *servire* (taking *populo Romano* as dative object) and *imperare* (taking *aliis* as dative object).

non sine causa: the phrase belongs to the indirect statement. A double negative (*non* + *sine*) makes a positive. The rhetorical device is called litotes.

maiores suos: the reflexive possessive adjective *suos* identifies the ancestors in question as those of the provincials (the implied subject of *intellegunt*).

tum, cum ea temperantia magistratus habebamus: another potentially tricky use of *cum*, given that it is followed by an ablative (*ea temperantia*). This may well give one the (wrong) idea that it is the preposition. In fact, it

---

is the conjunction: *cum* here introduces a temporal clause in the imperfect indicative (*habebamus*). It is set up by *tum*: 'at the time (*tum*) when (*cum*)'. (Note that this is not the correlation *cum – tum* discussed above.)

ea temperantia: an ablative of quality, which does not take any preposition.

magistratus: a fourth declension noun in the accusative plural: the accusative object of *habebamus*.

servire ... maluisse: as noted above, the most striking illustration of this unusual preference occurred in 133 BC, when the King of Pergamum, Attalus III, died leaving no heir but a will in which he left his kingdom to the people of Rome. Note, however, that the transfer of power occurred after his death, so did not affect him personally, and that other members of the royal family were not quite as keen to relinquish their independence as the deceased king: a rebellion of one of his more distant relatives ensued, which was, ironically, quelled with the help of the King of Pontus at the time, Mithridates V Euergetes, the father of Mithridates Eupator, against whom Rome is now fighting. Cicero of course has no interest in rehearsing any such details; he nonchalantly generalizes and, moreover, ascribes the unprecedented act of a single king to a widespread appreciation of Roman morals among Eastern provincials. The antithesis between *servire* and *imperare* heightens the hyperbole: the dramatic declaration that entire nations gladly gave up their own freedom in order to enjoy Roman rule underscores the alleged strategic advantage of *innocentia* in the context of imperial expansion. If, so Cicero seems to be implying here, provincials did not have to live in fear of marauding Roman generals and their armies, they would become part of the Roman empire of their own accord.

Iam vero ita faciles aditus ad eum privatorum, ita liberae querimoniae de aliorum iniuriis esse dicuntur, ut is qui dignitate principibus excellit, facilitate infimis par esse videatur: the verb is the passive *dicuntur*, which governs a nominative + infinitive (*esse*) construction. There are two plural subjects, *aditus* and *querimoniae*, each with a predicative complement, *faciles* and *liberae*, with the infinitive *esse*. The two subjects follow each other asyndetically, an effect re-inforced by the anaphora of *ita*, which sets up the consecutive *ut*-clause that concludes the sentence.

aditus ad eum privatorum: *privatorum* is a subjective genitive dependent on *aditus*: *who* has access? Private individuals. The power of a Roman magistrate or pro-magistrate in a province, especially when he was in command of an army, was quasi-autocratic. It is therefore hardly surprising that a steady stream of visitors – and not just official delegates from civic communities such as the Cretan ambassadors Cicero mentioned in § 35 but also private individuals – would seek him out to gain his support: for all intents and purposes, he represented the law. Cicero suggests that Pompey made himself available to all and sundry and used his extraordinary powers with a keen sense of justice.

de aliorum iniuriis: *aliorum* is a subjective genitive dependent on *iniuriis*: *who* has committed harm? Others.

ut is qui dignitate principibus excellit, facilitate infimis par esse videatur: the *ut*-clause and the relative clause embedded therein map out two complementary qualities situated at the opposite ends of Rome's socio-political spectrum. In terms of social rank (*dignitas*) Pompey is at the very top of Roman society; in terms of his accessibility (*facilitas*), his behaviour does not differ from those who are at the very bottom. The syntax reinforces the perfect, paradoxical match of Pompey's *dignitas* and *facilitas*:

	ut-clause	relative clause
Subject (Pompey)	*is*	*qui*
Ablative of respect	*dignitate*	*facilitate*
Whom he surpasses/matches	*principibus*	*infimis*
Verb, indicating Pompey's relative position	*excellit*	*par esse videatur*

42: PEACE FOR OUR TIME

In the previous paragraph, Cicero started with four sentences that dealt with Pompey's *temperantia*, constituted also stylistically as a unit by the quadruple anaphora of *nunc*. In the last sentence of § 41, he moved on to *facilitas* – a switch in focus marked by the particles *Iam vero* – which he treats in one sentence. § 42 continues this approach: we get another list of sentences, introduced by either *iam* or *vero*, to do with (mainly) 'soft' *virtutes*:

> (i) *Iam* quantum *consilio*, quantum *dicendi gravitate et copia* valeat, in quo ipso inest quaedam dignitas imperatoria, vos, Quirites, hoc ipso ex loco saepe cognovistis.
>
> (ii) *Fidem vero* eius quantam inter socios existimari putatis, quam hostes omnes omnium generum sanctissimam iudicarint?
>
> (iii) *Humanitate iam* tanta est, ut difficile dictu sit, utrum hostes magis virtutem eius pugnantes timuerint an mansuetudinem victi dilexerint.

Consilium is a quality Cicero included in his list of *virtutes imperatoriae* commonly recognized as such (see § 29: *labor in negotiis, fortitudo in periculis, industria in agendo, celeritas in conficiendo, consilium in providendo*). Like *facilitas*, *fides* and *humanitas* figure in the list of handmaidens to martial *virtus* Cicero enumerated in § 36: *Ac primum quanta innocentia debent esse imperatores! quanta deinde in omnibus rebus temperantia! quanta fide, quanta facilitate, quanto ingenio, quanta humanitate!* In that list, *innocentia* and *temperantia* took pride of place, corresponding to the lengthy treatment they receive in §§ 36-41, whereas *fides*, *facilitas*, *ingenium*, and *humanitas* occur in the form of a checklist, corresponding to their swift treatment in §§ 41-42. A word on *ingenium* and *dicendi gravitas et copia*: if you recall, we expressed a certain amount of bafflement in our commentary on § 36 that Cicero included *ingenium* in his list of *virtutes*. And he does indeed not mention the term again in his discussion of the perfect general. Instead, what we get here in § 42 is the somewhat surprising inclusion of powerful oratory among the qualities that define the *summus imperator*. We mentioned at the time that *ingenium* is a key technical term in rhetorical theory (innate talent complementing *ars*, or 'exercise', in constituting the perfect orator, the *summus orator*); and it now emerges that Cicero included a reference to *ingenium* to set up his pitch for *dicendi gravitas et copia* as an important characteristic of an outstanding military leader. Once we see this correspondence, all the *virtutes* mentioned in § 36 are accounted for, and the reference to oratory no longer comes (entirely) out of the blue.

In his sentence on *humanitas*, Cicero claims that Rome's enemies are as appreciative of Pompey's *virtus* (here used unequivocally in its 'primary' meaning of 'martial prowess') while fighting as they are of his mild disposition (*mansuetudo*) when defeated. He thereby elegantly sums up the full spectrum of *virtutes*, from tough-as-nail courage on the battlefield to humane treatment of vanquished foes, that he covered in §§ 29-42 and claimed for Pompey's rich portfolio of excellences – just before the final, concluding sentence of his discussion of *virtus*, in which he argues the paradoxical point that putting this uniquely able individual in charge of *war* will soon result in permanent *peace*, a boon of such proportions that it resembles a divine charter: *et quisquam dubitabit quin huic hoc tantum bellum permittendum sit, qui ad omnia nostrae memoriae bella conficienda divino quodam consilio natus esse videatur?*

Iam quantum consilio [sc. valeat], **quantum dicendi gravitate et copia valeat, in quo ipso inest quaedam dignitas imperatoria, vos, Quirites, hoc ipso ex loco saepe cognovistis**: the main verb is *cognovistis* which governs the indirect question (hence the subjunctive) *quantum ... valeat*. The antecedent of the relative clause introduced by *in quo ipso* is ambiguous, not least since *quo* and *ipso* could be either masculine or neuter. It could be Pompey, the subject of the indirect question implied in *valeat*: 'in whom there is anyhow a certain dignity characteristic of a general'. It could be *dicendi* – understood either specifically in the sense of 'Pompey's way of speaking' or more generally 'powerful oratory'. Or it could hark back to the indirect question in its entirety, i.e. the powerful display of political wisdom eloquently articulated. In this last sense in particular, Cicero implicitly claims *dignitas imperatoria* also for himself.

Lexically and thematically, Cicero here harks back to the opening of § 29, the beginning of his discussion of *virtus*: *Iam vero* <u>*virtuti*</u> *Cn. Pompei quae potest* <u>*oratio*</u> <u>*par*</u> *inveniri? Quid est quod quisquam aut illo* <u>*dignum*</u> *aut vobis* <u>*novum*</u> *aut cuiquam* <u>*inauditum*</u> *possit adferre? Neque enim illae sunt solae virtutes* <u>*imperatoriae,*</u> *quae volgo existimantur...* Arguably, his claim that *dicendi gravitas et copia* belongs to a discussion of (Pompey's) *virtus* and possesses *quaedam dignitas imperatoria*, apart from solving the tension between excellence and its recapitulation in discourse (insofar as discourse itself emerges as a field of excellence), constitutes something new and unheard of – and worthy not just of Pompey, but also of Cicero!

quantum consilio, quantum dicendi gravitate et copia valeat: Cicero uses the anaphora of *quantum* to differentiate between Pompey's political intelligence (*consilio*) and his eloquence (*dicendi gravitate et copia*).

consilio ... gravitate ... copia: ablatives of respect or specification.

vos, Quirites: the direct appeal to the audience makes this part more vivid: Cicero appeals to the experience of his audience as evidence for his argument.

hoc ipso ex loco: the preposition that governs the ablative phrase (*ex*) comes second, in this case after the two pronominal adjectives *hoc* and *ipso*, a phenomenon called 'anastrophe'. Cicero refers to the place from which he is speaking, i.e. the *rostra* or 'speaker's platform'. A keen sense of place is a distinctive feature of Cicero's oratory, and the very first sentence of the *pro lege Manilia* contains a programmatic reference to the location of delivery (§ 1): *Quamquam mihi semper frequens conspectus vester multo iucundissimus, hic autem locus ad agendum amplissimus, ad dicendum ornatissimus est visus, Quirites, tamen hoc aditu laudis, qui semper optimo cuique maxime patuit, non mea me voluntas adhuc, sed vitae meae rationes ab ineunte aetate susceptae prohibuerunt* ('Even though it has at all times given me a special pleasure to behold your crowded assembly, and this place in particular has seemed to me to afford the amplest scope for action, the fairest stage for eloquence, nonetheless, fellow-citizens, this approach to fame, which the best have ever found most widely open, has hitherto been barred to me, not certainly by any wish of mine, but by that scheme of life which, from my earliest years, I had laid down for myself'). The reference to the sphere of domestic politics sets up one of many contrasts operative in this passage. Cicero draws attention to Pompey's proven excellence *at home*, as basis for encouraging his audience to make reliable inferences about his reputation *abroad* (see further below: *inter socios, omnes hostes*).

Fidem vero eius quantam inter socios existimari putatis, quam hostes omnes omnium generum sanctissimam iudicarint?: The main verb of the question is *putatis* which governs *fidem vero eius quantam inter socios existimari* in *oratio obliqua*. The subject accusative is the interrogative pronoun *quantam*, the infinitive is *existimari*. *fidem* stands in predicative position to *quantam*, but is pulled up front for emphasis. It is also the antecedent of the relative pronoun *quam*.

Cicero works his way up from the domestic sphere in the previous sentence to Rome's allies in the main clause here (*inter socios*) to Rome's enemies in the relative clause (*hostes omnes omnium generum*), but he inverts allies and enemies chronologically: *iudicarint* is in the perfect (Rome's enemies have *already* judged Pompey's trustworthiness completely inviolable), which serves Cicero as basis for an *a-fortiori* argument that he casts as a rhetorical question: if already Rome's *enemies* have demonstrated the highest possible esteem for Pompey's *fides* (note the superlative *sanctissimam*), then the esteem in which it is held by Rome's *allies* is, surely, off the scale.

eius: the genitive of the demonstrative pronoun *is*, dependent on *fidem*: 'his [sc. Pompey's] trustworthiness'.

hostes omnes omnium generum: a hyperbole, reinforced by juxtaposition, polyptoton, and chiasmus (noun + adjective :: adjective + noun), designed to recall earlier universalizing statements about Pompey's comprehensive experience of warfare.

iudicarint: the contracted form of *iudica-ve-rint*, i.e. 3rd person plural perfect subjunctive active. The subjunctive is perhaps best explained as a case of so-called *attractio modi* ('attraction of mood'): it is a subordinate clause within indirect speech (*fidem ... existimari*) introduced by *putatis*.

Humanitate iam tanta est, ut difficile dictu sit, utrum hostes magis virtutem eius pugnantes timuerint an mansuetudinem victi dilexerint: the subject of *est* is Pompey. *humanitate ... tanta* is an ablative of characteristic or quality: 'he is of such human kindness that...'

ut difficile dictu sit: a consecutive *ut*-clause set up by *tanta*. *dictu* is a supine.

[Extra information:
The Latin 'supine' is a verbal substantive that follows the 4th declension in those cases in which it occurs. There are two forms: one ending in *-um*,

the other in *-u*. The supine in *-um* (originally an accusative of direction) expresses purposes with verb of motion. Here is an example from Ovid's *Ars Amatoria* on why women frequent the theatre: <u>spectatum</u> *veniunt, veniunt, spectentur ut ipsae*: 'they come in order to see, they come so that they themselves are seen' – or, more elegantly, 'they come to see and be seen'. The supine ending in *-u*, as here, derives originally from the dative (expressing purpose) and occurs mainly with a range of adjectives such as *fas*, *nefas*; *facilis*, *difficilis*; *incredibilis*; or *mirabilis*. It is best translated in English with the infinitive: *mirabile visu*: 'wondrous to behold', *difficile dictu*: 'difficult to say'.]

utrum hostes magis virtutem eius pugnantes timuerint an mansuetudinem victi dilexerint: after positioning Pompey in relation to the citizens and the allies, Cicero considers his impact on the enemy in what amounts to a magnificent play with antitheses (*virtutem* v. *mansuetudinem*, *pugnantes* v. *victi*, *timuerint* v. *dilexerint*) in two acts. Initially, while they are still involved in combat (*pugnantes*) the enemies fear (*timuerint*) Pompey's martial prowess (*virtus*); once vanquished (*victi*), they love (*dilexerint*) his leniency (*mansuetudinem*). Whether their initial fear or their subsequent love is stronger Cicero finds it difficult to say. The switch from present active participle (*pugnantes*) in the *utrum*-half to the perfect passive participle in the *an*-half presents the outcome of a war against Pompey as a foregone conclusion: all foes will be vanquished. As pointed out above, *virtus*, in the 'primary' sense of martial prowess/courage on the battlefield, and *mansuetudo* map out the full spectrum of Pompey's excellences, from the 'hard' to the 'soft'. The sense of closure thereby generated sets up the last sentence in the section on *virtus*:

Et quisquam dubitabit quin huic hoc tantum bellum permittendum sit, qui ad omnia nostrae memoriae bella conficienda divino quodam consilio natus esse videatur?: Cicero finishes with a rhetorical question (that requires a resounding 'no-one' as answer) and a concluding endorsement of Pompey that again asserts his special relationship with the divine sphere. Pompey, Cicero asserts, has been born for a purpose: to bring all wars to a successful conclusion. He uses the formulation *natus ad...* (with the preposition *ad* expressing purpose) to elevate certain individuals such as Pompey or Milo (who, according to Cicero, was born to rid the *res publica* of Clodius) into figures of destiny. They come into existence with a divine charter (cf. *divino quodam consilio*) to perform certain deeds for the wellbeing of the commonwealth.[46] This is particularly remarkable since Fate (with a capital F) is by and large a negative, four-letter word for Cicero: he usually doesn't hold with notions of historical destiny or necessity, only flirting with them occasionally (as here) to score rhetorical points.

Et quisquam dubitabit quin...: after negated expressions of doubt or hesitation (here the negation is built into the rhetorical question which demands 'no-one' as an answer), *quin* is a conjunction meaning 'that'. Such *quin*-clauses are in indirect speech and hence take the subjunctive (*permittendum* <u>*sit*</u>).

---

46 Begemann (2012) 249 labels this rhetorical ploy '*ad natus*-formula'.

43: RUMOUR AND RENOWN: POMPEY'S *AUCTORITAS*

Cicero here reaches the third of the four qualities that distinguish his perfect general: *auctoritas*. See the blueprint he gave his audience in § 28: *Ego enim sic existimo, in summo imperatore quattuor has res inesse oportere:* (i) *scientiam rei militaris,* (ii) *virtutem,* (iii) *auctoritatem,* (iv) *felicitatem.* After his lengthy treatment of *virtus* (§§ 29-42), Cicero devotes §§ 43-46 to his treatment of *auctoritas* before moving on to *felicitas* in §§ 47-48. Unlike *scientia militaris* and *virtus, auctoritas* is not an 'innate' quality. It captures the prestige and respect (and hence the 'commanding influence') that others accord an individual on the basis of his previous achievements – and the 'commanding influence' that he can therefore exercise. *auctoritas*, then, implies a socio-political context. It is a specifically Roman notion (and form of power). Yet unlike *potestas* or *imperium*, which are formalized modes of power linked to social roles (such as that of *pater familias*, 'father of a household', which comes with *patria potestas*) or public office (election to the consulship gives the individual consular *potestas* and the right to command an army, i.e. *imperium*), *auctoritas* is more diffuse, if no less potent: it enables those who have it to get things done without needing to flex their muscle, simply on the basis of the authoritative respect they command. In this and the following paragraph, Cicero argues that the *auctoritas* enjoyed by Pompey among friends and foes alike has no equal and illustrates its strategic value in warfare (and not least the ongoing war against Mithridates).

Et quoniam auctoritas quoque in bellis administrandis multum atque in imperio militari valet, certe nemini dubium est quin ea re idem ille imperator plurimum possit. The main clause is *certe nemini dubium est*; it is preceded by a causal subordinate clause introduced by *quoniam* (*quoniam ... valet*) and followed by a *quin*-clause. *dubium* governs the dative *nemini*: 'doubtful *to* nobody'.

multum: a so-called 'adverbial accusative': with certain adjectives such as *multus* or *plurimus* (for which see below) the neuter accusative singular serves as adverb; it goes with the verb of the *quoniam*-clause, i.e. *valet*.

quin ... possit: after negated expressions of doubt or hesitation (here the negation is *nemini* and the expression of doubt *dubium*), *quin* is a conjunction meaning 'that'. Such *quin*-clauses are in indirect speech and hence take the subjunctive (*possit*).

ea re: an ablative of respect that refers back to *auctoritas*: 'in this matter'.

idem ille imperator: the subject of the *quin*-clause.

plurimum possit: *plurimum*, the neuter accusative singular of *plurimus* (the superlative of *plus*) is another 'adverbial accusative': see above on *multum*. It goes with *possit*: note the alliteration. There is a nice step-up in intensity from <u>*multum*</u> *valet* to <u>*plurimum*</u> *possit*.

Vehementer autem pertinere ad bella administranda, quid hostes, quid socii de imperatoribus nostris existiment, quis ignorat, cum sciamus homines in tantis rebus, ut aut contemnant aut metuant, aut oderint aut ament, opinione non minus et fama quam aliqua ratione certa commoveri?: The main clause is the question *quis ignorat...? ignorat* governs an indirect statement with (the impersonal verb) *pertinere* as infinitive and the *quid*-clauses functioning as subject accusatives. *quis ignorat* is followed by a causal *cum*-clause (*cum ... commoveri*). It explains why Cicero considers this to be a rhetorical question. The verb of the *cum*-clause is *sciamus*, which governs an indirect statement with *homines* as subject accusative and *commoveri* as infinitive. *ut* introduces a result clause set up by *tantis*.

ad bella administranda: a gerundive governed by the preposition *ad*, which here expresses purpose.

quid hostes: supply *de imperatoribus nostris existiment* from what follows.

cum sciamus homines in tantis rebus, ut aut contemnant aut metuant, aut oderint aut ament, opinione non minus et fama quam aliqua ratione certa commoveri?: Cicero here states a generally agreed truth (cf. the first person plural verb *sciamus*) about human nature: *homines*, the generic term for 'human beings', elevates his discourse to the level of universalizing reflections about humanity, subsuming in the process the two categories he specified previously, i.e. *hostes* and *socii*. Notionally, the subject of *contemnant*, *metuant*, *oderint*, and *ament* is *homines*, but *contemnant* and *metuant* refer back to *hostes* (enemies despise a weak and are afraid of a strong, authoritative general), whereas *oderint* and *ament* pick up *socii* (allies hate a weak and love a strong, authoritative general). By associating *auctoritas* with *fama* and *opinio*, and contrasting these social phenomena with *ratio*, Cicero pinpoints the irrational element inherent in *auctoritas*. (See also the end of § 45, where Cicero affiliates *auctoritas* with *nomen* and *rumor*, all of which are, however influential they might be, less substantial than *virtus*, *imperium*, and *exercitus*.)

opinione non minus et fama quam aliqua ratione certa: *opinione, fama,* and *ratione* are all ablatives of means or instrument.

Quod igitur nomen umquam in orbe terrarum clarius fuit? *quod* is an interrogative adjective agreeing with *nomen* ('which name...'). The question it introduces is rhetorical. *clarius* is the comparative form of the adverb. Cicero leaves the comparison implicit: no name is more famous than that of Pompey.

cuius res gestae pares [sc. *fuerunt*]? The verb is elided but can easily be supplied from the previous clause. Again Cicero does not spell out the comparison: *nobody's* deeds are equal to those of Pompey.

de quo homine vos, id quod maxime facit auctoritatem, tanta et tam praeclara iudicia fecistis? *quo* is another interrogative adjective agreeing with *homine*. The parenthetical *id quod maxime <u>facit</u> auctoritatem* states a general principle (hence the present tense), which finds its historical application in the main clause (*vos tanta et tam praeclara iudicia <u>fecistis</u>*). For Cicero's identification of the *populus* as a source of special *auctoritas*, see the Introduction 2.4.

44: CASE STUDY I: THE SOCIO-ECONOMICS OF POMPEY'S *AUCTORITAS*

After the introductory paragraph on *auctoritas*, Cicero now offers the circumstances surrounding the passing of the *lex Gabinia* (the bill proposed by the tribune Aulus Gabinius in the previous year, which gave Pompey the extraordinary command against the pirates) as an illustration of Pompey's *auctoritas*. He proceeds in three steps:

> (i) *An vero … imperatorem depoposcit?*: a rhetorical question that invokes scenes from the legendary day on which the *lex Gabinia* was passed, asserts its universal fame (in the same idiom in which Cicero earlier described the ubiquitous presence of piracy in the Mediterranean), and recalls the tremendous popular support this piece of legislation enjoyed;
>
> (ii) *Itaque … exempla sumantur*: a moment of exhortative reflection, in which Cicero reiterates what this paragraph is about: the demonstration of *quantum auctoritas valet in bello* (the theory) with specific reference to Pompey (its application).
>
> (iii) *qui quo … efficere potuisset*: description of the economic consequences of Pompey's appointment.

Neither the syntax nor the phrasing in this paragraph is necessarily straightforward.

[Extra information:
Dio Cassius imagines Catulus, the old patrician war-horse, as making several pertinent points against the bill proposed by Gabinius: firstly, that the concentration of too much power in individuals' hands had led to the war between Sulla and the Marians; secondly, that power-sharing gave the Roman elite as a whole more experience; thirdly, that there were plenty of pro-magistrates around who could do the job instead of Pompey; and fourthly, that the office of dictator already existed to deal with crises. These arguments applied just as much to the *lex Manilia*, which gave Pompey yet more power and authority, but Cicero is eager to stress that the *lex Gabinia* was a miraculous success. Merely by mentioning the Gabinian law, therefore, Cicero implies that Catulus and Hortensius – the opponents of the present piece of legislation – are wrong now because they were wrong then. Pompey, after all, defeated the pirates in three months to popular acclaim.]

An vero ullam usquam esse oram tam desertam putatis, quo non illius diei fama pervaserit, cum universus populus Romanus referto foro completisque omnibus templis, ex quibus hic locus conspici potest, unum sibi ad commune omnium gentium bellum Cn. Pompeium imperatorem depoposcit?: Cicero again challenges his audience with a rhetorical question, introduced by *an*, that calls for a resounding 'no, we don't' as an answer. The main verb is *putatis*, which governs an indirect statement with *ullam ... oram* as subject accusative and *esse* as infinitive. *(tam) desertam* is the predicative complement. What follows is a *consecutive* relative clause, set up by *tam* (hence the subjunctive) and introduced by *quo* and a fairly intricate temporal *cum*-clause that works as follows:

- Subject: *universus populus Romanus*

- Two ablative absolutes linked by *-que: referto foro + completis omnibus templis*

- Relative clause: *ex quibus hic locus conspici potest*

- Accusatives: *unum* (agreeing in predicative position with) *Cn. Pompeium* (the accusative object, leading up to the predicative accusative) *imperatorem*

- A dative of advantage: *sibi*

- A prepositional phrase: *ad commune omnium gentium bellum*

- The verb: *depoposcit*

ullam usquam ... oram tam desertam: the adjective attribute *ullam* and the adverb *usquam* are pleonastic – *any* coast *anywhere*. The phrasing recalls §§ 31-32, where Cicero traced the entire Mediterranean world to illustrate the extent of the pirate problem (31: *Testes nunc vero iam omnes orae atque omnes exterae gentes ac nationes, denique maria omnia cum universa, tum in singulis oris omnes sinus at portus....*; 32: *quam multas existimatis insulas esse desertas?*).

quo: the relative pronoun in the ablative, which introduces the consecutive relative clause, stands for *ut* (= the normal conjunction to introduce result clauses) + the ablative of *is*, i.e. *eo*, used adverbially ('to that place', 'thither'): *ut eo > quo*.

illius diei fama: Cicero refers to the widespread fame of the day on which the Roman people passed the *lex Gabinia* that gave control of the war against the pirates to Pompey, together with extraordinary powers.

referto foro completisque omnibus templis: the *-que* after *completis* links two circumstantial ablative absolutes: *referto foro* and *completis omnibus templis*. In each case the participle (*referto, completis*) precedes the corresponding noun (*foro, templis*), perhaps in an enactment of the crowd flowing quickly into every available space to witness and celebrate the appointment of Pompey to a war of great concern to everybody, and especially the people of Rome, who relied on (cheap) corn imported from various places across the Mediterranean.

referto foro completisque omnibus templis ... hic locus: *hic locus* refers to the speaker's platform, or Rostra, from which Cicero is addressing the people. In the very first sentence of the speech he calls it *hic ... locus ad agendum* [sc. *cum populo*] *amplissimus* ('this place affording the amplest scope of action'). The platform was located on the forum, the big open space in the centre of the city, flanked by the Capitoline and Palatine Hills. There were several temples located on these two hills, which would have afforded a good view of the proceedings in the forum.

ad commune omnium gentium bellum: the preposition *ad* here expresses purpose ('for a war...'). *commune*, which stands in predicative position to *bellum* ('a war shared...' and NOT 'a shared war'), here governs the possessive genitive *omnium gentium* (its construction with dative is more frequent).

depoposcit: the verb governs two accusatives: the direct object *unum ... Cn. Pompeium* and the predicative accusative *imperatorem*, best coordinated with 'as' in English: 'the people demanded Gnaeus Pompeius alone *as* general' (and NOT 'the people demanded the general Gnaeus Pompeius'). It picks up a passage from the beginning of the speech where Cicero imagines Rome's allies in the region not daring to demand (*deposcere*) a specific general from the Roman people for the war against Mithridates (though implicitly hoping that Pompey would end up in charge). See § 12: *civitates autem omnes cuncta Asia atque Graecia vestrum auxilium exspectare propter periculi magnitudinem coguntur; imperatorem a vobis certum deposcere, cum praesertim vos alium miseritis, neque audent, neque se id facere sine summo periculo posse arbitrantur* ('it is to you that every state in Greece and Asia is, by the magnitude of its peril, forced to look for help: to demand from you one particular general (especially as you have sent someone else) they neither dare nor do they think that they could do so without extreme danger').

Itaque, ut plura non dicam neque aliorum exemplis confirmem, quantum auctoritas valeat in bello: the main verb – *sumantur* – is in the third person plural present subjunctive passive, with *exempla* as subject. The subjunctive is iussive: '*let there be* taken examples...'. *ut* introduces a result clause ('so that...'), not a purpose clause ('in order to...'), as the negations *non* and *neque* make clear. (Negated purpose clauses are introduced by *ne*.) *quantum* introduces an indirect question.

ab eodem Cn. Pompeio omnium rerum egregiarum exempla sumantur: a very compressed way of saying that Cicero intends to take his examples *from the public career of* Pompey.

qui quo die a vobis maritimo bello praepositus est imperator, tanta repente vilitas annonae ex summa inopia et caritate rei frumentariae consecuta est unius hominis spe ac nomine, quantum vix in summa ubertate agrorum diuturna pax efficere potuisset: another intricate sentence, best broken down into its constituent bits:

- The opening relative clause: *qui quo ... imperator*
- The main clause: *tanta ... spe ac nomine*
- The *quantum*-clause (set up by *tanta*): *quantum vix ... efficere potuisset*

Cicero adduces an interesting phenomenon that interlinks political decision-making with economic behaviour as evidence of Pompey's prestige. As soon as he was appointed general, the price of corn in Rome seems to have plummeted. Why? Because everyone just knew that Pompey would secure the supply routes and thereby alter the logic of supply and demand very much in favour of the former. It also suggests that the grain-merchants were using the pirates to raise their price for corn sky-high – much higher than necessary if the mere appointment of Pompey forced them to reduce their prices to the kind of bargain levels common in times of peace and agricultural fertility. There could thus be a subtle dig at those who profiteer from the misfortunes of others. But maybe this is a little too cynical. Perhaps grain prices would have fallen no matter who was appointed to the command, because of an expectation of an immediate glut based on the idea that someone was going to do something about the pirates (perhaps not necessarily that this was going to be a long-term solution, but at least that supply routes would be cleared in the short-term with negative results for anyone who had been keeping back grain against future shortages). Cicero, of course, makes it all about Pompey, but it could simply be a consequence of there being a command at all. One has to be sympathetic towards those merchants: transporting goods by sea is risky enough without adding pirates into the bargain.

qui quo die a vobis maritimo bello praepositus est imperator: the double relative *qui quo* at the start of the sentence is difficult. To make sense of the construction think of *qui* as a connecting relative (= *et is*), with *is* belonging to the relative clause introduced by *quo*, and *quo* as a relative pronoun with its antecedent (*eo die*) sucked into the relative clause. In other words, translate as if the Latin read: *et eo die, quo is a vobis maritimo bello praepositus est imperator...* ('And on the day [in which] this man was put in charge by you of the war against the pirates as general...').

tanta repente vilitas annonae ex summa inopia et caritate rei frumentariae consecuta est unius hominis spe ac nomine: the subject of the main clause is *tanta ... vilitas*, the verb *consecuta est*. The two genitives *annonae* (dependent on *vilitas*) and *rei frumentariae* (dependent on *ex summa inopia et caritate*) are virtually synonymous: both refer to the corn stored and sold in Rome.

unius hominis spe ac nomine: *spe* and *nomine* are causal ablatives. The genitive *unius hominis* goes with both, but is a different one in each case: *unius hominis spe* refers to 'the expectations *others* have towards this one man' (and not Pompey's own expectations), so it is an objective genitive, whereas *unius hominis nomine* refers to the name Pompey himself has, so it is a possessive genitive.

quantum vix in summa ubertate agrorum diuturna pax efficere potuisset: *quantum* picks up *tanta*: *such* a low price ... followed *as* prolonged peace ... could hardly have achieved. The pluperfect subjunctive *potuisset* indicates an unreal condition in the past: '*even if there had been* a prolonged period of peace with rich yield of produce, the price of corn would hardly have dropped lower than it did after the appointment of Pompey.'

45: CASE STUDY II: POMPEY'S *AUCTORITAS* AND PSYCHO-LOGICAL WARFARE

As his second case study to illustrate Pompey's *auctoritas*, Cicero chooses the impact of his presence in Asia after Mithridates' crushing defeat of the Roman forces under the command of C. Triarius at the battle of Zela in 67 BC. He invokes the possibility of a 'worst-case scenario': Rome's loss of the province of Asia. This, Cicero submits, would have been the outcome of the defeat had it not so happened by divine dispensation that Pompey was in the region at the time, as a result of his command against the pirates. The *auctoritas* accorded to him even by Rome's bitter foes Mithridates and Tigranes (the king of Armenia and Mithridates' son-in-law) sufficed to prevent them from exploiting their victory – or so Cicero argues. Without doing anything Pompey thus managed to check the enemy in an act of 'psychological warfare': his *auctoritas* in the eyes of the royal beholders. This scenario forms the basis for Cicero's conclusion: if Pompey's *auctoritas* has such a positive impact on Roman interests in the region, an opportunity to bring his *virtus* to bear on the war against Mithridates would surely yield the desired result.

Iam accepta in Ponto calamitate ex eo proelio, de quo vos paulo ante invitus admonui, cum socii pertimuissent, hostium opes animique crevissent, satis firmum praesidium provincia non haberet, amisissetis Asiam, Quirites, nisi ad ipsum discrimen eius temporis divinitus Cn. Pompeium ad eas regiones fortuna populi Romani attulisset. This is a complex sentence, best taken piece by piece.

> (i) We begin with an ablative absolute: the participle is *accepta* and the noun is *calamitate*. But unlike 'standard' ablative absolutes, this one is not self-contained. *ex eo proelio* belongs to the ablative absolute, just as much as the relative clause *de quo vos paulo ante invitus admonui* (the antecedent of *quo* is *proelio*) and a quick-fire sequence of three asyndetic *cum*-clauses: (a) *cum socii pertimuissent*, (b) [*cum*] *hostium opes animique crevissent*, (c) [*cum*] *satis firmum praesidium provincia non haberet*.
> (ii) This sets up the main clause: *amisissetis Asiam*...
> (iii) *amisissetis Asiam* forms the apodosis of a conditional sequence and is followed by the protasis, the dependent clause that specifies the condition, here introduced by *nisi*, which takes us to the end of the sentence (*attulisset*).

Overall, this is a highly dramatic syntax – the sentence is designed to generate a sense of crisis, evoke, if counterfactually, an ultimate disaster (the loss of Asia), before resolving the crisis with reference to our hero Pompey. By having the initial ablative absolute used to present the Roman defeat in battle 'overflow' into further constructions, Cicero gives an impression of the disastrous repercussions of the military disaster, an effect further enhanced by the use of asyndeton in the sequence of *cum*-clauses (and the elision of the conjunction after the first), which lead up to the centre of the sentence: the main clause *amisissetis Asiam* and a direct address to the audience (*Quirites*). By inverting the usual order of the conditional sequence (protasis followed by apodosis), Cicero can use the negated protasis to specify why the loss of Asia ultimately did not happen: according to him, it was the arrival of Pompey in the nick of time that turned an imminent into an averted catastrophe. Great stuff!

ex eo proelio: the reference is to the battle between the forces of Mithridates and a part of the Roman army that Lucullus had left under the command of C. Triarius near the city of Zela in 67 BC (the same year in which Pompey held the command against the pirates). The Romans were soundly defeated.

paulo ante: *ante* is an adverb, preceded by an ablative of the measure of difference: a little bit (*paulo*) earlier (*ante*). Cicero already touched upon the defeat in § 25.

invitus: even though it happens to serve his rhetorical agenda, Cicero is keen to stress, for obvious reasons, that he mentions this military disaster only with the greatest reluctance.

nisi ad ipsum discrimen eius temporis divinitus Cn. Pompeium ad eas regiones fortuna populi Romani attulisset: Cicero ascribes Pompey's presence in the region to divine agency. *fortuna* here should probably be capitalized: see our discussion of the phrase *fortuna rei publicae* in § 28. Together with the adverb *divinitus*, which means something akin to 'by divine providence or influence', the phrase *Fortuna populi Romani* implies that the appointment of Pompey to his command against the pirates happened according to a supernatural plan, chartered by Rome's patron deity.

ad ipsum discrimen eius temporis: a somewhat pleonastic expression of time to enhance the significance of the crisis: *ipsum discrimen* refers to the actual moment of crisis, *eius temporis* to the larger period of time within which it occurred.

Huius adventus et Mithridatem insolita inflatum victoria continuit et Tigranem magnis copiis minitantem Asiae retardavit.: The subject of the sentence is *adventus* – one of the various 'arrivals' by Pompey (who is of course meant with the demonstrative pronoun *huius*) that Cicero recalls at different moments in the speech: see also §§ 13 and 30. It goes with both verbs (*continuit, retardavit*), each with its own accusative object (*Mithridatem, Tigranem*). Both enemies of Rome receive further specification by means of a participle construction. Cicero portrays Mithridates as 'puffed up' (*inflatum*) because of his rare victory (*insolita ... victoria* is an ablative of cause), whereas Tigranes is threatening Asia with his troops: *minitor*, a deponent verb, takes the dative of the person or object under threat, here the Roman province of Asia (*Asiae*). *magnis copiis* is an instrumental ablative.

The sentence here reiterates an observation already made in § 13: *cuius adventu ipso atque nomine, tametsi ille ad maritimum bellum venerit, tamen impetus hostium repressos esse intellegunt* [sc. Rome's friends and allies in the region] *ac retardatos* ('the fact of his arrival, his reputation alone, although it is for a naval war that he has come, they feel to have checked and restrained the onslaughts of their foes').

Et quisquam dubitabit, quid virtute perfecturus sit, qui tantum auctoritate perfecerit? aut quam facile imperio atque exercitu socios et vectigalia conservaturus sit, qui ipso nomine ac rumore defenderit?: The main clause is *et quisquam dubitabit*, which governs two indirect questions each leading up to a relative clause of characteristic.

Main Clause	Indirect questions	Relative clauses of characteristic
Et quisquam dubitabit	(i) *quid virtute perfecturus sit* [aut] (ii) *quam facile imperio atque exercitu socios et vectigalia conservaturus sit*	(i) *qui tantum auctoritate perfecerit* (ii) *qui ipso nomine ac rumore defenderit*

The subject of the two verbs in the indirect question (*perfecturus sit, conservaturus sit*) and the relative clauses of characteristic (*perfecerit, defenderit*) is Pompey.

perfecturus sit ... conservaturus sit: indirect questions in Latin take the subjunctive, but here the actions to which Cicero is referring lie in the future – and Latin does not have a straightforward future subjunctive. To indicate future intent, he therefore uses the so-called 'future active periphrastic subjunctive', which consists of the future active participle form (*perfecturus, conservaturus*; note that Latin doesn't have a future passive participle) and the present subjunctive of *sum* (*sit*). (It's called 'periphrastic' because *separate* words, rather than inflection, are being used to express the grammatical form.) The problem does not arise in the relative clauses of characteristic: here Cicero is referring to past deeds and can use the perfect subjunctive (*perfecerit, defenderit*).

virtute ... auctoritate ... imperio atque exercitu ... nomine ac rumore: ablatives of means or instrument.

46: *AUCTORITAS* SUPREME

Cicero now sums up his discussion of *auctoritas*, using some of the same pieces of evidence he mustered to illustrate Pompey's *virtus*. The geographical sweep in the first sentence (*quod ex locis tam longinquis tamque diversis tam brevi tempore omnes huic se uni dediderunt*) recalls similar formulations in § 31 (*Hoc tantum bellum, tam turpe, tam vetus, tam late divisum atque dispersum, quis umquam arbitraretur aut ab omnibus imperatoribus uno anno aut omnibus annis ab uno imperatore confici posse?*) and § 35 (*Ita tantum bellum, tam diuturnum, tam longe lateque dispersum, quo bello omnes gentes ac nationes premebantur, Cn. Pompeius extrema hieme apparavit, ineunte vere suscepit, media aestate confecit*) among others. Also in § 35, Cicero had already brought the Cretan embassy to Pompey into play (*idem Cretensibus, cum ad eum usque in Pamphyliam legatos deprecatoresque misissent, spem deditionis non ademit, obsidesque imperavit*), which he revisits here in some more detail. The *illos reges* Cicero mentions at the end of the paragraph hark back to his discussion of Mithridates and Tigranes in § 45. And his concluding reference to the amplification of Pompey's *auctoritas* through his own deeds and *magnis vestris iudiciis* reiterates the socio-political economy that Cicero outlined at the beginning of the section (§ 43: *de quo homine vos, – id quod maxime facit auctoritatem, – tanta et tam praeclara iudicia fecistis?*).

Age vero illa res quantam declarat eiusdem hominis apud hostes populi Romani auctoritatem, quod ex locis tam longinquis tamque diversis tam brevi tempore omnes huic se uni dediderunt: the subject of the sentence is the vague *illa res* ('that matter'); Cicero explicates what 'that matter' is in the *quod*-clause ('namely that...'). The main verb is *declarat*, which takes *quantam ... auctoritatem* as accusative object: the hyperbaton is massive! The genitive *eiusdem hominis* (of course referring to Pompey) depends on *auctoritatem*.

age vero: the opening *age vero* is a transitional phrase, with *age*, the second person singular imperative active of *ago*, not impacting on the syntax of the sentence. Cicero already used this transition in § 40 (see above).

ex locis *tam* longinquis *tam*que diversis *tam* brevi tempore: Cicero here merges a prepositional phrase (*ex ... diversis*) to do with geography and an ablative of time (*tam brevi tempore*) into a tricolon of sorts by means of the three adjectives (agreeing with two nouns), which are further emphasized by the triple anaphora of *tam*. The -*que* after the second *tam* links *longinquis* and *diversis*, the two attributes of *locis*. The phrasing asserts a control over space and time perfectly suited to Rome's imperial needs.

omnes *huic* se *uni* dediderunt: *omnes* is the subject, the reflexive pronoun *se* the accusative object of *dediderunt*. Interspersed between is the dative *huic ... uni*: 'to him alone'.

quod a communi Cretensium legati, cum in eorum insula noster imperator exercitusque esset, ad Cn. Pompeium in ultimas prope terras venerunt eique se omnes Cretensium civitates dedere velle dixerunt!: This *quod*-clause too stands in apposition to *illa res* at the beginning of the paragraph. The subject is *legati*, the verbs are *venerunt* and *dixerunt*, linked by the -*que* after *ei*. Cicero here refers to the fact that the Cretans preferred to send legates after Pompey who was in Pamphylia at the time instead of turning to the Roman general in command of the army on their island (*noster imperator* is Quintus Metellus). He makes it out that the reason was Pompey's *auctoritas*. The truth of the matter is more complex: Pompey offered more favourable terms of peace, in part because he did not fancy prolonged fighting on the island. See further § 35.

a communi Cretensium: *communi* is the ablative singular of the neuter noun *commune*.

cum in eorum insula noster imperator exercitusque esset: the *cum* has concessive force: 'even though'.

eique se omnes Cretensium civitates dedere velle dixerunt: the subject continues to be *legati*, the verb is *dixerunt*. It introduces an indirect statement with *omnes ... civitates* as subject accusative and *velle* as infinitive. *dedere* is a supplementary infinitive with *velle*, which takes the reflexive pronoun *se* as accusative object and *ei* (i.e. Pompey) as dative object: they want to hand over themselves (*se*) to him (*ei*).

Quid? idem iste Mithridates nonne ad eundem Cn. Pompeium legatum usque in Hispaniam misit?: In 75 BC, Pompey was in Spain fighting against Sertorius (see above § 28). Mithridates reached out to Sertorius as a potential ally in his fight against Rome. See Plutarch, *Life of Sertorius* 23:

> His negotiations with king Mithridates further argue the greatness of his mind. For when Mithridates, recovering himself from his overthrow by Sulla, like a strong wrestler that gets up to try another fall, was again endeavouring to reestablish his power in Asia, at this time the great fame of Sertorius was celebrated in all places and when the merchants who came out of the western parts of Europe, bringing these, as it were, among their other foreign wares, had filled the kingdom of Pontus with their stories of his exploits in war, Mithridates was extremely desirous to send an embassy to him, being also highly encouraged to it by the boastings of his flattering courtiers, who, comparing Mithridates to Pyrrhus, and Sertorius to Hannibal, professed that the Romans would never be able to make any considerable resistance against such great forces, and such admirable commanders, when they should be set upon on both sides at once, on one by the most warlike general, and on the other by the most powerful prince in existence. Accordingly, Mithridates sends ambassadors into Spain to Sertorius with letters and instructions, and commission to promise ships and money towards the charge of the war, if Sertorius would confirm his pretensions upon Asia, and authorize him to possess all that he had surrendered to the Romans in his treaty with Sulla. Sertorius summoned a full council which he called a senate, where, when others joyfully approved of the conditions, and were desirous immediately to accept his offer, seeing that he desired nothing of them but a name, and an empty title to places not in their power to dispose of in recompense of which they should be supplied with what they then stood most in need of Sertorius would by no means agree to it; declaring that he was willing that king Mithridates should exercise all royal power and authority over Bithynia and Cappadocia, countries accustomed to a monarchical government, and not belonging to Rome, but he could never consent that he should seize or detain a province, which, by the justest right and title, was possessed by the Romans, which Mithridates had formerly taken away from them, and had afterwards lost in open war to Fimbria, and quitted upon a treaty of peace with Sulla. For he looked upon it as his duty to enlarge the Roman possessions by his conquering arms, and not to increase his own power by the diminution of the Roman territories.

idem iste Mithridates: the very Mithridates that the *lex Manilia* is about.

nonne: the interrogative particle introduces a question expecting an answer in the affirmative.

eum quem Pompeius legatum semper iudicavit, ii quibus erat molestum ad eum potissimum esse missum, speculatorem quam legatum iudicari

maluerunt: the subject is *ii*, the verb *maluerunt*; it introduces an indirect statement with *eum* as subject accusative and *iudicari* as infinitive; *speculatorem quam legatum* modify *eum* in predicative position: '... that he is considered a spy rather than an ambassador'. The sentence confirms that *someone* from Mithridates made it to Pompey in Spain, but also that there was considerable controversy about the status of this person. Pompey claimed that the individual in question was an official ambassador tasked specifically with seeking out Pompey. Others, who found this a self-aggrandizing claim, argued that the person had no official diplomatic brief whatsoever and was rather a spy (*speculatorem*). But the whole sentence is odd and does not fit particularly well into Cicero's discourse at this point: it reminds everyone that within the ruling elite Pompey's achievements and self-promotion were highly controversial, whatever their popularity among the populace. Why should Cicero draw attention to this fact here? One could therefore consider bracketing the sentence as a marginal gloss on *legatum* in the previous sentence that then got included in the body of the text.

ii quibus erat molestum ad eum potissimum esse missum: *ii* is the antecedent of the relative pronoun *quibus* (in the dative following *molestum*: 'to whom it was irksome...'). It is unclear to whom Cicero is referring (as in the previous sentence he refrains from naming Pompey's rivals), but it is not unreasonable to suppose that the consul in charge of operations in Spain, Q. Metellus Pius, was one of them. *erat molestum* governs an indirect statement with the subject accusative (*eum* = the person sent by Mithridates) suppressed and *esse missum* as (perfect passive) infinitive.

ad eum: sc. Pompey.

potissimum: *potissimum* is an adverb (even though it may look as if it agrees with *ad eum*) and underscores the notion that Mithridates' man sought out Pompey, who only had the rank of quaestor at the time, *above all others* – including much higher-ranking officers, such as Quintus Metellus Pius, the consul of 80 BC, and in overall charge of the war against Sertorius until Pompey appeared on the scene.

Potestis igitur iam constituere, Quirites, hanc auctoritatem, multis postea rebus gestis magnisque vestris iudiciis amplificatam, quantum apud illos reges, quantum apud exteras nationes valituram esse existimetis.:

constituere sets up two indirect questions both introduced by *quantum* in asyndetic sequence. The verb of both *quantum*-clauses is *existimetis*, which governs an indirect statement with *hanc auctoritatem* as subject accusative and *valituram esse* as infinitive. For emphasis, Cicero pulls *hanc auctoritatem* out of the clauses into which it belongs and places it up front, right after the address to the citizens, an effect further enhanced by the participle phrase *multis postea rebus gestis magnisque vestris iudiciis amplificatam*. To appreciate the emphasis, economy, and elegance achieved by Cicero's word order, it may help to write out the sentence in the painful prolixity that would result if one were to restore normal word order and avoid all ellipses:

> *potestis igitur iam constituere, Quirites,*
>> *quantum hanc auctoritatem, multis postea rebus gestis magnisque vestris iudiciis amplificatam, apud illos reges valituram esse existimetis,*
>> *quantum hanc auctoritatem [multis postea rebus gestis magnisque vestris iudiciis amplificatam] apud exteras nationes valituram esse existimetis.*

The placement of *hanc auctoritatem* and the two indirect questions introduced by *quantum* recall the hyperbaton *quantam ... auctoritatem* at the beginning of the paragraph.

multis postea rebus gestis magnisque vestris iudiciis amplificatam: Cicero here specifies Pompey's deeds (*res gestae*) and the perceptive decisions and evaluations about him made by the Roman people (*vestra iudicia*), which resulted in the election of Pompey to *honores* ('public offices'), as the two sources that have jointly enhanced Pompey's *auctoritas*. The two *iudicia* that stand out are Pompey's election to the consulship of 70 BC and his appointment to fight the pirates under the *lex Gabinia* in 68 BC. The sentence looks back to § 43: see our commentary there. It neatly encapsulates Cicero's attempt to weld together the past deeds of an individual and their public recognition by means of constitutional procedures (which are vested in the people) in his notion of *auctoritas*, thereby uniting Pompey and the *populus*.

apud illos reges: Cicero refers back to Mithridates and Tigranes, whom he mentioned by name in § 45.

valituram esse: *valituram* is the future active participle in the feminine accusative singular (agreeing with *auctoritatem*) of *valeo*.

47: *FELICITAS*, OR HOW NOT TO 'SULL(A)Y' POMPEY[47]

Cicero has reached the last of the four qualities he considers essential attributes of the perfect general: after *scientia rei militaris*, *virtus*, and *auctoritas*, he turns his attention to *felicitas*, which signifies 'divinely sponsored success'. As we already had occasion to note in our commentary on § 41, an outstanding individual's special relationship with the gods (or, indeed, his semi-divine status) was difficult to reconcile with the principle of oligarchic equality, which underwrote the senatorial tradition of republican government. After Sulla's dictatorship, no-one in Rome needed a reminder of this fact: in his autobiography, the autocrat professed to confer with supernatural beings rather than his *consilium* before making important decisions, considered himself to be in a special relationship with Aphrodite/Venus, and added the attribute *'felix'* to his name, thereby claiming *felicitas* ('divine support') as a permanent, personal possession.[48] This act of nomenclature went down in the annals of Rome as a revolting outrage. Pliny the Elder (AD 23-79), writing more than a century after the fact, still remonstrates as follows when commenting on it (*Natural History* 7.137):

> unus hominum ad hoc aevi Felicis sibi cognomen adseruit L. Sulla, civili nempe sanguine ac patriae oppugnatione adoptatus. et quibus felicitates inductus argumentis? quod proscribere tot milia civium ac trucidare potuisset? o prava interpretatio et futuro tempore infelix!

> [The only human being who has so far added 'Felix' to his name was L. Sulla, who, sure enough, secured it through civil bloodshed and an attack on his country. Indeed, what evidence for his luck led him on? That he had been able to put so many thousands of citizens on hit lists and have them slaughtered? A disgraceful justification, with evil consequences for the future!]

It was precisely the fear that Pompey would turn into another Sulla (who, after all, had established his dictatorship upon his return from a war against Mithridates) that fuelled opposition to the *lex Manilia* and the appointment of Pompey among aristocratic circles. At the same time, divine support was an absolutely crucial element in the panegyric promotion of a military commander. In the early portion of his speech, Cicero himself had made this point, when he praised Lucullus for his

---

47 The following is adjusted from Gildenhard (2011) 268-69.
48 Steel (2001) 135.

virtus, but lamented the absence of *fortuna* from his military operations. One of the most fascinating aspects of §§ 47-48 is accordingly how Cicero tries to square the circle of claiming extraordinary *felicitas* for Pompey while avoiding the impression that Pompey is an *alter Sulla* in the making. A key ploy, at least initially, is his differentiation of *felicitas* into a traditional variant and its permutation (indeed perversion) by Sulla. The differences may be tabulated as follows:

	Traditional *felicitas*	**Sullan** *felicitas*
Verbal acknowledgement	Gingerly, by others	Boastful self-ascription
Status	Precarious quality	Secure possession
Duration	Temporary (hostage to fortune)	Permanent (fortune taken hostage) (*perpetuum*)
Examples from history	Maximus, Marcellus, Scipio, Marius and others	Sulla (unmentioned, but clearly implied)

In § 47 Cicero speaks out strongly in favour of the traditional conception, within general reflections on the discursive protocols to be observed when *felicitas* becomes the topic of public speech. Given that *felicitas* belongs properly to the supernatural domain (it is a gift from the gods), human beings, he argues, should observe the same reverent respect owed to divine matters in other contexts. In the light of these considerations, Cicero brands any attempt on the part of a human being to claim *felicitas* for himself as an intolerable act of *hubris*, liable to provoke the anger of the gods. The target of his criticism is easy to idenify: Sulla. The dictator did what Cicero claims must not be done, i.e. proclaim himself *felix* and to consider *felicitas* a personal and permanent possession. Remaining conspicuously unnamed in Cicero's list of Roman statesmen who were blessed with divine support, Sulla nevertheless looms large in these paragraphs, an *exemplum malum* best condemned to oblivion, a spectre called up only to be exorcised. After thus sketching out the range of possibilities, from the positive *exempla* of generals that were blessed with special fortune according to some divine plan (*divinitus*) to the unidentified *exemplum malum* Sulla, Cicero proceeds to suggest that Pompey is a special case that does not fit conventional categories. He does not share in Sulla's *hubris* of making *felicitas* an aspect of his self-promotion; but his luck significantly outclasses that enjoyed by any other Roman general. Indeed, in § 48 it emerges as unprecedented and off the scale.

Reliquum est ut de felicitate, quam praestare de se ipso nemo potest, meminisse et commemorare de altero possumus, sicut aequum est homines de potestate deorum [sc. dicere], **timide et pauca dicamus.**: The main clause *reliquum est* signals the transition from the treatment of *auctoritas* to the last quality to be covered, *felicitas*. The *ut*-clause that follows is consecutive: it explicates what remains to be discussed. Within the *ut*-clause, Cicero has added a relative clause that falls into two antithetical halves juxtaposed asyndetically: (i) *quam ... potest*; (ii) *[quam] meminisse ... possumus*. The antecedent of *quam* is *felicitate*. A further subordinate clause introduced by *sicut* glosses the two adverbs that go with the verb of the *ut*-clause (*dicamus*), i.e. *timide et pauca*: 'we speak about divinely sponsored luck in the same way as it is fit that human beings speak about the power of the gods, namely apprehensively (*timide*) and briefly (*pauca*).' Here is the sentence set out schematically:

Main clause: *Reliquum est*
   Ut-clause: *ut de felicitate,*
      Relative-clause: *quam praestare de se ipso nemo potest,*
                    [quam] meminisse et commemorare de altero possumus,
     Sicut-clause: *sicut aequum est homines de potestate deorum [sc. dicere],*
   Ut-clause (cont.): *timide et pauca dicamus.*

The intricate syntax and the adversative asyndeton in the relative clause reflect the fact that praising someone for his *felicitas* is a potential minefield in late-republican Rome.

sicut aequum est homines de potestate deorum [sc. *dicere*]: *aequum est* introduces a indirect statement with *homines* as subject accusative; the infinitive needs to be supplied from *dicamus*.

Ego enim sic existimo, Maximo, Marcello, Scipioni, Mario, et ceteris magnis imperatoribus non solum propter virtutem, sed etiam propter fortunam saepius imperia mandata atque exercitus esse commissos: the main verb is *existimo*, which governs an indirect statement, with *imperia* and *exercitus* as subject accusatives and *mandata* (sc. *esse*) and *esse commissos* as infinitives. *Maximo, Marcello, Scipioni, Mario, et ceteris magnis imperatoribus* are dative objects with both infinitives.

Maximo, Marcello, Scipioni, Mario: Cicero here invokes a pantheon of Roman heroes, with high degree of 'name recognition' (not least since Cicero proceeds in chronological order), which enables him to keep the nomenclature short and to the point:

Name as mentioned by Cicero	Full name	Dates and offices	Best known for
Maximo	Quintus Fabius Maximus Cunctator	c.280-203 BC consul 233, 228, 215, 214, 209 dictator 221, 217	Managed to wear down Hannibal in Italy during the Second Punic War by consistently avoiding battle (hence *cunctator* = 'the delayer')
Marcello	Marcus Claudius Marcellus	268-208 BC consul 222, 215, 214, 210, 208	222: killed the Gallic king Viridomarus in hand-to-hand combat during the battle of Clastidium, winning the so-called *spolia opima* 212: sacked Syracuse during the Second Punic War
Scipioni	Publius Scipio Aemilianus Minor ('the Younger')	185-129 BC consul 146, 134	146: The destruction of Carthage in the Third Punic War
Mario	Gaius Marius	157-86 BC consul 107, 104, 103, 102, 101, 100, 86	Defeat of the Germanic tribes of the Cimbri and Teutones who threatened to invade Italy

Cicero's inclusion of these generals adds weight of evidence to his point about good fortune as well as subtly ranking Pompey alongside (or even above) them. The inverse is also true, for one name is conspicuously absent from this list: Sulla. He was the general who hitherto had made most of *felicitas* in his self-promotion, but in doing so overstepped certain boundaries that Pompey, as Cicero is keen to stress, painstakingly observes.

saepius: the comparative form of the adverb *saepe*; the object of comparison isn't mentioned explicitly, hence it is best translated with 'rather frequently', and *not* 'more often'.

Fuit enim profecto quibusdam summis viris quaedam ad amplitudinem et ad gloriam et ad res magnas bene gerendas divinitus adiuncta fortuna: the absence of Sulla from Cicero's list of *summi viri* becomes even more conspicuous, given that Sulla adopted the epithet *Felix*, thereby claiming permanent affinity with divinely sponsored success. This, however, took matters a step too far. What Cicero is willing to concede is the existence of some providential force (cf. *divinitus*) that attached *fortuna* (here used synonymously with *felicitas*) to these outstanding individuals – which is something quite different from these outstanding individuals claiming to have a special purchase on *fortuna*.

ad **amplitudinem** <u>et</u> *ad* **gloriam** <u>et</u> *ad* **res magnas bene gerendas**: the triple *ad* here expresses purpose. Cicero uses a tricolon crescens, anaphora, and polysyndeton, swelling his rhetoric in line with his theme.

De huius autem hominis felicitate, de quo nunc agimus, hac utar moderatione dicendi, non ut in illius potestate fortunam positam esse dicam, sed ut praeterita meminisse, reliqua sperare videamur, ne aut invisa dis immortalibus oratio nostra aut ingrata esse videatur.: After stressing how carefully one has to tread when it comes to *felicitas*, Cicero here specifies how he will moderate his discourse so that it meets his own protocols of restraint. The idiom recalls the beginning of the paragraph. *non ut in illius potestate fortunam positam esse dicam* harks back to *(felicitate) quam praestare de se ipso nemo potest* and *sicut aequum est homines de potestate deorum (dicere)*; and *sed ut praeterita meminisse, reliqua sperare videamur* reworks *meminisse et commemorare de altero possumus*. Put differently, Cicero indeed does not claim *felicitas* for himself, and even when he talks about the *felicitas* of someone else, i.e. Pompey, he does not declare it his permanent, personal possession – rather, he observes that Pompey had *felicitas* in the past (*praeteritia meminisse*) and *hopes* that he will have further *felicitas* in the future (*reliqua sperare*). This kind of careful calibration, he suggests, will prevent his oration from drawing the ire of the gods. (At the same time, one may wonder about the force of the *praeteritio*. After all, his moderation consists in the fact of not *saying* that Pompey holds fortune hostage: *hac utar moderatione dicendi, non ut in illius potestate fortunam positam esse dicam*. The statement could imply, however, that Pompey's power over fortune is a fact – only Cicero refrains from spelling this out. Something similar could be said about his use of *videor*. The focus on what he *appears* to be doing (with two uses of *videor*) suggests that what he is *actually* doing is something quite different.

hac utar moderatione dicendi: *uti* (like *frui, fungi, vesci,* and *potiri*) belongs to a number of deponent verbs (best memorized as a group) that take an *ablative* object (here *hac ... moderatione*). *utar* is first person singular future indicative (though in form it could also be present subjunctive).

non ut in illius potestate fortunam positam esse dicam, sed ut praeterita meminisse, reliqua sperare videamur: a bipartite consecutive *ut*-clause (hence the subjunctives *dicam* and *videamur*), with the negation *non* pulled up front in structural parallel to *sed*, to bring out the antithesis. *dicam* introduces an indirect statement with *fortunam* as subject accusative and *positam esse* as infinitive.

praeterita meminisse, reliqua sperare: *praeterita* and *reliqua*, the accusative objects of, respectively, *meminisse* and *sperare*, are adjectives in the neuter plural used here in lieu of nouns: 'things that have passed' (*praeterita*); 'things that are left, i.e. will come to pass' (*reliqua*).

48: THE DARLING OF THE GODS[49]

Cicero continues using *praeteritio* to deal with Pompey's apparent power over fortune, with even nature doing his bidding. His use of the verb *obsecundare* (with *venti* and *tempestates* as subjects) in particular is striking and quite unparalleled: it personifies forces of nature and endows them with a mind of their own that Pompey is somehow able to bend to his will. This remarkable hyperbole assimilates him to a divine being capable of controlling the physical environment – though in the next sentence (*hoc brevissime dicam...*) Cicero stresses, however obliquely, that the gods remain the ultimate source of Pompey's luck: he is the recipient of such lavish divine favours (*quot et quantas di immortales ad Cn. Pompeium detulerunt*) that it would be an act of *hubris* for others to even dream about them. This sets up the concluding thought: Cicero suggests to the people that it would be in their interest to pray (as, he alleges, they anyway do so already) that the gods transform the *felicitas* he has ascribed to Pompey into its Sullan variant, by turning it into his personal and ever-lasting possession (*quod ut illi proprium ac perpetuum sit*). Both the *salus* and *imperium* of Rome and the man himself (*homo ipse*) justify such prayers – though the programmatic reference to Pompey as a human being (*homo ipse*) is designed to reassure those members of the audience who would have balked at Cicero's idiom of quasi-deification. Pompey, Cicero continues to suggest, is unlike Sulla: his luck does not serve as a source of self-empowerment beyond the remits of the republican constitution, but benefits the commonwealth at large. Cicero thus manages to attribute to Pompey luck of Sullan proportions without turning it into an undesirable quality reminiscent of a tyrant. The concluding emphasis on the benefits that the Roman people derive from Pompey's luck picks up on one of the main themes of the speech: the felicitous congruence of Pompey's appointment to the generalship and the interests of the people.

The section on *felicitas*, then, offers a precarious balancing act: it is as much about defining and delimiting 'divine support' as it is about claiming the quality for Pompey. Cicero makes a significant concession to the Sullan variant, trying to harness its appeal for his argument in favour of Pompey, while at the same time reworking it in a republican key. As Kathryn Welch

---

49 The following is adjusted from Gildenhard (2011) 269-70.

puts it: 'Pompey's *felicitas* is a personal attribute (Sullan) but he acts in harmony with his fellow-citizens and for their benefit (not-Sullan).'[50]

itaque non sum praedicaturus, quantas ille res domi militiae, terra marique, quantaque felicitate gesserit, ut eius semper voluntatibus non modo cives adsenserint, socii obtemperarint, hostes oboedierint, sed etiam venti tempestatesque obsecundarint: the main verb, *non sum praedicaturus*, governs the indirect question *quantas ... gesserit* (hence the subjunctive). *quantas* and *quanta* set up the consecutive *ut*-clause that concludes the sentence. Cicero enumerates four different entities who comply with Pompey's wishes. They are arranged climactically: we start with Roman citizens (*cives*), move on to allies (*socii*), which are followed, surprisingly, by enemies (*hostes*), and conclude hyperbolically with forces of nature (*venti tempestatesque*). Cicero enhances the effect by how he places *non modo* (followed by a tricolon of simple subject + verb phrases) and *sed etiam* (the last, climactic item and the only one that features two subjects – *venti tempestatesque*). *eius ... voluntatibus* and *semper* go with all four verbs.

itaque non sum praedicaturus: stating that one will not talk about something while doing so is called *praeteritio* – the rhetorical equivalent of having your cake and eating it.

quantas ille res domi militiae, terra marique, quantaque felicitate gesserit: *quantas* is an interrogative adjective agreeing with *res*, the accusative object of *gesserit*. Between accusative object, subject (*ille*) and verb, Cicero places a tricolon of ablative phrases: the first two (*domi militiae; terra marique*) are locatives; the third, *quanta felicitate*, is an ablative of means. The arrangement is climactic: Cicero moves from 'bipolar' mapping of geography, which includes consideration of both social (*domi militiae*) and physical (*terra marique*) space to the abstract quality of *felicitas*. The *-que* after *quanta* links *terra marique* and *quanta felicitate*.

domi militiae, terra marique: all four nouns are in the locative case. *domi militiae* refers to the Roman practice of dividing the world into a (demilitarized) zone of peace (*domi*) and a zone of (potential) warfare

---

50   Welch (2008) 194.

(*militiae*). Initially, the sacred boundary of the city of Rome, the *pomerium*, demarcated the two spheres. (The only occasion when an *imperator* with his soldiers was allowed to cross the *pomerium* was the triumph: in the course of the ritual, the general and his army would follow a prescribed route through the city to the Capitol, where he would sacrifice to Jupiter Optimus Maximus and lay down his *imperium*.)

obtemperarint: the syncopated form of *obtempera-ve-rint*.

venti tempestatesque obsecundarint: contrast § 40, where Cicero discusses the reasons for Pompey's seemingly special speed of movement: he disclaims the help of the winds as well as other external factors and, with deliberate bathos, grounds Pompey's velocity instead in his outstanding character.

obsecundarint: the syncopated form of *obsecunda-ve-rint*.

hoc brevissime dicam, neminem umquam tam impudentem fuisse, qui ab dis immortalibus tot et tantas res tacitus auderet optare, quot et quantas di immortales ad Cn. Pompeium detulerunt: after saying in *praeteritio* what he had allegedly no intention of saying, Cicero continues with what he will say – if very briefly (*brevissime*). *dicam* introduces an indirect statement with *neminem* as subject accusative and *fuisse* as infinitive, with *tam impudentem* in predicative position. *tam* sets up a relative clause of characteristics (hence the subjunctive of *auderet*).

hoc brevissime dicam, neminem umquam tam impudentem fuisse: Latin authors frequently add a demonstrative pronoun to verbs of thinking and stating that introduce an accusative + infinitive construction to give special emphasis to the indirect statement: '*This* I shall say, however briefly, namely that nobody...' The demonstrative pronoun is particularly pronounced here, coming as it does after a *praeteritio*: 'I won't be commenting on x; but *this* I will say...'

quod ut illi proprium ac perpetuum sit, Quirites, cum communis salutis atque imperii, tum ipsius hominis causa, sicuti facitis, velle et optare debetis.: *quod* is a connecting relative (= *et id*), referring back to Pompey's unparalleled *felicitas*. It is the subject of the nominal *ut*-clause dependent on (*velle et*) <u>*optare*</u> *debetis; proprium ac perpetuum* agree with *quod* in predicative position.

cum communis salutis atque imperii, tum ipsius hominis causa: this is one long prepositional phrase dependent on the postpositive preposition *causa*, which governs the genitives *communis salutis atque imperii* and *ipsius hominis*. They are coordinated by *cum ... tum*. See our commentary on § 31.

sicuti facitis, velle et optare debetis: Cicero takes the normative sting out of *debetis* ('you ought...!'), by claiming that the people do so already anyway: *sicuti facitis*, namely *velle et optare*.

49: SUMMING UP

§ 49 concludes Cicero's discussion of the war (§§ 6-26) and the choice of general (§§ 27-49), which involved him in outlining the ideal of the perfect military commander and demonstrating that Pompey is its living embodiment. As such, the paragraph systematically revisits the main themes of the argument.

Quare cum et bellum sit ita necessarium, ut neglegi non possit, ita magnum, ut accuratissime sit administrandum, et cum ei imperatorem praeficere possitis, in quo sit eximia belli scientia, singularis virtus, clarissima auctoritas, egregia fortuna, dubitatis Quirites, quin hoc tantum boni, quod vobis ab dis immortalibus oblatum et datum est, in rem publicam conservandam atque amplificandam conferatis?: This paragraph consists of one long sentence. It begins with an extensive *cum*-clause that contains within itself three further subordinate clauses: two *ut*-clauses and a relative clause (*in quo...*). The main verb is *dubitatis*, which sets up the concluding *quin*-clause, within which we get a further relative clause (*quod...*).

In the opening *cum*-clauses (*Quare cum... egregia fortuna...*) Cicero looks back to the tripartite argument he announced in § 6:

primum mihi videtur de genere belli, deinde de magnitudine, tum de imperatore deligendo esse dicendum.

He reiterated the blueprint at the beginning of the section devoted to the choice of *imperator* (§ 27):

Satis mihi multa verba fecisse videor, qua re esset hoc bellum genere ipso necessarium, magnitudine periculosum. Restat ut de imperatore ad id bellum deligendo ac tantis rebus praeficiendo dicendum esse videatur.

The design of the *cum*-clauses in § 49 mirrors the design of § 27: in both cases, Cicero groups together the first two items to do with the war and sets apart the choice of general as the climactic third topic to be treated. The first *cum*-clause covers the type and magnitude of the war, the second the appointment of the commander-in-chief:

(i)   *cum et bellum sit ita necessarium,*
         ut neglegi non possit,
     [cum bellum sit] ita magnum,
         ut accuratissime sit administrandum, et

(ii) *cum ei imperatorem praeficere possitis,*
         in quo sit eximia belli scientia, singularis virtus, clarissima
         auctoritas, egregia fortuna...

Cicero enhances the immediacy and vividness of his discourse by shifting from the impersonal passive constructions in the *ut*-clauses (*neglegi non possit; sit administrandum*) to a direct address of the audience in (ii): *praeficere possitis*. This shift generates a chiasmus of sorts: in (i) the verb in the *cum*-clause is *esse*, stating a fact, whereas the verbs in the *ut*-clauses indicate the action to be taken; in (ii) the verb in the *cum*-clause indicates the action to be taken and the verb in the subsequent relative clause (*in quo*) is *esse*, stating a fact.

§ 49 also sums up the section on the perfect general, harking back to § 28 in particular. Compare:

§ 28 (the ideal): Ego enim sic existimo, in summo imperatore quattuor has res inesse oportere: scientiam rei militaris, virtutem, auctoritatem, felicitatem.

with

§ 49 (its incarnation): imperatorem ..., in quo sit eximia belli scientia, singularis virtus, clarissima auctoritas, egregia fortuna

The following table shows how Cicero reiterates key words in those paragraphs that flag up the structure of his discourse. If § 6 introduces the main themes and functions almost like a table of contents, §§ 27, 28, 49 offer repetitions, variations, and elaborations:

	§ 6	§ 27	§ 28	§ 49
The type of war	de *genere belli*	*bellum genere ipso necessarium*		*bellum sit ita necessarium, ut...*
Its magnitude	de *magnitudine* [sc. *belli*]	[*bellum*] *magnitudine periculosum*		[*bellum sit*] ita *magnum, ut...*
The choice of general	de *imperatore deligendo*	de *imperatore ad id* bellum *deligendo* ac tantis rebus *praeficiendo*	in summo *imperatore* quattuor has res inesse oportere: *scientiam rei militaris, virtutem, auctoritatem, felicitatem*	cum ei *imperatorem praeficere* possitis, in quo sit eximia belli *scientia,* singularis *virtus,* clarissima *auctoritas,* egregia *fortuna*

Note in particular how the notional perfect general of § 28 has become a flesh-and-blood exemplar in § 49 – indeed, how Pompey outdoes the theoretical specimen Cicero delineated in § 28. At the outset, he simply specified the four qualities that ought to be present in the *summus imperator*; by § 49 we have learned that Pompey possesses these four qualities not only in abundance, but to a unique degree: the four nouns *scientia, virtus, auctoritas* and *felicitas/fortuna* recur with reference to Pompey, each preceded by a panegyric attribute: *eximia, singularis, clarissima, egregia.*

cum et bellum sit ita necessarium, ut neglegi non possit, [sc. bellum sit] **ita magnum, ut accuratissime sit administrandum, et cum...:** both *ut*-clauses are consecutive, set up by a preceding *ita*. The subject throughout (of *sit, possit,* and *sit administrandum*) is *bellum*. The anaphora (*ita... ita...*), the asyndeton (the two parts of the *cum*-clause follow on each other without connectives), and the ellipsis of *bellum sit* before *magnum* generates a sense of urgency, perhaps even impatience: by now Cicero has set out the indisputable facts of the matter – there is now no reason to hesitate further. Note, though, that Cicero uses connectives to coordinate the two *cum*-clauses: *cum et ... et cum.*

et cum ei imperatorem praeficere possitis: the demonstrative pronoun *ei* (in the neuter dative singular) harks back to *bellum. praeficere* here takes both an accusative object (*imperatorem*) and a dative object (*ei*). The idiom is: 'to put the accusative in charge of the dative'.

in quo sit eximia belli scientia, singularis virtus, clarissima auctoritas, egregia fortuna: *in quo* introduces a relative clause of characteristics, hence the subjunctive (*sit*). By pulling the verb up front, Cicero clears space for the powerful, asyndetic enumeration of the four key qualities of his perfect general, all endowed with an amplifying attribute.

dubitatis, Quirites, quin...: one would expect an infinitive here, rather than a *quin*-clause (which is the regular construction with *negated* expressions of doubt).

quin hoc tantum boni, quod vobis ab dis immortalibus oblatum et datum est, in rem publicam conservandam atque amplificandam conferatis?: Cicero here casts his audience as the lucky recipients of divine favour – and challenges them to make the most of the windfall that is Pompey, for the greater good of the commonwealth. There is a notional chain from the gods to the *res publica*, via Pompey and the Roman citizens: the gods (*ab dis immortalibus*) gift the citizens (*vobis*) with Pompey (who hides behind the abstract formulation *hoc tantum boni*), whom they in turn should not hesitate to utilize for public service (*in rem publicam conservandam atque amplificandam*). The one who is rhetorically in charge of the sequence *di immortales* > Pompey > *Quirites* > *res publica* is of course Cicero; those who get sidelined in this sequence are all the other members of Rome's senatorial elite, which was technically in charge of handling all interactions with the divine sphere of political relevance in republican times.

hoc tantum boni: *hoc tantum* is the subject of the *quin*-clause and the antecedent of *quod*. *boni* is a partitive genitive dependent on *tantum*: 'so much of a boon'.

5. Further Resources

Chronological table: the parallel lives of Pompey and Cicero

Year	Pompey	Cicero
106	Born (29 September)	Born (3 January)
90-88		Military Service, including with Pompey's father Gnaeus Pompeius Strabo (one of the consuls of 89)
89-87	Military Service under his father Gnaeus Pompeius Strabo, who dies in 87.	
83-81	Various campaigns: in support of Sulla (in Italy, Sicily, Africa)	
81	First triumph	First surviving public speech (*pro Quinctio*)
79-77		Rhetorical and philosophical studies in Rhodes and Athens
76-71	Campaign in Spain against Sertorius as holder of a proconsular *imperium* (granted by a reluctant senate); contribution to the suppression of the slave revolt upon his return; second triumph for his victories in Spain	Active in the law courts
75		Quaestor in Sicily
70	Consul for the first time (with Crassus)	Prosecution of Verres
69		Aedile
67	Campaign against the pirates as holder of an extraordinary command sanctioned by the *lex Gabinia*	

66		Praetor; speech in favour of the *lex Manilia* (*de imperio Gn. Pompei*)
65-61	Campaign against Mithridates as holder of an extraordinary command sanctioned by the *lex Manilia*; third triumph	
63		Consul; suppression of the Catilinarian conspiracy
58		Pushed into exile on account of the execution of the Catilinarians (till 57)
55	Consul for the second time (with Crassus)	
52	Consul *sine collega* ('without colleague'), to restore order in the capital	
51		Pro-consul in Cilicia
48	Pompey assassinated in the course of the civil war against Caesar	
43		Proscription by Mark Antony; death

The speech in summary, or: what a Roman citizen may have heard in the forum

§

1 • So... I've never given a *contio* speech before...

2 • But, well, I'm a praetor now, so I guess I *probably* should.

3 • Happily enough, my topic would suit anyone – the wonders of Gnaeus Pompey.

4 • Let's start with the cause: Mithridates and Tigranes, and the war in Asia.

5 • The *publicani* are very, very worried. We need a new general. Guess who?

6 • Let's run through, in order, the nature of the war; its seriousness; the choice of a commander.
   • It's a very patriotic war! Lots of glory to be had!

7 • And since Romans have ever been glory-seekers, you should damn well go glory-seeking against Mithridates, which frankly has been a rather embarrassing mess so far.

8 • I mean, two triumphs have come out of this (for Sulla and Murena), but Mithridates remained on his throne. Shocking! (Not that Sulla and Murena didn't deserve their triumphs; both of them got called back early, after all: Sulla by domestic crisis, Murena by Sulla.)

9 • Mithridates used his grace period to rearm, the horror. Of course, we were distracted by the Spanish war then.

10 • But Pompey's sorted out Sertorius and out in the East, well... let me damn Lucullus with faint praise for a bit. Good qualities, right, but really: his luck's so awful, isn't it?

11 • Let me appeal to the ancestors (*maiores*)! They used to go to war to avenge the slightest insult against our citizens, not to mention envoys – surely we're not going to let pass the murder of thousands of citizens by Mithridates? and the horribly torturous death of a Roman consular envoy (Manius Aquilius)?

12   • What about your allies, eh? We want to protect Ariobarzanes, who's been driven into exile, and all the Greek and Asian states.
      • They don't dare ask for a specific general...

13   • ... but they totally would if they thought they could get away with it. Because he's so awesome!

14   • You are going to defend your allies, right, just like our ancestors did?
      • I mean, if nothing else, think how much we'll be financially screwed if we don't get Asia back...

15   • And I mean *seriously* screwed.

16   • Genuinely and horribly so.

17   • And we need to protect the interests of our citizens whose property is affected by this war.

18   • Not least since our economic recovery will be problematic if they can't e.g. bid for contracts to collect taxes. Etc.

19   • And we want to avoid a collapse of credit, such as happened with the first Mithridatic war.

20   • Let's talk about the magnitude of the war now.
      • It's very big.
      • I mean, *okay*, Lucullus has, like, relieved our good friends in Cyzicus...

21   • ... and sunk the massive fleet that was heading for Italy under Sertorian leadership...
      • ... and opened the way for our legions into Pontus...
      • ... captured Sinope and Amisus, plus countless other cities of Pontus and Cappadocia...
      • ... forced Mithridates into exile...

22   • But the war is still very big!
      • Analogy of Mithridates' flight with that of Medea, scattering her brother's limbs. Mithridates leaves scattered only his vast wealth, thereby escaping our soldiers.

23   • ... and is picked up by Tigranes of Armenia.

- In a way that upsets all sorts of new enemies. Oh dear.

24   • I'll just leave it at that, shall I?

25   • Result: Mithridates looks better placed than ever. And also goes home merrily and attacks our army again. I'll pass over the disaster (it was awful).

26   • And at this terrible moment, Lucullus was obliged to disband some troops and hand over others to Manius Glabrio, all because you insisted on customary practice!

27   • Let's talk about the choice of general now.
        • Pompey is pretty much head and shoulders above everybody else in the *world*.
        • He possesses the four necessary qualities of a perfect general: knowledge of warfare, ability, prestige, luck.

28   • Wow, he does have a great knowledge of warfare! Think of all the (civil) wars he's been involved in! What a range!

29   • And what amazing abilities!

30   • All these countries in which he's done battle are my witness!

31   • Plus every sea.

32   • Let me lament the days of yore, for… some reason involving pirates…

33   • Awful pirates, they are.
        • And good lord! Pompey has sorted them all out.

34   • And he did it very fast!
        • He's travelled to so many places.

35   • So very, very many places.
        • Sorting out pirates! All in half a year!

36   • And he has so many other awesome qualities!

37   • Truly glorious ones. He isn't avaricious at all, unlike *some* people, naming no names.

38   • I mean, *some* of our generals have been pretty destructive in touring with their armies.

39   • Whereas Pompey is pretty awesome!

40   • In, like, just about every way.

41   • People out in the provinces are starting to think of him as a god from heaven! They begin to believe in the existence of Ye Olde Roman!

42   • He's such a wonderful person, I just can't tell you.
     • So seriously, why would anyone hesitate to put him in charge of this war?

43   • Prestige matters too. Guess who has lots of it?

44   • And I mean *lots*.
     • Look how the price of wheat fell when he was appointed to the command of the naval war!

45   • And look how just his providential presence in Asia back after that disaster at Pontus restrained Mithridates and checked Tigranes!

46   • And how all Rome's enemies surrendered to him very suddenly! Even when there were closer Roman generals to whom they might have surrendered!

47   • Now let's talk about good luck.
     • It's very important. But also kind of difficult to talk about, what with not wanting to provoke the gods.

48   • Basically, Pompey has it as well. Lots of it.

49   • So why would you hesitate to put Pompey in charge of the war?

50   • You'd do it even if he was here (but as it is, he's there already) and a private citizen (he isn't)! So seriously, just give him all the other armies in the vicinity and let him get on with it.

51   • Catulus and Hortensius disagree with me.
     • Well, they're both very distinguished gentlemen; but that's not going to stop me damning them too with a bit of faint praise.

52   • Hortensius says we shouldn't give supreme command to one man (although if we were going to, the right man would be Pompey).
     • This argument is out of date. Hortensius argued against Gabinius' law re: pirates…

53 • … well, Pompey got the pirate command, thanks to the Roman people. They didn't agree with Hortensius then, quite rightly too.

54 • Those pirates were very mean people!

55 • Very, very mean!

56 • So the Roman people ignored Hortensius' well-intentioned advice and gave supreme command against the pirates to Pompey, with the result that those very mean pirates were sorted out within the year.

57 • The opposition to Gabinius (who proposed this law) serving as legate to Pompey as per Pompey's request is therefore terribly ungracious.

58 • There are other precedents that back me up!
   • Something should be done about it; and if the consuls won't do it, I will myself.

59 • About Catulus – wasn't that amusing, when he said 'Who will you put in command if something happens to Supreme Commander Pompey?' and you all said 'You!'
   • I mean, he is a pretty decent guy really, but I have to disagree with him here. Human life is very uncertain – that just means we should take advantage of the abilities of a great man while he's around for everyone else to exploit.

60 • Okay, so some people say we should just go along with what the *maiores* always did; but *I* shall ostentatiously refrain from pointing out a long list of precedents in which the *maiores* totally put all their trust in the hands of one man and thereby won the day.

61 • Think how many such precedents for Pompey himself have already been approved by Catulus among others!
   • Such novelties as can be seen from his early career.

62 • Seriously, his early career was *very* novel. As L. Philippus is said to have remarked, *non se illum sua sententia pro consule sed pro consulibus mittere* ('I give my vote to send him not in place of a consul but in place of both consuls!'). That's really helpful!

63 • So let everyone who agreed to those novelties understand that it would be terribly unjust for them not to agree now that the people want him to have full command, just as they did re: pirates.

64   • Since you made a perfectly sensible decision when you gave
        Pompey command against the pirates, you're obviously making
        a perfectly sensible one now.
     • After all, this war against an Asiatic monarch requires very
        special moral qualities!

65   • We are very, very unpopular abroad right now, thanks to the bad
        behaviour of our governors.

66   • As Catulus and Hortensius know.
     • So a general sent abroad to Asia needs to be *very* special.

67   • As Pompey is! How convenient.
     • That's why the coastal regions asked for him to be appointed.

68   • So let's not hesitate to give him full command.
     • If you want some serious *auctoritas* to agree with me, what about
        Gaius Curio? What about Gnaeus Lentulus? And Gaius Cassius!

69   • I therefore applaud and commend Gaius Manilius's law. It's a
        very good one. I'm behind you all the way.

70   • I call on the gods to witness that I'm acting in the interests of the
        state and definitely not e.g. in the hopes of winning Pompey's
        favour. *Oh no.* Definitely not!

71   • That's because it's my duty to place your wishes, the honour of
        the state and the well-being of the provinces and allies above my
        own advantages and interests.

Translation of §§ 27-49

[27] I think I have covered at sufficient length why this war is both inevitable given its kind and perilous given its immense scope. What remains to be covered is that one ought to speak, it seems, about the general to be chosen for this war and to be put in charge of such important matters. Citizens, if only you had such abundance of brave and upright men as to make difficult your deliberation over who above all ought, in your opinion, to be put in charge of such important matters and so great a war! But in fact – given that Gnaeus Pompeius alone has surpassed in excellence not only the fame of those men who live now but also the recorded achievement of past generations – what is it that could make the mind of anyone hesitant in this matter?

[28] I for my part think that in the perfect general the following four attributes ought to be present: knowledge of military matters, overall excellence, commanding prestige, and luck grounded in divine support. In that case, who has ever been, or should be, more knowledgeable than this man? He departed from school and from the lessons of childhood to his father's army and the discipline of warfare during a major war against extremely fierce enemies. At the end of his childhood he was a soldier in the army of a perfect general, at the onset of adolescence he was himself a general of a major army. He has fought more often with an *external* enemy than anyone else has argued with a *personal* enemy, has conducted more campaigns than the rest have read of, has held more public offices than others have desired. His youth [= In his youth, he] was instructed in knowledge of military matters not through teachings from others but through commands he held himself, not through setbacks in war but victories, not through seasons of military service, but the celebration of triumphs. Finally, what type of war can there be, in which the vicissitudes of our commonwealth have not trained him [or: in which the Fortuna (understood as a positive 'divine quality') of the Commonwealth has not given him practice]? The civil war, the wars in Africa, Transalpine Gaul, and Spain, the Slave war and the war at sea [sc. against the pirates], these varied and different types of wars and enemies, which were not only conducted by this one man but also brought to successful conclusion, prove that there is not a thing within the sphere of military experience that could escape this man's knowledge.

[29] Besides, to the (innate) excellence of Gnaeus Pompeius what discourse can be found that measures up? What is there that anyone could adduce either worthy of him or novel to you or unfamiliar to anyone? Nor, in fact, are *those* the only qualities distinctive of a general, which are commonly so considered, namely effort in public affairs, courage in dangers, care in operating, speed in finishing, good judgement in exercising forethought; these are present in this one man to such an extent as they have not been in all the other generals, whom we have either seen or heard of.

[30] Italy is my witness, which the great conqueror Lucius Sulla himself admitted was freed by the excellence and the assistance of this man. Sicily is my witness, which, when it was surrounded on all sides by many dangers, he rescued not by the horror of war but by the speed of his counsel. Africa is my witness, which, borne down upon by massive enemy forces, overflowed with the blood of the self-same foes. Gaul is my witness, through which – by the slaughter of the Gauls – a route has been opened up into Spain for our legions. Spain is my witness, which most frequently has seen great numbers of the enemy overcome and laid low by this man. Over and over again, Italy is my witness, which, when it was weighed down by a foul and dangerous slave war, sought assistance from him though he was far away; and this war was weakened and diminished in expectation of him [= his return] and crushed and buried upon his arrival.

[31] Witnesses, as it is, are now indeed all coasts and all foreign ethnicities and nations, finally all seas, both in their totality and, on every single coastline, all bays and ports. Which place on the whole sea either maintained a garrison throughout these years secure enough to keep it safe, or was so secluded that it escaped notice? Did anyone set to sea without exposing himself to the danger of either death or enslavement, seeing that he sailed either in winter or else on a sea teeming with pirates? Who would ever have supposed that so great a war – so shameful, so ancient, so widely spread and fragmented – could be brought to an end either by all generals in a single year or by a single general across an eternity?

[32] Which province did you keep free from pirates throughout these particular years? Which revenue was safe to you [= which of your revenues was safe]? Which ally did you protect? For whom were you a safeguard with your fleet? How many islands, do you think, have been deserted, how

many cities of your allies have either been abandoned because of fear or been captured by pirates? But why do I recall matters far away? Once this was the case, it was characteristic of the Roman people, namely to wage war far away from home and to defend, with the bulwarks of empire, the possessions of the allies rather than their own homes. Am I to say that for our allies the sea was off-limits throughout these years, when your own armies never crossed from Brundisium except in the middle of winter? Am I to lament that those were captured who came to you from foreign nations, when legates of the Roman people were ransomed? Am I to say that the sea was unsafe for merchants, when twelve axes fell into the power of the pirates?

[33] Am I to mention that Cnidus or Colophon or Samos, cities of greatest renown, and countless others, were captured, given that you know that your harbours and those harbours, from which you take your life and breath, were under the control of the pirates? Do you really not know that the harbour of Caieta, crowded and crammed full of ships, was plundered by pirates even though a praetor was watching? That the children of that very praetor, who had previously waged war against the pirates, were snatched by the pirates from Misenum? Why am I to lament the set-back in Ostia and that blot and disgrace of the republic when, almost with you witnessing it, that fleet of which a consul of the Roman people was in charge, was captured and crushed by the pirates? Oh immortal gods! Was the remarkable and divine excellence of one man able to bring so much light to the republic in such a short time, that you, who were recently watching the fleet of the enemy at the mouth of the Tiber, now hear that no ship of the pirates is within the Mediterranean [i.e. this side of the strait of Gibraltar]?

[34] And even though you see (sc. for yourselves) with what speed these things were accomplished, it still ought not to be passed over by me in my speech. For who, in their zeal for attending to business or making profit, was ever able to visit so many places, to complete such long journeys in as little time as it took for the force of such a massive military operation to sweep speedily across the sea under the leadership of Gnaeus Pompeius? He landed in Sicily on a sea not yet seasonable for sailing, reconnoitred Africa, came to Sardinia with his fleet, and safeguarded those three suppliers of the commonwealth's corn with the toughest garrisons and fleets.

[35] After he had returned from there to Italy – the two Spains and Gallia Cisalpina having been fortified with strongholds and ships, ships having likewise been sent to the coast of the Illyrian Sea, to Achaia, and all of Greece – he furnished both seas bordering on Italy with very large fleets and the toughest strongholds; he himself then added, on the forty-ninth day after he had departed from Brundisium, all of Cilicia to the empire of the Roman people. All pirates wherever they were, were either captured and killed or handed themselves over to the military command and magisterial power of this one man. The same man did not take away the hope of good terms of surrender from the Cretans, when they sent ambassadors and pleaders after him all the way to Pamphylia, but rather demanded hostages. Thus such a great war, so long drawn-out, so far-flung and widely scattered, a war by which all peoples and nations were oppressed, Pompey prepared for at the end of winter, took on at the beginning of spring, and brought to completion in the middle of summer.

[36] This, then, is his god-like and unbelievable excellence as general. Well? His other qualities, which I had begun to enumerate a little while ago – how great and how numerous are they! For in the consummate and perfect general not only excellence in waging war ought to be expected; rather, many qualities are assistants and associates of this his most conspicuous excellence. First, of what outstanding integrity generals must be! Further, of what outstanding moderation in every walk of life! Of what outstanding trustworthiness, outstanding ease in interpersonal relations, outstanding talent, outstanding human kindness! Let us hence consider these briefly, of what kind they are in Gnaeus Pompeius: all qualities are present to the highest degree, citizens; they can, however, be more easily discerned and appreciated through a comparison with others than in and of themselves.

[37] Whom can we believe to be a general of any esteem, in whose army the offices of the centurion are sold and have been sold? What [can we believe] a person of this kind to think about the commonwealth [that is] grand and edifying, who either, out of desire for a province, shared out among the magistrates the money that had been issued from the treasury to conduct a campaign or, out of greed, left it at interest in Rome? Your groans indicate, citizens, that you seem to recognize those who have done these things. For my part, I mention no-one by name. Hence nobody will be able to be angry with me unless he is willing to own up about himself beforehand. Who

does not know how great the disasters are that our armies bring along wherever they go because of this greed of our generals?

[38] Recall what marches in recent years our generals undertook in Italy through the fields and townships of Roman citizens! Then you will decide more easily on what you think is happening among foreign peoples. Do you believe that in recent years more cities were destroyed through the armed violence of your soldiers or more allied communities through their winter quarters? For a general, who does not control himself, is unable to control an army and someone who does not wish others to be strict judges of himself, is unable to be strict in passing judgment.

[39] In these circumstances are we surprised that this man so greatly surpasses all the others, whose legions [= given that his legions] have arrived in Asia in such a way that not only no hand, but not even a footstep, of so great an army is said to have harmed anyone peaceful? In addition, oral reports and letters announce on a daily basis how the soldiers pass the winter: not only is no violence inflicted on anybody to expend money on behalf of a soldier, but no-one is allowed to do so even if he wishes. For our ancestors wanted the houses of our allies and friends to be a refuge from the winter, not a refuge for greed.

[40] Come, consider what moderation he displays in other matters! From where, do you think, has come such surpassing speed and such unbelievable rapidity of motion? Not the exceptional strength of his oarsmen or some unheard-of art of navigation or some novel winds have borne him into the farthest lands; rather, those matters that are wont to delay the others did not hinder his progress: no greed diverted him from his planned path to any plunder; no lust to pleasure, no charming location to its enjoyment, no renown of a city to sight-seeing, and, finally, not even toil to rest. Moreover, the pictures and paintings and other adornments of Greek towns that others believe ought to be carried off, he thought that they ought not to be even looked at by him.

[41] And so now everyone in these locations regards Gnaeus Pompeius as someone not sent from this city, but descended from heaven. Now they finally start to believe that Roman men once had this (kind of) self-control,

something which by now was beginning to seem to foreign nations unbelievable and wrongly handed down to memory. Now the lustre of your empire begins to bring light to these peoples. Now they understand that it was not without reason that at a time when we had magistrates of such moderation, their ancestors preferred to serve the Roman people rather than to rule over others. Moreover, approaches to him by private individuals are said to be so easy, complaints about the wrongs suffered from others so freely received that he who outdoes the leading citizens in dignity seems equal in affability to the humblest.

[42] Besides, how strong he is in political wisdom, how strong in the weight and eloquence of his oratory, in which there is itself a certain dignity characteristic of a general, this, citizens, you have often come to know in this very place. How great indeed do you think his trustworthiness is reckoned (to be) among the allies, which all of his enemies of every type have judged utterly inviolable? He is of such human kindness that it is difficult to say whether the enemy feared his martial prowess when fighting more than they esteemed his gentleness once defeated. And will anyone doubt that such a great war should be given over to this man, who seems, by some divine plan, to have been born to end all wars in our time?

[43] And inasmuch as authority too is of great importance in waging war and in a military command, surely no-one doubts that in this matter that very same general is supremely capable? Who does not know that what the enemy, what the allies think of our general is greatly of relevance to waging war since we know that human beings are moved by belief and hearsay no less than by any specific reason in matters of such importance that they either despise or fear, either hate or love? Which name, then, has ever been more famous in the whole wide world? Whose deeds comparable? About which man have you passed such weighty and such glorious judgements, which is the greatest source of authority?

[44] Or do you really believe that any coast anywhere is so deserted that news of that day did not reach it, when the entire Roman people, with the forum full to bursting and all the temples from which this place here can be seen having been filled, demanded for itself Pompey alone as general for a war of shared concern to all peoples? Thus, to say no more or to strengthen my case with examples of others as to how much authority matters in war,

let examples of all extraordinary deeds be taken from [the career of] that self-same Gnaeus Pompeius. And on the day he was put in charge by you of the war against the pirates as general, such a low price for corn suddenly followed after the most severe shortage and sky-high prices for the corn-supply because of the expectation raised by, and the name of, one single individual as prolonged peace coupled with the greatest fertility of the soil could hardly have achieved.

[45] Now, after the disaster in Pontus had happened, as a consequence of that battle, of which against my will I reminded you a little earlier, when our allies were in a state of panic, when the power and spirits of our enemies had grown, and the province did not have a sufficiently strong safeguard, you would have lost Asia, citizens, if the fortune of the Roman people had not providentially brought Gnaeus Pompeius at that critical moment in time into those regions. His arrival checked Mithridates, puffed up by his unusual victory, and slowed down Tigranes, who was threatening Asia with a large number of troops. And will anyone doubt what he will accomplish by his excellence, who has accomplished so much by his authoritative prestige? Or how easily he will preserve allies and revenues with a command and an army, who has defended them by his mere name and reputation?

[46] Come now: that matter reveals the great prestige of this same individual among the enemies of the Roman people, namely that from locations so far away and so far apart they all surrendered themselves in so short a time to this man alone; that legates from the commonwealth of the Cretans, even though there was a general and an army of ours on their island, came almost to the ends of the earth to Gnaeus Pompeius and said that all the civic communities of the Cretans were willing to surrender themselves to him. And again: did not that Mithridates himself send an ambassador all the way to Spain to the same Gnaeus Pompeius? Pompeius always considered him an ambassador; those to whom it was irritating that [the man] had been sent to him [sc. Pompeius] especially, preferred him to be considered a spy rather than an ambassador. Hence you can now establish, citizens, how much you think that this commanding prestige, which has in the meantime been further enhanced by many deeds and by your own magnificent judgements, will have weight with those kings, how much it will have weight with foreign peoples.

[47] What remains is for me to say a few apprehensive words about good fortune, which no-one can vouch for concerning himself, but which we may recall and record concerning someone else, in the same way as is fitting for mortals to speak about the power of the gods. For I am of the opinion that commands were rather frequently assigned, and armies entrusted to Maximus, Marcellus, Scipio, Marius and the rest of the outstanding generals not only because of their excellence, but also because of their good fortune. For undoubtedly, a certain good fortune was by divine agency attached to certain most excellent men for distinction and fame and the performance of great deeds. But about the good fortune of this man here, with whom we are concerned now, I shall restrain my discourse, so that I will not claim fortune to be in his power, but that I seem to recall events in the past and am hopeful about those still to come, with the view to avoiding that my speech seem odious or displeasing to the gods.

[48] Therefore I shall not announce what deeds he carried out both at home and abroad, on land and on sea, and with what good fortune, so that not only the citizens always concurred with his plans, the allies complied with them, and the enemies obeyed them, but even the winds and storms supported them. I shall only mention most briefly this, that no-one has ever been so arrogant as to dare to wish privately successful deeds of such frequency and scale from the immortal gods as the immortal gods have granted to Pompey. You should wish and pray, as you do, that he retains this forever as a personal possession, citizens, both on account of the common good and the empire and because of the man himself.

[49] Why, then, given that the war is so essential that it cannot be ignored, so significant, that it ought to be waged with the greatest care, and given that you can put a general in charge of it in whom there is outstanding knowledge of warfare, nonpareil excellence, the brightest prestige, and exceptional good fortune, do you hesitate, citizens, to direct this magnificent boon, which was offered and given to you by the immortal gods, towards the preservation and enhancement of the commonwealth?

The Protagonists

Cicero

Born in 106 BC, Cicero was elected quaestor for 75, curule aedile for 69, praetor for 66 and consul for 63, during which crowning moment of glory he became the protagonist (or antagonist, depending on your point of view) of the Catilinarian crisis.[1] Cicero held each office *suo anno*, 'in his year', that is at the minimum age required by the *lex Villia annalis* ('the Villian Law on Minimum Ages'),[2] which was a remarkable achievement for a *homo novus*, a 'new man' from Arpinum, who lacked senatorial ancestors in his family tree. His heroics in 63, however, included the execution without trial of a number of the 'Catilinarian Conspirators', including the praetor Publius Cornelius Lentulus Sura. When Cicero's *inimicus* ('political enemy') Publius Clodius Pulcher was elected tribune of the plebs in 58 and promptly passed legislation to remind everyone about the *lex Sempronia*, which banished anyone who did precisely this, Cicero hurried off into exile and was only recalled in 57 by a vote of the senate.[3] For the rest of the decade, his political activity was constrained by the activities of the greater political monsters: Pompey, Marcus Licinius Crassus and Gaius Julius Caesar. Crassus fell in battle against the Parthians in 53 and civil war broke out when Caesar crossed the Rubicon to invade Italy in 49. After much dithering, Cicero took Pompey's side; stayed until Pompey's defeat at Pharsalus in 48; accepted Caesar's *clementia* ('mercy'), then praised Caesar's assassination during the Ides of March 44, and was finally chopped down in 43 as a prize scalp in the

---

1 Cicero, *in Catilinam* 1-4, Appian, *Bellum Civile* 2.2-6, Plutarch, *Life of Cicero* 10-23.
2 Promulgated in 180 BC, the *lex Villia annalis* seems to have fixed the sequence of compulsory magistracies that held, the so-called *cursus honorum* ('course of offices': first quaestorship, then praetorship, and finally consulship), the two-year gap (*biennium*) between tenure of each magistracy (and ten years between repeat holding of the consulship, which was then banned in 151 BC), and minimum age requirements at least for the praetorship and consulship. For further details, see e.g. Hopkins (1983) 47, Evans and Kleijwegt (1992) 181-82, Lintott (1999) 145, and Brennan (2000) 168-70. The conditions of the *lex Villia annalis* were reinstated and tightened up by Sulla's *lex annalis* of 81 BC (see Lintott (1999) 145 and Flower (2010) 123-24), so that by this point the minimum ages for each magistracy are thirty for the quaestorship, thirty-six for the non-compulsory aedileship, thirty-nine for the praetorship, forty-two for the consulship: Lintott (1999), Patterson (2000).
3 Appian, *Bellum Civile* 2.15-16, Plutarch, *Life of Pompey* 49 and *Life of Cicero* 28-33.

proscriptions of the 'Second Triumvirate' (consisting of Caesar Octavianus (the future Augustus), Marcus Antonius, and Marcus Aemilius Lepidus).[4]

Cicero's political career, which lasted from his first really prominent legal case in 80 (the defence of Sextus Roscius on a charge of parricide[5]) to his death in 43, was based not least on oratorical ability and way with words more generally. He left behind a corpus of more than 75 texts (and that's just the ones that have survived) including speeches, philosophical dialogues and treatises, some poetry, and a massive collection of letters to and from friends, family and political acquaintances.

Pompey (106-48 BC)

Family background: Pompey's father was Gnaeus Pompeius Strabo (135-87 BC), *homo novus* ('new man') and yet *consularis* ('a former consul, i.e. someone who has reached the consulship in his career') who for some less than obvious reason is regularly labelled sneaky and untrustworthy even though not noticeably showing a great deal more of either trait than your average successful Roman politician of this era. (Apparently the consul of 105 Publius Rutilius Rufus, known for his moral uprightness and commitment to Stoicism, had a go at him;[6] and Cicero slates him as cruel and money-grasping as well, *Brutus* 47.) He was consul in 89, i.e. the middle of the Social War, during which he was perfectly competent (see § 28 of the set text);[7] got involved in the political mess left behind by Sulla;[8] and died struck by lightning in 87, leaving his most interesting offspring to run the family's fiefdom in Picenum at the tender mid-twenties age.[9]

Pompey's Career till his first consulship (70 BC): strictly speaking, as the son of a *consularis*, Pompey was therefore *nobilis* from 88 onwards, but the family was far from distinguished at Rome and Strabo doesn't seem to have made

---

4   Plutarch, *Life of Cicero* 37-48.
5   Cicero, *pro Sexto Roscio Amerino*, Plutarch, *Life of Cicero* 3.
6   Plutarch, *Life of Pompey* 37.
7   Appian, *Bellum Civile* 1.40, 1.47-8, 1.50, 1.52.
8   Appian, *Bellum Civile* 1.63: benefits from the death-by-soldier-riot of successor and Sulla's colleague Quintus Pompeius; 1.66-7: is summoned by Octavius to deal with Cinna, but basically just sits next to the Colline Gate looking shifty while Cinna and Marius roll up; 1.68, does eventually give Octavius a hand expelling Cinna and Marius from Rome, to which they had been admitted by treacherous military tribune Appius Claudius.
9   Cf. Hillard (1996) for an overview and discussion of the sources on Strabo's death.

a great many friends during the course of his career. Pompey in fact was prosecuted during the 80s on account of some irregularity to do with Strabo's war booty; he got off with the help of a friendly praetor, whose daughter Antistia he married.[10] According to Plutarch, the lady's father was killed for his family-alliance with Pompey; her mother committed suicide.[11] Then Sulla came back from his war against Mithridates VI in 83, at which point Pompey, who was 23 years of age and a *privatus* at the time (i.e. someone who did not hold a public office), raised an army from his father's veterans in Picenum and joined Sulla (along, it must be said, with several other *privati* with private armies).[12] This proved to be a winning move, since Sulla won: Pompey divorced Antistia, married Sulla's stepdaughter Aemilia (already pregnant by her own divorced spouse, Aemilia died shortly afterwards in childbirth),[13] and was given a string of commands against Marian generals on the run in Sicily (82), Africa (81) and Spain (77-71). (Cicero glosses these appointments in §§ 28-30 of the set text). These commands he held as an unelected holder of (dummy) praetorian *imperium*. Along the way, he was involved in suppressing Lepidus' rising in 78, celebrated unprecedented triumphs as an equestrian (i.e. non-senator) in 81 or 80 and again in 71,[14] got married for the third time to Mucia, the relative of various prominent Romans,[15] contributed to Crassus's defeat of Spartacus's slave war, and was eventually elected to the consulship of 70 at the age of thirty-six, six years too young and (unlike Cicero) having held none of the prerequisite offices.[16] So much, then, for the stipulations of the various *leges annales* ('Laws of Minimum Age Requirements') detailed in footnote 2 above.

In addition to military successes, Pompey was popular with the people, not least because he got involved in removing the final restrictions Sulla had placed on the tribunate during his consulship.[17] (Sulla had removed the right of the tribunes of the plebs to veto the legislation of other magistrates, to summon the senate or propose legislation, and he had made the office a

---

10 Plutarch, *Life of Pompey* 4.
11 Plutarch, *Life of Pompey* 9; Leach (1978) 22, 27-8.
12 Cicero, *pro lege Manilia* 61; Appian, *Bellum Civile* 1.80.366; Plutarch, *Life of Pompey* 10; Seager (2002) 26.
13 Haley (1985) 50.
14 Cf. Leach (1978) 24-59, Greenhalgh (1980) 13-67, Seager (2002) 26-36.
15 Haley (1985) 50, Leach (1978) 34.
16 Cicero, *pro lege Manilia* 61-2; cf. Sherwin-White (1956) 5-8.
17 Stockton (1973) 209-12, Keaveney (1982) 54-61, Vasaly (2009) 101-02.

dead end on the *cursus honorum*.[18] In 75 the tribunate was put back on the *cursus honorum* and in 70 Pompey and Crassus restored its other functions.)

The wars against the pirates and Mithridates: Post-consulship, Pompey seems to have taken a break (as far as we can tell) for a few years. Then, when people started jumping up and down and crying to high heavens about the latest piratical incursions in 67, it was Pompey who was assigned the task of suppressing the menace thanks to the *lex Gabinia*. Ill-disposed people floating around on boats were a major issue for everyone living on the Mediterranean coast, and had been for centuries, not least because cities like Rome and Athens depended on imported grain from places like Egypt and the Black Sea region. You can be cynical about this if you want; Philip de Souza, for example, argues that in the third to second century BC, 'the Rhodians encouraged other Greeks to see Rhodes as their naval protector. By virtue of this role they claimed the right to intervene with their naval forces in order to suppress what they deemed to be acts of piracy. In effect they were using the suppression of piracy as a justification for making war'.[19] With the rise of Rome as a naval power in the second century, however, and the establishment of Delos as a free port in 166, Rhodes went into decline along with its 'naval protection racket',[20] leaving the policing of the Mediterranean up to the new boss. On Rome's progress in that area, we could do worse than quote Plutarch (*Life of Pompey* 24):

> The power of the pirates had its seat in Cilicia at first, and at the outset it was venturesome and elusive; but it took on confidence and boldness during the Mithridatic war, because it lent itself to the king's service. Then, while the Romans were embroiled in civil wars at the gates of Rome, the sea was left unguarded, and gradually drew and enticed them on until they no longer attacked navigators only, but also laid waste islands and maritime cities. And presently men whose wealth gave them power, and those whose lineage was illustrious, and those who laid claim to superior intelligence, began to embark on piratical craft and share their enterprises, feeling that the occupation brought them a certain reputation and distinction. There were also fortified roadsteads and signal-stations for piratical craft in many places, and fleets put in here which were not merely furnished for their peculiar work with sturdy crews, skilful pilots, and light and speedy ships; nay, more

---

18   Keaveney (1982) 169-70, Hantos (1988) 74-9, 130-47.
19   de Souza (2008) 76. On piracy in the Greco-Roman world see more generally de Souza (1999).
20   Gabrielsen (2001).

annoying than the fear which they inspired was the odious extravagance of their equipment, with their gilded sails, and purple awnings, and silvered oars, as if they rioted in their iniquity and plumed themselves upon it. Their flutes and stringed instruments and drinking bouts along every coast, their seizures of persons in high command, and their ransomings of captured cities, were a disgrace to the Roman supremacy. For, you see, the ships of the pirates numbered more than a thousand, and the cities captured by them four hundred.

Plutarch goes on to provide a list of sacked sanctuaries, abducted Romans (including two praetors and a daughter of the orator Marcus Antonius, c.143-87 BC), and the 'crowning insolence' of the pirates' mockery of anyone who thought Roman citizenship would save them. In addition, the pirates made travel and commercial activity by sea impossible.[21] Notably, Plutarch slots pirates into the 'side-effect of civil war' category, although he is probably just indulging in one of this particular *Life*'s running themes here, since a former Roman attempt to police the pirates out of the water had been run by M. Antonius, father of the abducted Antonia and grandfather of the future triumvir, Marcus Antonius, who had been fighting those pirates back in 102, well before the civil wars.[22] Antonius earned a triumph for his efforts in 100, but evidently those efforts were not very long-lasting, since P. Servilius Vatia Isauricus was active in Cilicia in 78-74,[23] then Antonius's son M. Antonius Creticus had an unsuccessful go as praetor in 74,[24] and finally in 67 the tribune Aulus Gabinius, Pompey's friend, proposed a law to give Pompey an extraordinary command against said pirates.

It might be tempting to think, with Philip de Souza, that these pirates sound less like 'pirates' and more like 'the navy of a country that Rome, for some reason, refuses to acknowledge as such': 'Roman campaigns against maritime enemies were presented as the suppression of piracy because that suited contemporary political needs, especially when the Roman aristocracy wanted to convince reluctant allies that they should fight with or for the Roman cause'.[25] He argues that the Cilician 'pirates' under attack here are not so much 'mundane pirates' (which certainly existed[26])

---

21 Plutarch, *Life of Pompey* 24.
22 Ehrenberg (1954) 116-17, de Souza (2008) 78.
23 de Souza (2008) 82.
24 Ehrenberg (1954) 117, Jameson (1970) 547, de Souza (2008) 82-3.
25 de Souza (2008) 71; cf. further 78-81, 84-5.
26 de Souza (2008) 85, defining 'mundane pirates' as 'armed robbers with ships who owed no particular political allegiance and whose actions were motivated only by thoughts of immediate material gain'.

as organised opponents of Roman power, and that Cicero in the *pro lege Manilia* transforms them into colourful pirate-stereotypes to justify Roman imperial aggression – the ancient equivalents, as it were, of 'Dread Pirate Roberts'.[27]

According to Plutarch, the *lex Gabinia* gave Pompey 'dominion over the sea this side of the Pillars of Hercules [cf. § 33 of the set text], over all the mainland to the distance of four hundred furlongs from the sea. These limits included almost all places in the Roman world, and the greatest nations and most powerful kings were comprised within them. Besides this, he was empowered to choose fifteen legates from the senate for the several principalities, and to take from the public treasuries and the tax-collectors as much money as he wished, and to have two hundred ships, with full power over the number and levying of soldiers and oarsmen'.[28] One classic question concerning the *lex Gabinia* is just what sort of command (*imperium*) Pompey received relative to the local pro-magistrates: whether, like Antonius in 74, he was given *imperium* equal (*aequum*) to that of the local proconsuls, or if it was greater (*maius*) and allowed him to overrule his colleagues in the region.[29] This is an issue that may never be resolved; the sources disagree and the great and influential nineteenth-century classicist Theodor Mommsen (1817-1903) did not help matters by taking a firm stance that has resulted in complications ever since. The war itself was over within a record three months[30] and Philip de Souza suggests that Pompey's secret was his 'remarkable willingness to come to terms with the enemy': unlike his predecessors, 'Pompey, wary of the demands such a campaign would make on Roman and allied resources yet anxious to obtain a quick victory to further his own political career, offered a general amnesty in return for immediate surrender'.[31] This stellar progress left Pompey with about two years outstanding on his *imperium* (whatever the precise nature of that *imperium*) and nothing much to do with it, putting him in an excellent position to usurp Lucullus's command against Mithridates with the help of another handy tribune, Manilius.[32]

---

27 de Souza (2008) 86. For 'Dread Pirate Roberts' see http://en.wikipedia.org/wiki/Dread_Pirate_Roberts
28 Plutarch, *Life of Pompey* 25.
29 Last (1947) 160-61, Ehrenberg (1954) 115-22, Jameson (1970), Seager (2008) 46.
30 Cicero, *pro lege Manilia* 34-5, de Souza (2008) 83-4.
31 de Souza (2008) 83-4.
32 Plutarch, *Life of Pompey* 30.

Lucullus had been having problems since 69 or so: it had been a long war and everyone was getting tired of it, not least Lucullus's soldiers.[33] Mithridates VI Eupator, the king of Pontus, had first made trouble while the Social War (90-88) was ongoing: in 89 he invaded Bithynia and Phrygia and in 88 he prompted the Asiatic Vespers, a genocidal slaughter of all the Italians (not just Roman citizens) in Asia Minor.[34] This, in addition to the defection of large parts of the Greek East was naturally inflammatory, but at the time Rome was distracted by (1) the end of the Social War and (2) the unexpected post-Social War outbreak of political discord sparked by the tribune Publius Sulpicius's attempt to transfer command of the war against Mithridates from the consul Lucius Cornelius Sulla to the *privatus* and six-times-consul Gaius Marius.[35] After Sulla and his colleague had occupied Rome, decapitated Sulpicius, put Marius and various friends on a 'kill on sight' list, laid down their preferred version of the law and overseen the election of consuls for the following year (Cinna and Octavius, who swore to uphold the new status quo), Sulla marched off to deal with Mithridates (88-84).[36] Since the situation back home very quickly went sour, however,[37] *his* iteration of the Mithridatic Wars ended in a deal,[38] leaving Mithridates in place to rearm while the Romans sorted out their own problems.

By 74, the Romans were back thinking about another Eastern war,[39] which (after some manoeuvring involving the then popular favourite Cethegus's disreputable girlfriend Praecia, if Plutarch is to be believed[40]) was handed over to the late Sulla's lieutenant Lucius Licinius Lucullus, a tough disciplinarian and highly competent general who knocked the local Roman troops into good shape[41] and spent the next four or five years hammering Mithridates and his friend/relative Tigranes one battle at a time.[42] Unfortunately Lucullus's soldiers weren't as tough as he was and turned against him (disaffected officers include Lucius Quinctius, who as praetor in 67 is stirring things up at Rome, and Cicero's future bête noire,

---

33 Seager (2008) 42.
34 Cicero, *pro lege Manilia* 37; Appian, *Bellum Civile* 1.55; Plutarch, *Life of Sulla* 11; Santangelo (2007) 31-2.
35 Appian, *Bellum Civile* 1.55-61, Plutarch, *Life of Sulla* 7-10.
36 Plutarch, *Life of Sulla* 11-21.
37 Appian, *Bellum Civile* 1.64-75.
38 Plutarch, *Life of Sulla* 22-4.
39 Plutarch, *Life of Lucullus* 5.
40 Plutarch, *Life of Lucullus* 6.
41 Plutarch, *Life of Lucullus* 7.
42 Plutarch, *Life of Lucullus* 7-32.

Publius Clodius),[43] while back at home, various people were at work on getting what remained of the command transferred to Pompey, hence our speech in favour of the controversial *lex Manilia,* which did just that.

The *lex Manilia* added to Pompey's existing *imperium* the provinces of Cilicia and Bithynia.[44] There was a chilly meeting between Pompey and Lucullus in a Galatian village;[45] Lucullus, not unreasonably, felt he had been robbed of his war and Pompey had sneaked in to snatch the credit after the heavy lifting had already been done (not for the first time, either, as Crassus might have pointed out: see our commentary on § 28 of the set text). Briefly (perhaps not quite as briefly as Appian's version at *Bellum Civile* 2.1, which may be summarised as 'Pompey beat up the pirates and then he beat up Mithridates'), Pompey spent several years out East, wrapping up the war and massively reorganising the whole area.[46] Then he came home. According to Plutarch, everyone back in Rome got very nervous over whether he might choose to march in and take over in true Sullan style,[47] but in fact he disbanded his army at Brundisium (and why not? There was no need to do anything else, despite various Italian troubles in his absence) and rolled home peacefully to a hero's reception.[48]

Till the beheading: It was at this point, when Pompey submitted his entire Eastern programme (and promises of public land for his veterans) for senatorial approval, that he ran into trouble. The senate was difficult.[49] Simultaneously, Pompey divorced his Metellan wife Mucia,[50] but without lining up a replacement; his attempt to marry into the Catonian faction was not very well received.[51] The senate dragged its heels; Pompey got frustrated; eventually he teamed up with his former colleagues Crassus and Caesar, whose attempt to stand for the consulship *in absentia* while waiting for a triumph for fighting various Spanish tribes as praetor (which meant he had to wait outside the official city boundary, the *pomerium,* in order to avoid forfeiting his *imperium* and thereby losing his triumphant army)

43 Plutarch, *Life of Lucullus* 33-5.
44 Ehrenberg (1954) 120, Jameson (1970) 558, Seager (2008) 49.
45 Plutarch, *Life of Lucullus* 36, *Life of Pompey* 31.
46 Plutarch, *Life of Pompey* 32-43.
47 Plutarch, *Life of Pompey* 43.
48 Plutarch, *Life of Pompey* 43.
49 Appian, *Bellum Civile* 2.9, Plutarch, *Life of Pompey* 46.
50 Plutarch, *Life of Pompey* 42.
51 Plutarch, *Life of Pompey* 44, Leach (1978) 112-13, Haley (1985) 52-3.

was maliciously delayed by Cato.[52] Caesar, giving up his triumph in the interests of gaining the consulship of 59, sorted out everyone's immediate problems in exchange for an extraordinary command in Gaul.[53] The deal was the so-called 'First Triumvirate', a wholly unofficial arrangement cemented by Pompey's marriage to Caesar's daughter Julia.[54]

In 57 Pompey picked up a specially contrived grain supply command (*Praefectus Annonae* for five years). Plutarch (probably unfairly) blames the post-exilic Cicero for showing his gratitude towards Pompey (whose involvement in Cicero's departure had not been altogether commendable[55]) by reconciling Pompey with the senate. Moreover, 'by his advocacy of the corn law he in a manner once more made Pompey master of all the land and sea in Roman possession. For under his direction were placed harbours, trading-places, distributions of crops – in a word, navigation and agriculture'.[56] The political agreement between Pompey, Crassus and Caesar, by now fraying, was renewed in 56 via the 'Conference at Luca',[57] following which Crassus and Pompey stood successfully for the consulship of 55. They arranged the extension of Caesar's command, allotted Spain and Africa to Pompey (but to be governed by proxy), and gave Crassus a chance to distinguish himself with yet another extraordinary command, this time against the Parthians.[58] Unfortunately this bombed at the Battle of Carrhae in 53,[59] with Crassus' death collapsing the triad; and once Julia had died in 54,[60] Pompey's ties to Caesar were weakened.[61] Pompey's next wife, married in 52, was a Cornelia, the daughter of Metellus Scipio and the widow of Crassus's son (slain with his father at Carrhae), indicating a political shift away from Caesar (who had failed to convince Pompey to marry his niece Octavia) and towards Caesar's senatorial enemies.[62]

The political situation in Rome generally was chaotic. To quote Appian (*Bellum Civile* 2.19),

---

52 Appian, *Bellum Civile* 2.8, Plutarch, *Life of Pompey* 47, *Life of Caesar* 13.
53 Appian, *Bellum Civile* 2.10-14, Plutarch, *Life of Pompey* 47-8, *Life of Caesar* 14.
54 Plutarch, *Life of Pompey* 47, *Life of Caesar* 14, Appian, *Bellum Civile* 2.43, Leach (1978) 126.
55 Plutarch, *Life of Pompey* 46.
56 Plutarch, *Life of Pompey* 49.
57 Appian, *Bellum Civile* 2.17, Plutarch, *Life of Pompey* 51, *Life of Caesar* 21.
58 Appian, *Bellum Civile* 2.18.
59 Plutarch, *Life of Pompey* 52.
60 Appian, *Bellum Civile* 2.19, Plutarch, *Life of Pompey* 52.
61 Leach (1978) 151-52.
62 Plutarch, *Life of Pompey* 55, Leach (1978) 154, Haley (1985) 55.

The magistrates were chosen by means of money, and faction fights, with dishonest zeal, with the aid of stones and even swords. Bribery and corruption prevailed in the most scandalous manner. The people themselves went already bought to the elections. A case was found where a deposit of 800 talents had been made to obtain the consulship. The consuls holding office yearly could not hope to lead armies or to command in war because they were shut out by the power of the triumvirate. The baser among them strove for gain, instead of military commands, at the expense of the public treasury or from the election of their own successors. For these reasons good men abstained from office altogether, and the disorder was such that at one time the republic was without consuls for eight months, Pompey conniving at the state of affairs in order that there might be need of a dictator.[63]

And then Titus Annius Milo (canvassing for the consulship) killed the *popularis* darling Publius Clodius Pulcher (canvassing for the praetorship) on the Appian Way.[64] The situation exploded; indeed, the riotous people burnt down the senate-house along with Clodius's body.[65] Riots ensued. 'The Senate assembled in consternation and looked to Pompey, intending to make him dictator at once, for they considered this necessary as a remedy for the present evils; but at the suggestion of Cato they appointed him consul without a colleague, so that by ruling alone he might have the power of a dictator with the responsibility of a consul. He was the first of consuls who had two of the greatest provinces, and an army, and the public money, and autocratic power in the city, by virtue of being sole consul'.[66]

This unprecedented sole consulship was arguably the crowning moment of Pompey's career. We recap Sherwin-White's summary of Pompey: he 'would bluff up to the limits of legality, but he never marched on Rome or crossed a Rubicon in his life. He disbanded his legions at Brundisium on his return from the East. In his own phrase he would take a sword, but only if the consuls placed it in his hands; if someone else drew a sword he would raise a shield'.[67] The consuls *did* place a sword ceremoniously into his hand when Caesar crossed the Rubicon in 49, thereby handing Pompey command of 'the Republicans' against Caesar. Pompey, whose real strength was in his foreign *clientela* ('networks of dependents'), made the strategically sound but politically upsetting choice to evacuate Rome,

63 Cf. also Plutarch, *Life of Pompey* 54.
64 Appian, *Bellum Civile* 2.20-22, Plutarch, *Life of Cicero* 35.
65 Appian, *Bellum Civile* 2.21.
66 Appian, *Bellum Civile* 2.23; cf. also Plutarch, *Life of Pompey* 54.
67 Sherwin-White (1956) 8.

and fought a good campaign until he lost the battle of Pharsalus, chose the wrong former client to run to, and was unceremoniously murdered and decapitated thanks to the young Ptolemy XIII's advisers when he disembarked in Egypt.[68] (Caesar is said to have shed crocodile tears when presented with Pompey's head and seal ring: unlike Sulla, he did not go in for decapitation. Well, not the decapitation of fellow Roman citizens, at any rate.[69])

Manilius

Compared with Cicero and Pompey, Gaius Manilius, the proposer of the *lex Manilia*, casts a very slight shadow. This has something to do with the fact that he was a *popularis* tribune of obscure family who proposed two controversial laws: a law to distribute freedmen throughout the 35 voting tribes of the *comitia tributa* (they were currently confined to the four urban tribes, thus limiting the value of their votes): it was passed through violence and afterwards annulled;[70] and the law that forms the subject of the *pro lege Manilia*, that is the transfer of Lucullus's command against Mithridates to Pompey, which was also passed and remained in place. Towards the end of his term as tribune (and Cicero's as praetor), Manilius found himself facing a charge of extortion. Plutarch reports as follows (*Life of Cicero* 9):

> Two or three days before Cicero's term of office expired, Manilius was brought before him on a charge of fraudulent accounting. This Manilius had the good will and eager support of the people, since it was thought that he was prosecuted on Pompey's account, being a friend of his. On his demanding several days in which to make his defence, Cicero granted him only one, and that the next; and the people were indignant because it was customary for the praetor to grant ten days at least to the accused. And when the tribunes brought Cicero to the rostra and denounced him, he begged for a hearing, and then said that he had always treated defendants, so far as the laws allowed, with clemency and kindness, and thought it an unfortunate thing that Manilius should not have this advantage; wherefore, since only one day was left to his disposal as praetor, he had purposely set this day for the trial, and surely it was not the part of one who wished to help Manilius to defer it to another praetor's term. These words produced a wonderful change in the feelings of the people, and with many expressions of approval

---

68 Plutarch, *Life of Pompey* 77-80.
69 Plutarch, *Life of Caesar* 48.
70 Phillips (1970) 595, Ward (1970) 546.

they begged Cicero to assume the defence of Manilius. This he willingly consented to do, chiefly for the sake of Pompey, who was absent, and once more mounting the rostra harangued the people anew, vigorously attacking the oligarchical party and those who were jealous of Pompey.

It may be that the extortion charge was connected to Manilius's totally unknown quaestorship rather than his tribunate, since tribunes generally lacked the opportunity to extort anything (a charge of public violence, *vis*, would be more likely, especially given Manilius's activities).[71] Cicero's role in the affair remains unclear: whether his excuse to the tribunes was sincere or whether he had been caught out trying to hamstring Manilius's case is a matter of debate.[72] Manilius's first trial in 65 was riotous (literally)[73] and the senate passed a *senatus consultum* instructing the consuls to keep the peace during the second trial.[74] Cicero perhaps refused to defend Manilius the second time round and Manilius was condemned.[75] Following which, we hear no more of Manilius.

---

71 Phillips (1970) 597, Ramsey (1980) 325-26.

72 Phillips (1970) 597-601, Ward (1970) 546-47, Ramsey (1980) 323-24, 328-31.

73 Phillips (1970) 603, Ward (1970) 548-49.

74 Phillips (1970) 603-05 argues that this trial was for the same charge, rather than 'treason' (*maiestas*) as had sometimes been thought; cf. also Ward (1970) 548 n.15.

75 Phillips (1970) 607, Ward (1970) 552-54, Ramsey (1980) 331.

The Historical Context

The contio-setting

There were three principal settings for speeches in the late Roman republic: (1) the law-courts; (2) the senate; (3) the *contio*, a public meeting called by certain magistrates. *Contiones* were held for a variety of purposes: to inform the *populus Romanus* ('the people of Rome') of proposed legislation or important events, to debate controversial issues of the day, and very often for senior politicians to be held to account (or hauled over the coals, depending on your perspective) by the tribunes of the plebs. The plebeian tribunate was one of the magistracies with the right to call *contiones* and tribunes are often found in the *contio* setting in our sources; as the principal place to address the *populus*, the *contio* was the natural habitat for these most *populares* magistrates. The important point for the *pro lege Manilia* is how audience influences oratory: in a law-court the speaker addresses the jury, in the senate he addresses his fellow senators (his peers), and in a *contio* speech he addresses (or affects to address) the *populus Romanus*, the Roman people, generally called *Quirites* to their face. (In this oration, Cicero addresses his audience with the appellation *Quirites* twenty-three times, five times in the set text alone: § 27: *utinam, Quirites, ...*; § 36: *summa enim omnia sunt, Quirites, ...* § 37: *Vestra admurmuratio facit, Quirites, ...* § 42: vos, Quirites, hoc ipso ex loco saepe cognovistis*; § 45: *amisissetis Asiam, Quirites, ...* See also § 46: *Potestis igitur iam constituere, Quirites, ...* § 48: *Quod ut illi proprium ac perpetuum sit, Quirites, ...* § 49: *dubitatis Quirites, quin...*)

Cicero had not held the plebeian tribunate, which was an optional office on the *cursus honorum*, but (as noted above) at the time of the *pro lege Manilia* he was one of that year's praetors. His previous speeches had all been legal cases; he opens the *pro lege Manilia* with the observation that this was his first-ever *contio* speech.[76] The expressed purpose of the speech is to encourage people to vote for the *lex Manilia*, a proposed law intended to transfer command of the campaign against Mithridates to Pompey. The secondary purpose of the speech, as we may infer from reading between the lines and from its publication after the event, is to promote Cicero himself, both as an orator and as a Friend of Pompey. Cicero's interests are

---

76 Cic. *Man.* 1.

long-term: he needs not just to buff the reputation of Marcus Tullius Cicero, praetor, but also to anticipate his next political campaign, the canvass for the consulship. By speaking at all, Cicero publicises his support of Pompey, which Pompey himself may appreciate and which will hopefully gain Cicero some of the reflected glow from Pompey's popularity; and by publishing the speech he preserves testimony to the occasion and also enables those deprived souls who missed the performance to enjoy his oratory second-hand (this includes you!). (He no doubt revised the script before its dissemination in writing, though how much Cicero revised any given speech for publication is one of those eternally debated issues that keep modern scholars occupied and safely off the streets.)

Rome's imperial expansion

Rome began as just one city-state among a quarrelsome bunch in the Italian peninsula. Disregarding the historically doubtful wars of the regal period and very early Republic, Rome's winning ways with its neighbours resulted in:

- war with the Samnites (1) (343-341);

- war with the Latins and Volscians (340-338);

- war with Neapolis (328);

- war with the Samnites (2) (326-321, 316-304) *and* with the Etrurians and Umbrians (311-309);

- war with the Samnites (3) (298-290);

- war with the Sabines (290);

- war with the Etruscans and Gauls (284-280) *and* war with Tarentum (284);

- war with Pyrrhus of Epirus (280);

- war with Carthage (1) (264-241);

- war with Gauls (225);

- war with Carthage (2) (216-201) *and* war with Macedonia (1) (215-205);

- war with Macedonia (2) (200-197);

- war with Antiochus of Syria (192-188);

- war with Macedonia (3) (171-168);

- war in Spain ('Celtiberian War') (153-151);

- war with Carthage (3) (149-146) *and* war with Macedonia (4) (149-148);

- war with Achaea (146);

- war with Spanish/Celtiberian city of Numantia (133);

- war with King Jugurtha of Numidia (109-105);

- war with the migrating Cimbri (105-100);

- war with Mithridates of Pontus (1) (89-85);

- war with Mithridates of Pontus (2) (74-66).

In the course of successfully prosecuting several centuries of sustained warfare the *populus Romanus* expanded their territory from the ordinary hinterland of an average city-state to a territorial empire embracing chunks of Spain, Greece, Asia Minor, the Near East (mod. Middle East) and Africa. One unforeseen by-product of this remarkable imperial expansion has been the modern debate over how to explain it. Broadly speaking, there are three academic views:

- The classic view, 'defensive imperialism': that the Romans were constantly pressed to defend themselves against external powers, and in the course of reluctantly defending themselves somehow ended up with an empire (mysterious!).[77]

- The 'aggressive imperialism' view, propounded in the first place as a revisionist perspective by W. V. Harris: that the Romans were extraordinarily aggressive and took out their anger management issues on their neighbours, prosecuting a deliberate policy of expansion via the ferocious contest for *laus* and *gloria* among their top politicians and their unusual capacity for deeply unpleasant behaviour. ('In my view it is more likely that the regular harshness of Roman war-methods sprang from an unusually pronounced

---

77 E.g. Walbank (1963), Brunt (1964).

willingness to use violence against alien peoples, and this willingness contributed to Roman bellicosity.'[78])

- The 'realist' view, representing the inevitable backswing against the initial revisionist perspective: certainly the 'defensive imperialism' idea is untenable, derived as it is from our self-justifying and mostly late Republic/imperial Roman sources. On the other hand, it seems unlikely that the Romans were a uniquely violent people (or, presumably, uniquely xenophobic). Rather, the ancient world was a violent place (and, at the time of writing, nothing much seems to have changed since) in which nations and city-states were *constantly* going to war with each other, and Roman social and political structures just happened to be uniquely suited to coping with decades-long wars and the occasional catastrophic defeat (or, better, *evolved* into being able to do so).[79]

We (this is probably no surprise) favour the 'realist' take,[80] but it doesn't really matter too much for present purposes. What *does* matter is that in the course of systematically rendering their neighbours down for soup stock, the Romans fell prey not to an enemy power but instead, in the end, to internal political dissensions, thereby kicking off the sequence of civil wars that eventually transformed the Republic into the monarchic Empire.

Civil wars

The first *formal* civil war (defined as 'war between Roman citizens') is generally taken to be Sulla's first march on Rome in 88. However, this

---

78 Harris (1979) 51; cf. also Rowland (1983).
79 E.g. North (1981); cf. also Adler's critique (2008a), (2008b) of the idea that the 'defensive imperialism' version is pro-imperialistic, pro-Roman apologia: what it boils down to is that anyone who is or feels themselves to be vulnerable to accusations of being in possession of an empire actually gets very uncomfortable about comparisons with Rome and tends to denigrate whatever they think the Roman version of imperialism is. In contrast, 'anti-imperialists'/critics of hawkish foreign policies/etc. jump straight for (often inappropriate and shockingly inaccurate) comparisons with Rome, which is once again the villain of the piece due to negative popular preconceptions. (This is a separate issue from the point that Victorian/Edwardian classicists tended to rely innocently on literary sources, which are generally self-justifying Roman ones, of course.) For more on modern (re)conceptions of ancient empires, cf. Harrison (2008).
80 Persian expansion, for instance, was unambiguously aggressive. So were the Assyrians: just look at their friezes. And how about Alexander? And when Rome turned up in Sicily, was Carthage already there because the Sicilians had decided to invite them round for tea?

came at the tail-end of a lengthy history of political violence starting in 133, when the tribune Tiberius Gracchus's controversial legislation to divvy up public land for the benefit of the landless (with the good of the Roman army in mind: at this point, only men in possession of a certain amount of property could serve in the army) ended in the death of Tiberius and some 300 followers in a minor bloodbath on the Capitol when the senior senator and *pontifex maximus* ('chief pontiff') Publius Scipio Nasica led a mob of senators there to disrupt Tiberius's dubiously legal re-election as tribune.[81] Further political violence took place in 121, when Tiberius's younger brother Gaius Gracchus, who had followed in Tiberius's political footsteps and was seeking to be tribune for the *third* time, was slaughtered along with his allies in somewhat more organised fashion by the sitting consul, L. Opimius;[82] then in 100, the tribune L. Appuleius Saturninus and the praetor C. Servilius Glaucia were lynched in the *Curia Hostilia*, despite promises of safe conduct from the sixth-time consul and sometime *popularis* Gaius Marius.[83]

In 91, the murder of the *popularis* tribune M. Livius Drusus by persons unknown added to the various tensions that gave rise to the Social War, which we hesitate to call a civil war only due to a quibble of semantics: it was fought between Romans and their Italian allies (the *socii*), rather than between Roman citizens. However, citizenship issues were an important factor in the Social War, so it isn't actually too much of a stretch to describe the Social War as a civil war: on the traditional account, the Italian city-states decided to break with Rome and set up a separate federal state, *Italia*, out of the frustrated desire to become Roman citizens, as promised by the murdered Drusus.[84] (Henrik Mouritsen, it is worth noting, has proposed a wilfully post-colonial antidote to this traditional view arguing that the 'we want citizenship' version was superimposed on a 'down with evil oppressor Rome' original.[85]) In any case, whether you buy that or not, the Social War ran from 91-88; the (former) allies were defeated through a combination of military victory and political concessions: the Latins were granted citizenship, though the qualifications to this grant (especially confining them to the four urban tribes, like freedmen, thereby restricting the new citizens' political influence) became new sources of political tensions

---

81 Plutarch, *Life of Tiberius Gracchus*; Appian, *Bellum Civile* 1.9-16; Velleius Paterculus 2.3.
82 Plutarch, *Life of Gaius Gracchus*, Appian *Bellum Civile* 1.21-26. Cf. especially Stockton (1979) 114-61, Nippel (1995) 63-4, Flower (2006) 69, 76-8 and (2010) 86.
83 Appian, *Bellum Civile* 1.110ff.
84 E.g. Brunt (1965) 271, Gabba (1989), Salmon (1982) 128-29.
85 Mouritsen (1998).

immediately.[86] One of the tribunes of 88, P. Sulpicius Rufus, proposed laws to distribute the new citizens through all 35 voting tribes and sought to gain support for his legislation by transferring command of the impending war against Mithridates from the consul Lucius Cornelius Sulla to the ageing Gaius Marius.[87] This did not go down well: after open violence in the streets, Sulla escaped to his army, joined forces with his colleague, Quintus Pompeius, and together the consuls marched on Rome.[88]

There is an argument to be made that Sulla's first march on Rome was a police action, and Christian Meier, followed by Robert Morstein-Marx, has made it.[89] Well, perhaps. It *was* the first full-on military occupation of Rome by Roman consuls, who should technically have forfeited their *imperium* as soon as they crossed the formal city boundary (the *pomerium*). Once in possession of Rome, they revoked Sulpicius's laws and handed out a 'kill on sight' list that included Sulpicius (who got it in the neck, rather literally) and Marius (who escaped to Africa and enjoyed several pathetic adventures of the sort that later became *de rigueur* for Sulla's enemies). It isn't clear what other legislation was promulgated at this point, because there's a suspicion that the sources are retrojecting the legislation of Sulla's second march on Rome.[90] Sulla did hold the elections for the following year and upheld the results even though he disapproved of one of the winners, Lucius Cornelius Cinna; both consuls-designate were obliged to swear an oath to uphold Sulla's settlement and Sulla himself headed out East to take the first of several inconclusive hacks at Mithridates.[91]

As soon as Sulla was out of the way, things broke down in Rome. The consuls Cinna and C. Octavius fell out with each other and the senate backed Octavius, who drove Cinna out of Rome. Marius reappeared; Cinna and Marius together marched on Rome; both got to be consuls (Marius for the seventh time) and Marius died a natural death later that year. The four years or so that followed are generally known as the *Tempus Cinnae* ('the

---

86 Salmon (1982) 130.
87 On the events of 88 generally, cf. Katz (1977), Mitchell (1979) 54-76. On Sulpicius and his activities, cf. Badian (1969) 481-90, Lintott (1971), Mitchell (1975), Keaveney (1979), Powell (1990), Lewis (1998), Lovano (2002) 1-18. Luce (1970) argues that much of the 90s should be seen in the light of Marius's ambitions for another great command and his opponents' attempts to prevent him from getting one.
88 Keaveney (1982) 60-4, Levick (1982) 508, Lovano (2002) 19-21, Santangelo (2007) 6-7.
89 Morstein-Marx (2011) 272, Meier (1966) 224; for a similarly sympathetic perspective cf. Mitchell (1979) 68-76.
90 Flower (2010) 120.
91 Keaveney (1982) 66-8, Levick (1982) 508, Lovano (2002) 31.

time of Cinna') or the *Dominatio Cinnae* ('the tyranny of Cinna') or something on those lines; meanwhile Sulla, out East, was obliged to manoeuvre around not just Mithridates but also the senatorial/Cinnan candidate for the command.[92] Eventually he decided he'd had enough of this and came to terms with Mithridates, which allowed him to head back to Italy for his second march on Rome in 83. This time he did things thoroughly: relevant details are supporters, dictatorship, legislation, proscriptions, resignation, a natural death.[93] Although it's tempting to cut off 'Sulla's civil wars' with Sulla's victory at Rome, in fact the civil wars continued down through the 70s, as the various 'Marians' who had fled Rome continued to fight the good fight in Sicily, Africa and, most determinedly, Sertorius in Spain.[94] Additionally, Italy itself continued to be troubled, first by M. Aemilius Lepidus, one of the consuls of 78,[95] and then by whatever was going on with Catiline in 63.[96] (Whatever *was* going on in Rome, there was certainly an uprising out in the field.) And we might throw in Spartacus and the slave war in Italy in the 70s for good measure.

In short, we are looking at twenty years of civil war from the Social War in 91 to the end of Sertorius in Spain in 72; then the 60s, when Pompey is out East, then the 50s, when Caesar is out west; and then the return of civil war in 49, when Caesar crosses the Rubicon and marches on Rome. This civil war lasted from 49 to Actium in 31 – another twenty years, from which Caesar's doubtfully adopted heir Octavian/Augustus emerged triumphant and everyone still standing went and had a nice quiet lie down for several years. But as far as the *pro lege Manilia* is concerned, all of that remains safely in the future and the main shadow in everyone's tragic backstory is Sulla.

The shadow of Sulla

Why is this a relevant category? In general terms, because the unfinished war against Mithridates is one of Sulla's legacies, and anything with Sulla's fingerprints on it is potentially a sticky issue. It's less than ten years since

---

92 Lovano (2002) 32-45; on the *Cinnae dominatio* generally cf. Badian (1962), Bulst (1964), Mitchell (1979) 76-80, Lovano (2002).
93 Keaveney (1982) 169-75, Hantos (1988).
94 Plutarch, *Life of Sertorius*, Spann (1987).
95 Weigel (1992) 12-19.
96 Salmon (1935), Allen (1938), Yavetz (1963) 496, Phillips (1976), Smith (1966) 105-31, Waters (1970), Stockton (1971) 110-42, Seager (1973), Mitchell (1979) 232-42.

the last major Marian (Sertorius) was disposed of, less than fifteen years since Sulla's death, all those currently engaged in politics had *some* level of complicity in Sulla's regime, and Mithridates remained free to make trouble because Sulla left the war early so he could sort out his enemies in Rome. Cicero soft-pedals this point in the actual speech: two triumphs have so far been won for wars with Mithridates, even though those wars left Mithridates bloody but unbowed, but Sulla and L. Murena, the *triumphatores* in question, both 'deserve praise for what they did, pardon for what they left undone, since both were recalled to Italy from the war, Sulla by a crisis at home and Murena by Sulla'.[97] Moreover, Cicero goes on to point out that the rearming Mithridates did his best to link up with Sertorius in Spain so that Rome might be attacked on two fronts,[98] thereby linking the defeated side of the *civil* war with the current *external* enemy.[99]

This awkward Sullan background perhaps plays into Cicero's 'damn with faint praise' strategy in this speech, which applies most noticeably in his treatment of Lucullus, who features as a general who is great but not *quite* great enough. Lucullus is a *fortis vir*, a *sapiens homo* and a *magnus imperator* who relieved Cyzicus from siege, defeated a Sertorian fleet, opened the way into Pontus, occupied Sinope, Amisus and countless other cities of Pontus and Cappadocia, drove out Mithridates and did all this without endangering Rome's *socii* or revenues.[100] However, he was hamstrung by the avarice of his troops, the hostility of Mithridates' neighbours and the adherence to petty precedent on the part of the senate,[101] leaving a war (says Cicero) so great that only a truly extraordinary *imperator* (sc. Pompey) can handle it.[102] Likewise, those who oppose the *lex Manilia* do so from sincere, if misplaced concerns: Hortensius opposed the *lex Gabinia* and now opposes the *lex Manilia*, and the *populus Romanus* recognises that he does so *bono animo* ('with good intention'), but nonetheless disagreed with him then and should disagree with him now.[103] Quintus Catulus, a respected patriot

---

97 Cic. *Man.* 8: *verum tamen illis imperatoribus laus est tribuenda, quod egerunt, venia danda, quod reliquerunt, propterea quod ab ea bello Sullam in Italiam res publica, Murenam Sulla revocavit.*

98 Cic. *Man.* 9.

99 It's possibly worth noting that he delays citing Sertorius by name until *Man.* 10; introduced in *Man.* 9, Sertorius is only 'that *imperator* over in Hispania we had all those problems with', which somewhat camouflages the civil war aspect.

100 Cic. *Man.* 20-1.

101 Cic. *Man.* 22-6.

102 Cic. *Man.* 27.

103 Cic. *Man.* 56.

(*amantissimus rei publicae*: *Man.* 51) argues against innovating in the face of the *exempla et instituta maiorum* by handing so much power to a *privatus* (*Man.* 60): not only were the *maiores* actually quite happy to innovate themselves, says Cicero, but Pompey's previous career is all the precedent he needs.[104] In the *pro lege Manilia*, the only villain is Mithridates; unlike in Cicero's legal speeches, where the need to find alternative candidates for the role of the defendant (or, in the case of the *Verrines*, where Cicero speaks for the prosecution) results in character assassinations and outright attacks, here Cicero presents us with a rational Rome where prominent figures disagree with one another in good faith and may be outvoted by a *populus* wiser than any of them.

In fact, this serene take on the Roman political sphere contrasts not just with Cicero's legal speeches but also with quite a lot of Cicero's later political speeches, which feature a gallery of super-villains, demagogic would-be tyrants and corrupt politicians to rival anything Marvel or DC has yet come up with. In particular, the speeches against Catiline from the second half of Cicero's consulship, the mid-50s invective *in Pisonem* and the *Second Philippic* against M. Antonius are all dominated by attacks on specific individuals and present a version of Rome that is divided, under attack and in extreme peril from political dangers. Now, one difference between the *pro lege Manilia* and those speeches is that after he reached the consulship Cicero no longer needed to canvass for office, having topped the *cursus honorum* (well, there was still the censorship, but that was far too irregularly held to count on at this point in time), and, being in a position to make real *inimici* ('political enemies'), henceforth did so, quite gratuitously in the case of his future arch-nemesis Clodius Pulcher. As a praetor in 66, however, Cicero was still obliged to calculate his position with regards both to his political peers and his future voting constituency: to lean too far towards the *populus* and/or demonize his eminent opponents could alienate people whose support/votes he was going to need, and so he treads carefully around Hortensius and Catulus. Similarly, if in a slightly different way, he treads rather carefully around Manilius, whose law he is ostentatiously supporting. We mentioned above that Manilius was a turbulent tribune and certainly Manilius's political future was not heading down the sort of career path that might make him a valuable *amicus* for a respectable gentleman like Cicero, which may explain why Manilius

---

104 Cic. *Man.* 59-62.

himself is markedly absent from the *pro lege Manilia*. Cicero appeals to the magnitude of the war, the excellence of Pompey and the wisdom of the *populus*, but he has very little to say about Manilius.

To tie all this back to Sulla, it is perhaps noteworthy that Cicero is so delicate in this speech *in contione*. Cicero's treatment of Sulla in his consular speeches *de lege agraria* 2 and 3, also delivered to the *populus*, suggests there were cheap points to be made by unkind references to Sulla (and even more so to the beneficiaries of Sulla's proscriptions and colony policies).[105] Sulla was not a popular (and certainly not *popularis*) figure, but his settlement did have to be upheld by those in power, since they were in power thanks to Sulla's settlement. Certainly Sulla's contribution to Roman political consensus remained contentious for quite a long time to come: the politics of the 70s had revolved around unpicking particular aspects of Sulla's political settlement, Manlius's uprising during the Catilinarian affair of 63 testifies to the grievances of Sullan veterans, Pompey in the 50s was apostrophised (famously) as *carnifex adulescentulus* as a call-back to his early career under Sulla, and the shadow of Sulla fell particularly heavily on both sides in the civil war that started when Caesar crossed the Rubicon in 49.

Speaking of Pompey's particular Sullan past, the other sticky issue for the *pro lege Manilia* was the extraordinary nature of the command being handed to Pompey. More on extraordinary commands below, but in aggregate Sulla's dictatorial settlement seems to have aimed at concentrating political power in the hands of the senate as a way to counteract the upsetting recent trend towards rogue magisterial action, whereas the *lex Manilia* doubles up the offence of the *lex Gabinia* in concentrating extraordinary power in the hands of a *privatus* whose early career necessarily invoked Sulla as mentor and role model. Pompey's remarkable career would not have been possible if not for Sulla's activities (and, presumably, his father Strabo dying before he could pick a side for his veterans) and Cicero's careful treatment of Pompey's previous career in this speech reflects the problems inherent in lauding victories gained in civil war. Pompey had gone from the games and lessons of childhood to his father's army in order to study military matters in a great war (*bellum maximum*) against the most savage enemies (*acerrimi hostes*); as a mere boy, he had served as soldier in

---

105 Cic. *Agr.* 1.21, 2.82, 3.5 (*Sullana dominatio*/Sulla the *tyrannus*), 2.52 (the proscriptions), 2.68-70, 3.3, 3.13 (Sullan profiteers), 3.6-7, 3.10 (Sullans and Marians, i.e. political positioning in relation to the Sullan regime).

a *summus imperator*'s army, and as an *adulescens* commanded a great army; he had 'more often clashed with his country's enemies (*cum hoste conflixit*) than any other man has quarrelled with his own (*cum inimico concertavit*), fought more wars than others have read of, discharged more public offices (*provinciae*) than other men have coveted; in his youth (*adulescentia*), he learned the lessons of warfare not from the instructions of others but under his own command (*suis imperiis*), not by reverses in war but by victories, not through campaigns but through triumphs'.[106] Pompey had engaged in all types of warfare and so gained universal competence: 'The civil war, the wars in Africa, Transalpine Gaul and Spain, the slave war and the naval war, wars different in type and locality and against foes as different, not only carried on by himself unaided but carried to a conclusion, make it manifest that there is no item within the sphere of military experience which can be beyond the knowledge of Pompeius'.[107] This glorious account tarnishes when rephrased as what it was: a series of victories achieved against Roman citizens. Cicero disguises this by portraying the wars waged outside Italy as foreign wars, rather than extensions of the initial civil war sparked by Sulla's return from the East.[108] His response to Hortensius and Catulus's criticisms of the *imperium* proposed for Pompey was similarly slippery: it was disingenuous of Cicero to dismiss as unimportant the problems Pompey's singular *cursus honorum* posed, as future events would show.

The lex Manilia and the problem of extraordinary commands

We spared a few words above for the academic problem that we don't really know what Pompey's *imperium* ('right of command') as per the *lex Gabinia* was. Whatever the details, it handed to Pompey, a private citizen, an extraordinary *imperium* for a set number of years. This plays into a theme of the late Republic, that of 'extraordinary commands'. 'Ordinary' commands were based on election to a magistracy with attached *imperium*, either the praetorship or the consulship, and either as a magistrate during your term in office or as a promagistrate after your term in office you get handed a *provincia* (this is really a sphere of operation, but – except

---

106 Cic. *Man.* 28.
107 Cic. *Man.* 28.
108 Steel (2001) 145 (see further 140-47).

for the urban praetor – generally one attached to certain geographical boundaries) in which to operate your *imperium*. But for certain military challenges that emerged in the late republic, not least as a result of Rome's imperial expansion, this system didn't quite work – and the Romans felt that in certain situations extraordinary measures proved necessary (if not desirable). We might start this trend with Marius's totally unprecedented repeat elections to six consulships to deal with the marauding Cimbri and Teutones, which is not technically an extraordinary command as we just defined it (because Marius was, indeed, elected), but which is at least an example of someone holding a command significantly past the usual expiration date and without requiring prorogation. Marius is also significant because he was the first to start (officially) raising levies from the *capite censi*, the poorest class of citizens who possessed less than a certain amount of property and were hence literally 'counted by the head'. We combine these details because the real issue here is that the longer you hold your command, and the more your men rely on you to reward them (usually with land) at the end of their time in service, the more opportunity you have to turn your army into one loyal to you personally.

This problem was exacerbated by extraordinary commands. By the time of the *lex Manilia*, the conferral of an *imperium extra ordinem* was by no means unprecedented, let alone unconstitutional. Erich Gruen, for instance, stresses that such commands were an integral part of Rome's political repertory, especially in situations of military crisis.[109] He does not, however, reckon with the possibility that even 'constitutional' acts could still have been perceived as profoundly problematic and may have had unintended and dysfunctional consequences as well. Such mandates provided high-profile aristocrats with further opportunities to distinguish themselves over and above their peers and tended to be longer and involve more grandiose forms of *imperium* than the usual sort. The increasing need for special commands due to imperial expansion and the ensuing accumulation of power and resources in the hands of outstanding individuals has often been recognized as one of the defining paradoxes of late republican politics. Moreover, the controversial nature of said commands led to political blowback in the form of the senate's refusal or quibbling over

---

109 Gruen (1974) 534-43 ('Appendix III: *imperia extra ordinem*'). Note that his heavy reliance on Cicero's speech *de Imperio* as evidence for the ordinary nature of extraordinary commands is circular: it is, of course, exactly what Cicero wishes his audience to believe, and he spins facts and *exempla* accordingly.

post-command settlements, especially the settlement of veterans on land. This, in turn, made soldiers more inclined to look to their commanders as the source of potential and actual rewards – and more willing to obey when, for example, their commanders proposed such dubious activities as fighting fellow citizens.

Pompey was pretty much the king of extraordinary commands in the late Republic: his early career, right up to his consulship, involved a string of commands given to a private citizen (as per citations from the *pro lege Manilia*, above), followed by a stint in Spain *non pro consule sed pro consulibus* (© L. Philippus, Cic. *Man.* 62). After his consulship, the *lex Gabinia* gave him the command against the pirates that the *lex Manilia* commuted into a command against Mithridates. In the 50s, as we pointed out above, he picked up a grain-related command and a Spanish pro-consulship-by-proxy, which is probably the most egregious, since he delegated the work to legates and lurked just outside Rome (so as not to abrogate his *imperium* by crossing the *pomerium*). The extraordinary commands that actually did it for the Republic, however, were those given to Caesar: a five year command in Gaul that was prorogued in 55 for a further five years, at the end of which a quarrel over whether Caesar should be allowed to stand for the consulship *in absentia* (thereby saving him any concern about being prosecuted in the interval between giving up his Gallic command and resuming a new office) sparked a civil war in which Caesar's army and officers were loyal, above all, to Caesar himself.

List of rhetorical terms

N.B.:

(i) The list contains some of the more frequent rhetorical figures but is far from complete. More comprehensive accounts are available in standard textbooks (e.g. Morwood (1999) 150-54: 'Some literary terms') or on the web (e.g. *Silva Rhetoricae: The Forest of Rhetoric*: http://rhetoric.byu.edu/).

(ii) Most of the terms derive from, or indeed are, either Greek or Latin; we have therefore provided an etymological explanation for each, not least to show that the terminological abracadabra makes perfectly good sense – even though it takes a smattering of ancient Greek and Latin to see this.

(iii) The English examples are from Shakespeare. Unless otherwise indicated they come from the Pyramus-and-Thisbe episode in Act 5 of *A Midsummer Night's Dream*. The main reason for drawing on the *oeuvre* of an (early) modern author for illustration is to convey a sense of the continuity of classical and classicizing rhetoric in the western cultural tradition. And using a Shakespeare text that engages in allusive dialogue with Ovid's *Metamorphoses* ought to generate some interesting cross-fertilization with the AS-level set text in verse (the Pentheus-episode from *Metamorphoses* 3).

alliteration: the repeated use of the same sound at the beginning of words in close proximity.

> *Etymology*: from (un-classical) Latin *alliterare*, 'to begin with the same letter'.
>
> *Examples*: 'O dainty duck! O dear!' 'When lion rough in wildest rage doth roar.' 'Whereat, with blade, with bloody, blameful blade/ He bravely broach'd his boiling bloody breast.'

anacoluthon: a sudden break in a sentence, resulting in an incomplete grammatical or syntactical unit; a change in construction in mid-sentence.

> *Etymology*: from Greek *anakolouthos*, 'inconsistent, anomalous, inconsequent'.
>
> *Example*: 'No, you unnatural hags,/ I will have such revenges on you both,/ That all the world shall – I will do such things…' (*King Lear*, Act 2, Scene 4).

anaphora: the repetition of the same word or phrase at the beginning of several successive syntactic units.

> *Etymology*: from Greek *anapherein*, 'to carry back, to repeat'.
>
> *Example*: 'O grim-look'd night! O night with hue so black! O night, which ever art when day is not! O night, O night, alack, alack, alack!'

antithesis: literally 'a placing against'; the (balanced) juxtaposition of contrasting ideas.

> *Etymology*: from Greek *antitithenai*, 'to place (*tithenai*) against (*anti-*)'.
>
> *Example*: ''Tide life, 'tide death, I come without delay.'

apo koinou: two constructions that have a word or phrase in common; or, put the other way around, a word or phrase shared by two different constructions.

> *Etymology*: from the Greek phrase *apo koinou lambanein*, used by ancient grammarians of two clauses taking (*apo ... lambanein*) a word in common (*koinou*, the genitive of *koinon* after the preposition *apo*).
>
> *Example*: 'There was a man – dwelt by the churchyard' (*The Winter's Tale*, Act 2, Scene 1).

asyndeton: the absence or omission of conjunctions (see also below *polysundeton*).

> *Etymology*: from Greek *asyndetos*, 'not (*a*-privativum) bound (*detos*, from *dein*, to bind) together (*sun*)'.
>
> *Example*: 'O Fates, come, come, cut thread and thrum; quail, crush, conclude, and quell!'

captatio benevolentiae: a Latin phrase that literally means 'the capture of goodwill', i.e. a rhetorical technique designed to render the audience kindly disposed towards the speaker.

> *(Botched) example*: 'If we offend, it is with our good will. That you should think, we come not to offend. But with good will.'[110]

---

110   Note that Shakespeare's character here, hilariously, 'translates' the Latin *benevolentia* of the rhetorical figure, but, perversely, refers to the 'good will' of himself, the speaker, rather than that of the audience.

chiasmus: the repetition of a grammatical pattern in inverse order: *a b – b a*.

Etymology: from Greek *chiasmos*, 'a placing crosswise', from the letter X (pronounced *chi*) of the Greek alphabet. (Imagine the two *a* at either end of the first diagonal line of X, and at either end of the second diagonal line the two *b*; then read the top half first and afterwards the bottom half and you get *a b – b a*.)

Example: '(a) Sweet Moon, (b) I thank thee ... (b), I thank thee, (a) Moon...'

climax: a series or sequence of units that gradually increase in import or force.

Etymology: from Greek *klimax*, 'ladder'.

Example: 'Tongue, lose thy light;/ Moon take thy flight: Now die, die, die, die, die' (Pyramus before stabbing himself).

ellipsis: the omission of one or more words in a sentence necessary for a complete grammatical construction.

Etymology: from Greek *elleipein*, 'to fall short, leave out'.

Example: 'I neither know it nor can learn of him' (*Romeo and Juliet*, Act 1, Scene 1).[111]

figura etymologica: a Latin phrase referring to words of the same etymological derivation used in close proximity to one another.

Example: 'So long <u>lives</u> this, and this gives <u>life</u> to thee'(*Sonnet* 18).

hendiadys: one idea expressed by two words joined by 'and', such as two nouns used in place of a noun and an adjective.

Etymology: from Greek *hen-dia-duoin*, 'one thing (*hen*) by means of (*dia*) two (*duoin*)'.

Example: 'The service and the loyalty I owe'(*Macbeth*, Act 1, Scene 4), for 'the loyal service'.

homoioteleuton: similarity of ending in words in close proximity to one another.

Etymology: from Greek *homoios*, 'like', and *teleute*, 'ending'.

Example: 'My mother weep<u>ing</u>, my father wail<u>ing</u>, my sister cry<u>ing</u>, our maid howl<u>ing</u>, our cat wring<u>ing</u> her hands'(*The Two Gentlemen of Verona*, Act 2, Scene 3).[112]

---

111 Filling in the items elided would results in something like 'I neither know it nor can I learn anything about it from him'.

112 Note that the last item in the list (wring-ing) contains the -ing sound twice, a stylistic

hyperbaton: dislocation of the customary or logical word order, with the result that items that normally go together are separated.

> *Etymology*: from Greek *huperbaino*, 'to step (*bainein*) over (*huper-*)'. (Imagine, for instance, that if an adjective is placed apart from the noun it modifies you have to 'step over' the intervening words to get from one to the other.)
>
> *Example*: 'Some rise by sin, and some by virtue fall' (*Measure for Measure*, Act 2, Scene 1).[113]

hyperbole: the use of exaggeration.

> *Etymology*: from Greek *huperballein*, 'to throw (*ballein*, from which derives *bole*, "a throwing") over or beyond (*huper*)'.
>
> *Example*: 'Will all great Neptune's ocean wash this blood/ Clean from my hand? No. This my hand will rather/ The multitudinous seas incarnadine,/ Making the green one red' (*Macbeth*, Act 2, Scene 2).[114]

husteron proteron: A Greek phrase, meaning 'the latter (*husteron*) first (*proteron*)', producing chronological disorder.

> *Example*: 'Th' Antoniad, the Egyptian admiral,/ With all their sixty, fly and turn the rudder' (*Antony and Cleopatra*, Act 3, Scene 10).[115]

litotes: a 'double negation', in which a statement, quality, or attribute is affirmed by the negation of its opposite; assertion by means of understatement, frequently for the purpose of intensification.

> *Etymology*: from Greek *litos*, 'simple, plain, petty, small'.
>
> *Example*: 'That I was <u>not ignoble</u> of descent' (*Henry VI*, Act 4, Scene 1).[116]

> climax that reinforces the climax in content achieved through the anthropomorphism of the cat and the unexpected switch from sound (weeping etc.) to silence (wringing).

113 Natural word order would require 'some fall by virtue'. Note that the hyperbaton also produces a chiasmus – Some (a) rise (b) by sin, and some (b) by virtue (a) fall – which is ideally suited to reinforce the elegant antitheses of sin and virtue, rising and falling. One could further argue that the hyperbaton, which produces disorder on the level of grammar and syntax, is the perfect figure of speech for the basic idea of the utterance: *moral* disorder, which manifests itself in the reward of sin and the punishment of virtue and implies that our universe is devoid of justice, i.e. as chaotic as the hyperbatic word order.

114 'To incarnadine' means 'to turn into the colour of flesh (Latin *caro/carnis, carnis*), dye red, redden'. A more familiar term with a similar etymology is 'incarnation'.

115 The logical sequence would require 'they turn the rudder and fly'. The example is a beautiful instance of enactment since the *husteron proteron* conveys a sense of how hastily ('heel over head' as it were) everyone is trying to get away.

116 Note that in modern literary criticism litotes is often used loosely to refer to simple negation (e.g. Shakespeare, *Sonnet* 130: 'My mistress' eyes are nothing like the sun...').

onomatopoesis/onomatopoeia: expressions where the sound suggests the sense.

> *Etymology*: from Greek *onoma* (genitive *onomatos*), 'word, name', and *poiein* (noun: *poesis*), 'to make'.

> *Example*: 'Sea-nymphs hourly ring his knell/ Hark! now I hear them, – Ding-dong, bell' (*The Tempest*, Act 1, Scene 2).

oxymoron: a 'pointedly foolish' expression, resulting from the juxtaposition or combination of two words of contradictory meaning.

> *Etymology*: from Greek *oxus*, 'sharp', and *môros*, 'stupid'.

> *Examples*: '"A tedious brief scene of young Pyramus/ And his love Thisbe; very tragical mirth." Merry and tragical! tedious and brief!/ That is, hot ice and wondrous strange snow./ How shall we find the concord of this discord?'

paronomasia: a play upon words that sound alike; a pun.

> *Etymology*: from Greek *para-*, '...', and *onoma*, 'word, name'.

> *Examples*: 'Our sport shall be to <u>take</u> what they mis<u>take</u>'; 'You, ladies, you, whose gentle hearts do fear/ the smallest <u>monstrous mouse</u> that creeps on floor...'

pleonasm: a 'fullness of expression', that is, the use of more words than is strictly speaking necessary to convey the desired meaning.

> *Etymology*: from Greek *pleonazein*, 'to be more than enough or superfluous'.

> *Example*: 'the most unkindest cut of all' (*Julius Caesar*, Act 3, Scene 2, about Brutus' stabbing of Caesar). [117]

polyptoton: the repetition of the same word, variously inflected.

> *Etymology*: from Greek *poluptoton*, 'many (*polu*) cases (from *ptôsis*, i.e. fall, grammatical case)'.

> *Example*: 'Then know that I, one Snug the joiner, am/ A <u>lion</u>-fell, nor else no <u>lion's</u> dam.'

polysyndeton: the frequent use of conjunctions such as 'and' or 'or' even when they are not required.

> *Etymology*: from Greek *polusyndetos*, 'many times (*polu*) bound (*detos*, from *dein*, to bind) together (*sun*)'.

---

117 Shakespeare expresses the degree to which Brutus' unkindness outdid that of all the others pleonastically by using both the adverb 'most' and the superlative ending -est.

Example: 'Peering in maps for ports <u>and</u> piers <u>and</u> roads' (*The Merchant of Venice*, Act 1, Scene 1).

praeteritio: a Latin term that means 'passing over'; as a rhetorical figure it refers to the practice of mentioning something by not meaning to mention it.

Example: 'Soft you; a word or two before you go./ I have done the state some service, and they know't –/ No more of that' (*Othello*, Act 5, Scene 2).

tautology: the repetition of the same idea in different ways.

Etymology: from Greek *tauto*, 'the same', and *logos*, 'word, idea'.

Example: 'The ... mouse ... may now perchance <u>both quake and tremble</u> here.'

tmesis: the 'cutting apart' of a compound word by the interposition of others.

Etymology: from Greek *temnein*, 'to cut'.

Example: 'that man – <u>how dearly ever</u> parted' (*Troilus and Cressida*, Act 3, Scene 3).

tricolon: the use of three parallel grammatical units (words, phrases, clauses).

Etymology: from Greek *tri-*, 'three', and *kôlon*, 'limb, member, clause, unit'.

Example: 'Tongue, not a word;/ Come, trusty sword;/ Come, ! ...de, my breast imbue.'

6. Bibliography

A note on translations: The translation of the set text provided in 'Further Resources' is our own. It is solely meant as an aid to understanding the original and stays as close to the Latin as possible. As such, it has limited literary value, though we hope that you'll find the occasional formulation felicitous. For translations cited elsewhere in the volume we have for the most part relied on those available in the Loeb Classical Library (frequently with minor adjustments).

Adler, E. (2008a), 'Late Victorian and Edwardian Views of Rome and the Nature of "Defensive Imperialism"', *International Journal of the Classical Tradition* 15.2, 187-216.

— (2008b), 'Post-9/11 Views of Rome and the Nature of "Defensive Imperialism"', *International Journal of the Classical Tradition* 15.4, 587-610.

Albrecht, von M. (2003), *Cicero's Style: A Synopsis Followed by Selected Analytic Studies*, Leiden and Boston.

Allen, W. (1938), 'In Defense of Catiline', *Classical Journal* 34.2, 70-85.

Badian, E. (1969), 'Quaestiones Variae', *Historia* 18.4, 447-91.

— (1962), 'Waiting for Sulla', *Journal of Roman Studies* 52, 47-61.

— (1996), 'Alexander the Great between two Thrones and Heaven', in A. M. Small (ed.), *Subject and Ruler: The Cult of the Ruling Power in Classical Antiquity*, Ann Arbor, 11-26.

— (2009), 'From the Iulii to Caesar', in M. Griffin (ed.), *A Companion to Julius Caesar*, Oxford, 11-22.

Balsdon, J. P. V. D. (1951), 'Sulla Felix', *Journal of Roman Studies* 41, 1-10.

— (1960) '*Auctoritas, dignitas, otium*', *Classical Quarterly* 10, 43-50.

Beard, M. (2007), *The Roman Triumph*, Cambridge, Mass.

Beard, M., North, J., and Price, S. (1998), *Religions of Rome*, 2 vols, Cambridge.

Begemann, E. (2012), *Schicksal als Argument. Ciceros Rede vom fatum in der späten Republik*, Stuttgart.

Bendlin, A. (2004), 'Deification', in *Brill's New Pauly*, Leiden.

Berry, D. H. (2003), '*Equester ordo tuus est*: Did Cicero Win his Cases Because of his Support for the *equites?*', *Classical Quarterly* 53.1, 222-34.

Brennan, T. C. (2000), *The Praetorship in the Roman Republic*, vol. I, Oxford.

Brown, R. (2003), 'The Terms *Bellum Sociale* and *Bellum Ciuile* in the Late Republic', in C. Deroux (ed.), *Studies in Latin Literature and Roman History*, Brussels, 94-120.

Brunt, P. A. (1965), 'Reflections on British and Roman Imperialism', *Comparative Studies in Society and History* 7.3, 267-88.

Bulst, C. M. (1964), '"Cinnanum Tempus": A Reassessment of the "Dominatio Cinnae"', *Historia* 13.3, 307-37.

Champeaux, J. (1982-87), *Fortuna: recherches sur le culte de la Fortune à Rome et dans le monde romain des origines à la mort de César*, 2 vols, Rome.

Chaniotis, A. (2003), 'The Divinity of Hellenistic Rulers', in A. Erskine (ed.), *A Companion to the Hellenistic World*, Oxford, 431-45.

Clark, A. (2007), *Divine Qualities*, Oxford.

Classen, J. (1963), 'Gottmenschentum in der römischen Republik', *Gymnasium* 70, 312-38.

Cole, S. (2014), *Cicero and the Rise of Deification at Rome*, Cambridge.

de Souza, P. (1999), *Piracy in the Graeco-Roman World*, Cambridge.

— (2008), 'Rome's Contribution to the Development of Piracy', *Memoirs of the American Academy in Rome. Supplementary Volumes, Vol. 6, The Maritime World of Ancient Rome*, 71-96.

Ehrenberg, V. (1953), '*Imperium Maius* in the Roman Republic', *American Journal of Philology* 74.2, 113-36.

Enenkel, K. A. E. (2005), 'The Propagation of *fortitudo*: Gladiatorial Combats from ca. 85 BC to the Times of Trajan and their Reflection in Roman Literature', in K. A. E. Enenkel and I. L. Pfeijffer (eds.), *The Manipulative Mode: Political Propaganda in Antiquity – A Collection of Case Studies*, Leiden and Boston, 275-93.

Erkell, H. (1952), *Augustus, Felicitas, Fortuna*, Gothenburg.

Evans, R. J. and Kleijwegt, M. (1992), 'Did the Romans like Young Men? A Study of the *Lex Villia Annalis*: Causes and Effects', *Zeitschrift für Papyrologie und Epigraphik* 92, 181-95.

Fears, J. R. (1981), 'The Theology of Victory at Rome', *Aufstieg und Niedergang der Römischen Welt* 2.17.2, 737-826.

Feeney, D. C. (1998), *Literature and Religion at Rome: Cultures, Contexts, and Beliefs*, Cambridge.

Fishwick, D. (1987), *The Imperial Cult in the Latin West*, vol. I, Leiden.

Flower, H. I. (1996), *Ancestor Masks and Aristocratic Power in Roman Culture*, Oxford.

— (2006), *The Art of Forgetting: Disgrace and Oblivion in Roman Political Culture*, Chapel Hill.

— (2010), *Roman Republics*, Princeton.

Gabrielsen, V. (2001), 'Economic Activity, Maritime Trade and Piracy in the Hellenistic Aegean', *Revue des Études Anciennes* 103, 219-40.

Gabba, E. (1989), 'Rome and Italy in the Second Century B.C.', in A. E. Astin, F. W. Walbank, M. W. Frederiksen and R. M. Ogilvie (eds.), *The Cambridge Ancient History Vol. VIII* (2nd ed.), Cambridge, 197-243.

Galinsky, K. (1996), *Augustan Culture: An Interpretive Introduction*, Princeton.

Gavoille, L. (2007), *Oratio ou la parole persuasive: étude sémantique et pragmatique*, Paris.

Gildenhard, I. (2011), *Creative Eloquence: The Construction of Reality in Cicero's Speeches*, Oxford.

Goldsworthy, A. (1998), '"Instinctive genius": The Depiction of Caesar the General', in K. Welch and A. Powell (eds.), *Julius Caesar as Artful Reporter: The War Commentaries as Political Instruments*, Swansea, 193-219.

Gotter, U. (2008), 'Cultural Differences and Cross-Cultural Contact: Greek and Roman Concepts of Power', *Harvard Studies in Classical Philology* 104, 179-230.

Gradel, I. (2002), *Emperor Worship and Roman Religion*, Oxford.

Greenhalgh, P. (1980), *Pompey. The Roman Alexander*, London.

Gruber, J. (1988), 'Cicero und das hellenistische Herrscherideal: Überlegungen zur Rede *De imperio Cn. Pompei*', *Wiener Studien* 101, 243-58.

Gruen, E. S. (1974), *The Last Generation of the Roman Republic*, Berkeley, Los Angeles and London.

Haake, M. (2003), 'Warum und zu welchem Ende schreibt man *peri basileias*? Überlegungen zum historischen Kontext einer literarischen Gattung im Hellenismus', in K. Piepenbrink (ed.), *Philosophie und Lebenswelt in der Antike*, Darmstadt, 83-138.

Habicht, C. (1970), *Gottmenschentum und griechische Städte*, Munich.

Haley, S. P. (1985), 'The Five Wives of Pompey the Great', *Greece & Rome* 32.1, 49-59.

Harris, W. V. (1979), *War and Imperialism in Republican Rome*, Oxford.

Harrison, T. (2008), 'Ancient and Modern Imperialism', *Greece & Rome* 55.1, 1-22.

Hantos, T. (1988), *Res Publica Constituta*, Stuttgart.

Hillard, T. W. (1996), 'Death by Lightning, Pompeius Strabo and the People', *Rheinisches Museum für Philologie* 139.2, 135-45.

Hodgson, L. (2014), 'Appropriation and Adaptation: Republican Idiom in *Res Gestae* 1.1', *Classical Quarterly* 64, 254-69.

Hopkins, K. (1983), *Death and Renewal*, Cambridge.

Hurlet, F. (2010), 'Pouvoirs extraordinaires et tromperie: La tentation de la Monarchie à la fin de la République romaine (82-44 av. J.–C.)', in A. J. Turner, J. H. Kim On Chong-Gossard and F. J. Vervaet (eds.), *Private and Public Lies: The Discourse of Despotism and Deceit in the Graeco-Roman World*, Leiden, 107-29.

Hutchinson, G. O. (2013), *Greek to Latin: Frameworks and Contexts for Intertextuality*, Oxford.

Jameson, S. (1970), 'Pompey's *Imperium* in 67: Some Constitutional Fictions', *Historia* 19.5, 539-60.

Kaster, R. A. (2007), 'Review of McDonnell (2006)', *Bryn Mawr Classical Review* 2007.02.08.

Katz, B. R. (1977), 'Caesar Strabo's Struggle for the Consulship – And More', *Rheinisches Museum für Philologie, Neue Folge* 120.1, 45-63.

Keaveney, A. (1979), 'Sulla, Sulpicius and Caesar Strabo', *Latomus* 38.2, 451-60.

— (1982), *Sulla. The Last Republican*, London.

Koortbojian, M. (2013), *The Divinization of Caesar and Augustus: Precedents, Consequences, Implications*, Princeton.

Last, H. (1947), '*Imperium Maius*: A Note', *Journal of Roman Studies* 37, 157-64.

Lavan, M. (2013), *Slaves to Rome: Paradigms of Empire in Roman Culture*, Cambridge.

Leach, J. (1978), *Pompey the Great*, London.

Leschhorn, W. (1985), 'Ausdrücke der übermenschlichen Ehrung bei Cicero', in A. Alföldi (ed.), *Caesar in 44 v. Chr.*, Bonn, 387-97.

Levene, D. (1998), 'God and Man in the Classical Latin Panegyric', *Proceedings of the Cambridge Philological Society* 43, 66-103.

— (2012), 'Defining the Divine in Rome', *Transactions of the American Philological Association* 142.1, 41-81.

Levick, B. (1982), 'Sulla's March on Rome in 88 B.C.', *Historia* 31.4, 503-08.

Lewis, R. G. (1991), 'Sulla's Autobiography: Scope and Economy', *Athenaeum* n.s. 69, 509-19.

— (1998), 'P. Sulpicius' Law to Recall Exiles, 88 B.C.', *Classical Quarterly, New Series* 48.1, 195-99.

Lintott, A. (1971), 'The Tribunate of P. Sulpicius Rufus', *Classical Quarterly, New Series* 21.2, 442-53.

— (1999), *The Constitution of the Roman Republic*, Oxford.

Loader, W. R. (1940), 'Pompey's Command under the Lex Gabinia', *Classical Review* 54.3, 134-36.

Lovano, M. (2002), *The Age of Cinna: Crucible of Late Republican Rome*, Stuttgart.

Luce, T. J. (1970), 'Marius and the Mithridatic Command', *Historia* 19.2, 161-94.

Ma, J. (1999/2002), *Antiochos III and the Cities of Western Asia Minor*, Oxford.

— (2003), 'Kings', in A. Erskine (ed.), *The Blackwell Companion to the Hellenistic Age*, Oxford, 177-95.

Macdonald, C. (1986), *Cicero: De Imperio*, Bristol.

MacKendrick, P. (1995), *The Speeches of Cicero: Context, Law, Rhetoric*, London.

Mayor, A. (2009), *The Poison King: The Life and Legend of Mithridates, Rome's Deadliest Enemy*, Princeton.

McDonnell, M. (2006), *Roman Manliness: Virtus and the Roman Republic*, Cambridge.

Meier, C. (1966), *Res Publica Amissa*, Wiesbaden.

Mikalson, J. D. (1998), *Religion in Hellenistic Athens*, Berkeley, Los Angeles and London.

Mitchell, T. N. (1975), 'The Volte-Face of P. Sulpicius Rufus in 88 BC', *Classical Philology* 70.3, 197-204.

— (1979), *Cicero. The Ascending Years*, New York and London.

Momigliano, A. D. (1987), 'How Roman Emperors Became Gods', *American Scholar*, Spring, 181-93.

Morstein-Marx, R. (2004), *Mass Oratory and Political Power in the Late Roman Republic*, Cambridge.

— (2011), 'Consular Appeals to the Army in 88 and 87: the Locus of Legitimacy in Late-Republican Rome' in H. Beck, A. Duplá, M. Jehne and F. Pina Polo (eds.), *Consuls and Res Publica: Holding High Office in the Roman Republic*, Cambridge, 259-78.

Morwood, J. (1999), *A Latin Grammar*, Oxford.

Mouritsen, H. (1998), *Italian Unification*, London.

Nippel, W. (1995), *Public Order in Ancient Rome*, Cambridge.

— (2007), 'The Roman Notion of *auctoritas*', in P. Pasquino and P. Harris (eds.), *The*

Concept of Authority. A Multidisciplinary Approach: From Epistemology to the Social Sciences, Rome, 13-34.

North, J. A. (1975), 'Praesens Divus', *Journal of Roman Studies* 65, 171-77.

— (1981), 'The Development of Roman Imperialism', *Journal of Roman Studies* 71, 1-9.

Patterson, J. R. (2000), *Political Life in the City of Rome*, London.

Phillips, E. J. (1970), 'Cicero and the Prosecution of C. Manilius', *Latomus* 29.3, 595-607.

— (1976), 'Catiline's Conspiracy', *Historia* 25.4, 441-48.

Pina Polo, F. (1996), *Contra arma verbis: Der Redner vor dem Volk in der späten römischen Republik*, Stuttgart.

Pollini, J. (1990), 'Man or God: Divine Assimilation and Imitation in the Late Republic and Early Principate', in K. A. Raaflaub and M. Toher (eds.), *Between Republic and Empire: Interpretations of Augustus and his Principate*, Berkeley, 334-63.

Powell, J. G. F. (1990), 'The Tribune Sulpicius', *Historia* 39.4, 446-60.

— (2013), 'Cicero's Style', in C. Steel (ed.), *The Cambridge Companion to Cicero*, Cambridge, 41-72.

Price, S. R. F. (1984), *Rituals and Power: The Roman Imperial Cult in Asia Minor*, Cambridge.

Radice, K. and Steel, C. (2014), *Cicero, De Imperio: An Extract: 27-45*, London and New York.

Ramage, E. S. (1991), 'Sulla's Propaganda', *Klio* 73, 93-121.

Ramsey, J. T. (1980), 'The Prosecution of C. Manilius in 66 B.C. and Cicero's *pro Manilio*', *Phoenix* 34.4, 323-36.

Rowland, R. J. (1983), 'Rome's Earliest Imperialism', *Latomus* 42.4, 749-62.

Salmon, E. T. (1935), 'Catiline, Crassus, and Caesar', *The American Journal of Philology* 56.4, 302-16.

— (1982), *The Making of Roman Italy*, London.

Santangelo, F. (2005), 'The Religious Tradition of the Gracchi', *Archiv für Religionsgeschichte* 7, 198-204.

— (2007), *Sulla, the Elites and the Empire*, Leiden.

Seager, R. (1973), 'Iusta Catilinae', *Historia* 22.2, 240-48.

— (2002), *Pompey the Great: A Political Biography* (2nd ed.), London.

Sherwin-White, A. N. (1956), 'Violence in Roman Politics', *Journal of Roman Studies* 46, 1-9.

Silk, M., Gildenhard, I., and Barrow, R. (2014), *The Classical Tradition: Art, Literature, Thought*, Oxford.

Smith, R. E. (1966), *Cicero the Statesman*, Cambridge.

Spann, P. O. (1987), *Quintus Sertorius and the Legacy of Sulla*, Fayetteville.

Spencer, D. (2002), *The Roman Alexander: Reading a Cultural Myth*, Exeter.

Steel, C. E. W. (2001), *Cicero, Rhetoric and Empire*, Oxford.

Stevenson, T. R. (1996), 'Social and Psychological Interpretations of Graeco-Roman Religion: Some Thoughts on the Ideal Benefactor', *Antichthon* 30, 1-18.

Stockton, D. (1971), *Cicero. A Political Biography*, Oxford.

— (1973), 'The First Consulship of Pompey', *Historia* 22.2, 205-18.

— (1979), *The Gracchi*, Oxford.

Vasaly, A. (2009), 'Cicero, Domestic Politics, and the First Action of the Verrines', *Classical Antiquity* 28.1, 101-37.

Walbank, F. W. (1963), 'Polybius and Rome's Eastern Policy', *Journal of Roman Studies* 53, 1-13.

Wallace-Hadrill, A. (1990), 'Roman Arches and Greek Honours: The Language of Power at Rome', *Proceedings of the Cambridge Philological Society* 36, 143-81.

— (2008), *Rome's Cultural Revolution*, Cambridge.

Ward, A. M. (1970), 'Politics in the Trials of Manilius and Cornelius', *Transactions and Proceedings of the American Philological Association* 101, 545-56.

Waters, K. H. (1970), 'Cicero, Sallust and Catiline', *Historia* 19.2, 195-215.

Weigel, R. D. (1992), *Lepidus: The Tarnished Triumvir*, London.

Weinstock, S. (1971), *Divus Julius*, Oxford.

Welch, K. (2005), '*Lux* and *lumina* in Cicero's Rome: A Metaphor for the *res publica* and her Leaders', in K. Welch and T. W. Hillard (eds.), *Roman Crossings: Theory and Practice in the Roman Republic*, Swansea, 313-37.

— (2008), '*Nimium felix*: Caesar's *Felicitas* and Cicero's *Philippics*', in T. Stevenson and M. Wilson (eds.), *Cicero's Philippics: History, Rhetoric, and Ideology*, Auckland, 181-213.

Wilkinson, L. P. (1963), *Golden Latin Artistry*, Cambridge.

Winkler, L. (1995), *Salus: Vom Staatskult zur politischen Idee. Eine archäologische Untersuchung*, Heidelberg.

Wiseman, T. P. (1971), *New Men in the Roman Senate, 139 B.C. – 14 A.D.*, Oxford.

Yakobson, A. (2009), 'Public Opinion, Foreign Policy and "Just War" in the Late Republic', in C. Eilers (ed.), *Diplomats and Diplomacy in the Roman World*, Leiden, 45-72.

Yavetz, Z. (1963), 'The Failure of Catiline's Conspiracy', *Historia* 12.4, 485-99.

This book need not end here...

At Open Book Publishers, we are changing the nature of the traditional academic book. The title you have just read will not be left on a library shelf, but will be accessed online by hundreds of readers each month across the globe. We make all our books free to read online so that students, researchers and members of the public who can't afford a printed edition can still have access to the same ideas as you.

Our digital publishing model also allows us to produce online supplementary material, including extra chapters, reviews, links and other digital resources. Find *Cicero, On Pompey's Command (De Imperio), 27-49* on our website to access its online extras. Please check this page regularly for ongoing updates, and join the conversation by leaving your own comments:

http://www.openbookpublishers.com/isbn/9781783740772

If you enjoyed this book, and feel that research like this should be available to all readers, regardless of their income, please think about donating to us. Our company is run entirely by academics, and our publishing decisions are based on intellectual merit and public value rather than on commercial viability. We do not operate for profit and all donations, as with all other revenue we generate, will be used to finance new Open Access publications.

For further information about what we do, to donate to OBP, to access additional digital material related to our titles or to order our books, please visit our website: www.openbookpublishers.com.

OpenBook Publishers

Knowledge is for sharing

Lightning Source UK Ltd.
Milton Keynes UK
UKOW05f1531151014

240130UK00001B/10/P